CULTURE VULTURES

Conversations with Damon Dash

BY
DAMON DASH AND KENYATTA GRIGGS

Poppington LLC

Hip Hop Motivation

CULTURE VULTURES
Published 2017 in U.S.A by
Poppington LLC and Hip Hop Motivation LLC

All rights reserved. No Part of this book may be used of reproduced by any means, graphic, electronic, or mechanical, including photocopying, recording, taping, or by any information storage retreval system without the written permission of the publisher.

Edited by: Jacob Algier, Kenyatta Griggs, and Dr. Tyra Seldon
Transcribed by: Kenyatta Griggs, and Carolyn Gentle
Artwork by: Raquel M. Horn
Layout by: Michael Ziobrowski / @XIsTheWeapon
Photography: Raquel M. Horn & Carolyn Gentle
Contributing photographers from DD172 & Poppington Staff :
Shea Flynn, George A. Robels, Jonah Schwartz, & John Peets
Audio Recorded by: Michelle Gentle
Published by: Poppington LLC.

With love to my children Boogie, Ava, Lucky, Tallulah, and "wifey for lifey" Raquel M. Horn. This book is dedicated to independent like minded people who believe love is the ultimate currency and that is how they determine their wealth, and to all women in the struggle... #investinwomen
– Damon Dash

My work in this book is dedicated to the life and memory of Benjamin Griggs (Dad), Wynolia Robinson (Grandmaw), Frazier "Slow" Robinson (Paw Paw), William Griggs (Grandfather), Carolyn Griggs (Aunt), David McCoy Jr. (Friend), and Dorothy Moseley (Aunt).

A Shout with Love goes to my children Khari, Kalei, Kamaile, Karma, Krisna, Kenyatta, and of course their wonderful mothers. My "First Lady" Michelle Gentle. My #hiphopmotivation partner in inspiration Carolyn "Care" Gentle. My East Coast #hiphopmotivation homeboy's John Robinson, and Kirk Webber, and my #hiphopmotivation producers Marlon "Frost" Douglas, and Invizible Handz. To my sisters and brothers: Myisha Griggs, Sherie Griggs, Malik "Raymond" Griggs, and Yorel Griggs. My family: Aunt Betty, Aunt Barbara, Aunt Della, Grandmaw Sarah (100 years old), Uncle Shabaka, Uncle Phil, Uncle James, Sanjay, Mark, Malika, Dawn, Amili (P-Steel), Abike, Toddy, Freddy, Shana, Shaundra, and all my loved ones in California, North Carolina, Ohio, Tennessee, and Pennsylvania. I have to give an honorable mention to my Mother Mary Griggs for starting me off on the right path. Love you mom! Also a big Shout Out goes to all the barbers, beauticians, and clients on Crenshaw, and last but not least the entire culture of Hip Hop. God Bless Your Journey.

---Kenyatta Griggs #hiphopmotivation

Culture Vulture Chapters:

What Is a Culture Vulture? 9
Intro Damon Dash 17
Intro Kenyatta Griggs 23

1st Section: Reasonable Clout 27

Chapter 1. Reasonable Doubt Reflection. 29
Chapter 2. We Played Our Position (All Jay Had To Do Was Rap). . . . 37
Chapter 3. Lee Daniels Was Being Flagrant 45
Chapter 4. People That Cheat To Win 51
Chapter 5. Spiritual Business 57

2nd Section: Business Elevator. 65

Chapter 6. Suitable Lawsuits. 67
Chapter 7. Secure Business Insecurity 71
Chapter 8. Business Objective 77
Chapter 9. Culture Parasite 81
Chapter 10. Elevator Incident (Jay Z & Solange). 85
Chapter 11. Closet Racism. 91
Chapter 12. Black Business Dysfunction. 95

3rd Section: Radioactivity 101

Chapter 13. Funkmaster Flex 103
Chapter 14. Ebro. 109
Chapter 15. Is Dame Broke?. 115
Chapter 16. Definition Of A Man 123
Chapter 17. Rules To The Game 129

4th Section: Independent Cheese With Corporate Crackers 135

Chapter 18. Crackers With Cheese 137
Chapter 19. Weed, DMX, Hollywood, The Devil 143
Chapter 20. I Taught Jay Z & Kanye Self Sufficiency 153
Chapter 21. Politics As Usual. 163
Chapter 22. Corporate Options. 165
Chapter 23. Beach Chair Life 169

Chapter 24. Can't Knock The Blueprint 173
Chapter 25. Shame In The Game 179
Chapter 26. Friend Or Foe 185
Chapter 27. On To The Next One (The Octopus) 189
Chapter 28. The 360 Deal 193
Chapter 28. I'm A Businessman 197

5th Section: Online Business Health 203

Chapter 29. Tortious Interference & O.D.B. Lawsuit 205
Chapter 30. Being A Diabetic 211
Chapter 31. Aaliyah 217
Chapter 32. Internet Hustle 223
Chapter 33. Web Currency 229
Chapter 34. Culture Disrespect 237
Chapter 35. Warren Buffet 247

6th Section: A Friendly Game Of Life............... 255

Chapter 36. Culture Embarrassment 257
Chapter 37. Big Pimpin Apology 265
Chapter 38. Tupac (B.I.G.) 271
Chapter 39. Black Distributors? 275
Chapter 40. God & Religion 279
Chapter 41. The Fashion Game 285
Chapter 42. The Film Game 293
Chapter 43. Digital Benefits 301
Chapter 44. The Investment Game 305

Bonus Photo Gallery............................... 312

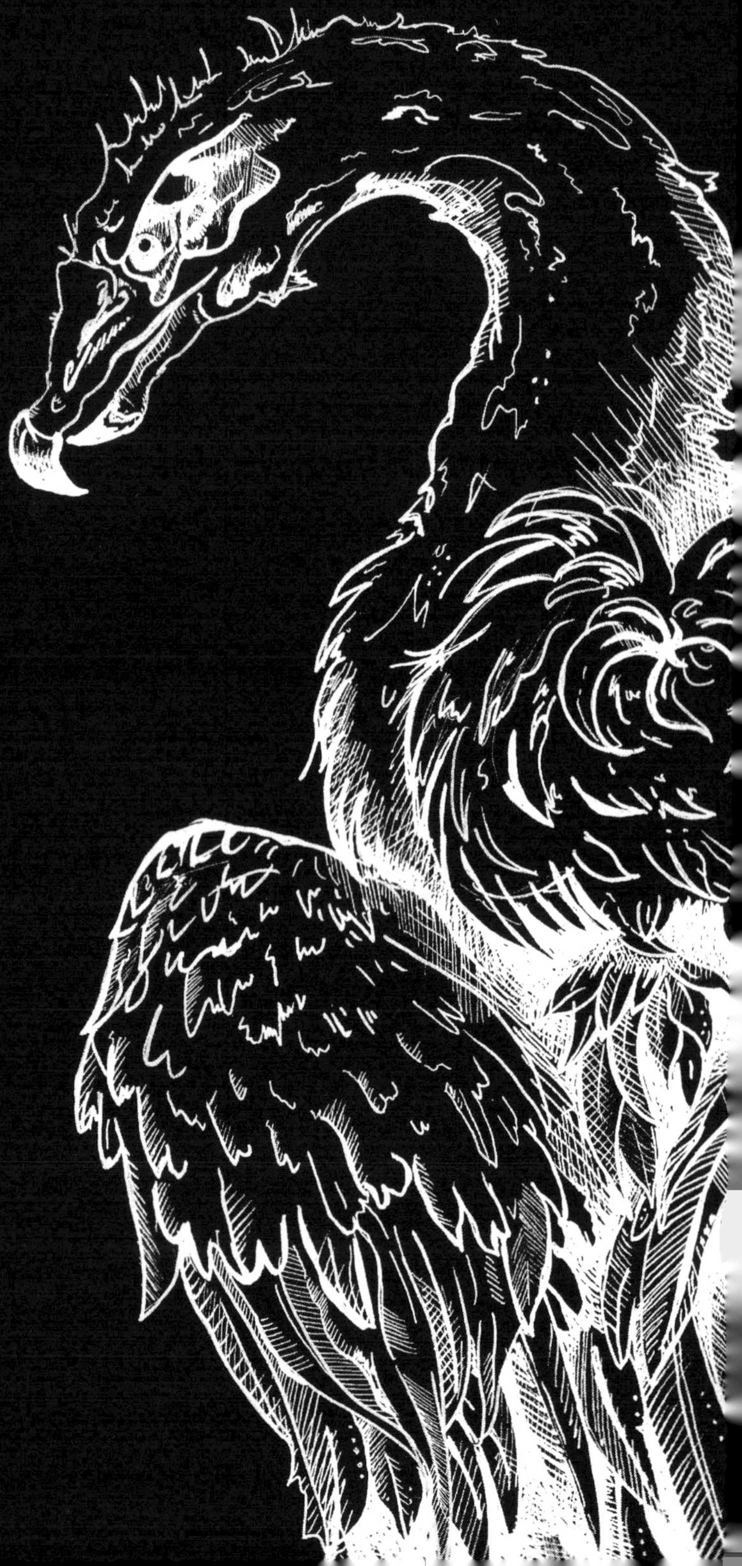

WHAT'S A CULTURE VULTURE?

You may be asking yourself, "What's a **Culture Vulture**?" A **Culture Vulture** isn't about skin color or race; it's about a person's state of mind and whether or not they live by the honor code. A **Culture Vulture** is someone who will exploit a life and culture they don't abide by, making money from it, while completely disrespecting it. It would be like a black man who's Christian making money off of the Jewish culture, and having one Jewish person fighting another Jewish person while that black man sits back and monetizes the situation without ever giving advice to the Jewish culture on how to respectfully further themselves and their community. If that were the case then that black man unapologetically would be defined as a **Culture Vulture**.

What I've witnessed is people of different races inside the culture of Hip Hop cheating to win like the black **Culture Vulture** Steve Stoute, and white **Culture Vultures** like Lyor Cohen. When I bring up certain people and label them as **Culture Vultures**, it's because of my personal experiences with them. I'm not saying that because it's a conspiracy or I assume something I don't know. This book is based on my personal experiences. For instance, the reason I call Lyor a **Culture Vulture** is because I've witnessed him make money from my culture while monetizing beefs without ever squashing them. Plus, he was the one who ended Rocafella. He gave Jay a choice saying, listen if you want to continue Rocafella without Dame and Biggs, I'll support you. I'm not saying that takes the blame away from the other parties involved, but I believe that if that option wasn't given then it wouldn't have ended the way it did. I've also heard similar stories from other people who have worked with him.

The reason why I called people like Charlie Walk and Alan Grunblatt **Culture Vultures** was because they took my idea and then went behind my back and made money off of someone from my culture. I had an idea and I shared it with them; it was about incubating an artist before taking him to a major label. The problem is that when you sign artists, they get an advance and that means that they won't make any money for two or three years because it takes that long to put out a record. So, for a major company if they don't get their money back, it becomes a loss at the end of the fiscal year. My idea was to incubate an artist because I don't really like to work with an artist after they've blown up; instead, I like the art of creating an artist and discovering the potential that others don't see. This means that I would film all of the videos and anything else that needs to be done, and when they're ready to hit the world stage, I would turn things up and release their music out through a major label. I was going to incubate artists through Koch. When I told Alan Grunblatt about that idea, he said he was unsuccessful in getting a meeting with Charlie Walk because he was trying to do the same thing. I told him that I'd get all of us in the same room for a meeting. So, I put Alan in the room with Charlie Walk, who, at the time, was the head of Epic, and we all spoke about doing it. They, then, went behind my back and executed my idea with Sean Kingston and Alan Grunblatt got paid over a million.

The reason I call Joie "Joey I.E." Manda and Todd Moscovitz **Culture Vultures** is because of their actions when Jim Jones had a beef with Max B. Joey I.E. gave Max B's camp my number without asking me, and not caring about the calamity of the situation that two people from the culture could've had. When he gave them my number, he told them he would give them money if they could get Max B off of Jim's label. For someone who doesn't have the best financial situation, they'll do anything to get that chip by any means necessary. So, instead of them sitting two black men down in a room to try and squash it and work things out, they put money on Jim's head, and that's really what they did. Things went down that got resolved, at least on my part because I didn't have anything to do with that, but if I wasn't a gentleman someone could've got killed; shit is real out there. I felt like, "Damn you're both trying to make money off my culture even if someone dies, even if somebody gets hurt!" No excuses—they knew how serious that situation was at the time. Joey I.E. and Todd Moscovitz are also who came between Currensy and I. See, the chances of someone getting hurt is always higher in the presence of any **Culture Vulture's** selfish mentality.

I call Steve Stoute a **Culture Vulture** because I've watched him talk about the people he worked with when they weren't doing well and all he would care about was making money off of them even if that meant a black person doing an ad for a company that waves a Confederate Flag. He's also the only man in the music business I've ever put my hands on because he ass bet me; he didn't pay the bet he lost. We all witnessed him tell on Puff and try to put Puff's bodyguard in jail so he could get a check after he got cracked in the head with a champagne bottle, and then advised Lance "UN" Rivera to use the same lawyer he used to sue Puff, and facilitating it for him when Jay got in that situation. The cloth I'm cut from labels him both a snitch and a **Culture Vulture**. It was crazy because he would be sitting around trying to chill with us. Steve Stoute is also the guy who, when we were initially going to do the Rocafella deal with Interscope, he told Jimmy Iovine not to mess with us, soon after that the Firm ended up there. Again, from my own experience, I've watched him do things like tell us all of LL Cool J, Will Smith, and Nas' business when it didn't appear that they were doing so well and he couldn't make money anymore off of them. I've also seen him compromise the brands of credible black artists by doing deals for them to sell fried chicken and put their full name on a twenty-dollar sneaker just so he could get a check. Steve Stoute, like other **Culture Vultures**, never liked the fact that I would always look out for the best interest of the artists by educating them. See, a **Culture Vulture** always wants the artists and everyone around them ignorant so they can manipulate them for their own selfish gain. This is not a conspiracy theory; this is based on my personal experiences. It's not based on what I've heard; instead, it's based on what I've witnessed.

Barry Klarberg, another **Culture Vulture**, was my accountant. He would tell me his other clients' business, then use my name to get other clients by telling them he worked for me. The IRS made me aware that he took a million dollars out of my account without telling me when we did the Rocawear deal, and he didn't pay my taxes when he told me he did, and he got paid two hundred and fifty thousand dollars that year for his services, which in my mind seems as if he jammed me up on purpose, pause. When I did the Rocawear deal, five million of the deal was in the form of a note, which was to be paid out over a period of time, and I told him I would only do the deal if I could immediately sell the note because I needed the cash for the Rachel Roy business. Barry Klarberg told me he sold the note so I would take the deal, come to find out he didn't sell the note, and to add insult to injury it was unsecure so when I did sell the note I had to sell it for half, which means my five million turned into two point five. He told me he was paying my taxes, and he didn't. I basically paid that **Culture Vulture** two hundred and fifty thousand dollars to thoroughly rob me so, I can only imagine his robbery tactics with other people. What's crazy is I personally know people in the industry from my culture that he's robbed, and he's still running around robbing people.

From my perspective, I always have to put my culture first. If someone did something bad to me, I feel like it's my obligation to warn my culture so those same Vultures can't continue to rob my culture. The thing that's crazy is that there are people from my culture who, when they talk to me, are conscious of what's going on, and they'll pretend like they're not with that but when they get a chance to talk to a **Culture Vulture**, who has even robbed them before, they never use their platform to question their validity. The right questions are never asked in front of **Culture Vultures**, but when they're interviewing me, they seem to get very militant; yet, they turn subservient when I'm not in the room, especially when a **Culture Vulture** is present, and they know who they are.

I feel that as a culture when you get to a certain point, it's your responsibility to warn other people so they don't have to get hurt, and stifled like you did. This is why I had to have more patience and move a little slower in order to achieve my goals. But because of these **Culture Vultures**, I've learned to make money off of myself because I can't depend on somebody's loyalty. From my own experience, I've learned that if I invest in somebody and they arrive at where they wanted to go, I know they're not going to want to have to pay me anymore. They're going to do things on their own. That's why there is no more Rocafella, but there is a Jay Z because Jay Z wanted Jay Z to be the brand and not Rocafella, and again, as you see, there is no more Rocafella. Every artist does that because they unconsciously only think about themselves before the bigger picture. For that reason, for the last ten years, I've created my own brands without the stress of disloyalty; I've created my own liquor Dusko, and brought it to the market place; I've created my own streaming service Dame Dash Studios, and brought it to the market place; I've directed and paid for my own movies like Loisadas and Too Honorable, and brought them to the market place; I've created my own fashion company Poppington, and brought it to the market place—from my point of view—with absolutely nothing to do with Rocafella. I did it my way because I'll never be disloyal to myself. The only person who can betray me is myself, and I think that's the way any real man would want to move. And, in that respect, I can also give the people who are cut from the same cloth a platform.

If I'm broke as they say I am then being broke never looked this good; it doesn't look bad to me. Throughout my journey, there have been a lot of different views from a lot of different places, but the blessings of my lifestyle have always been consistent and I'm thankful for that. See, the thing I want the people of the culture to understand is that you don't need them to live a certain life. Look at me; I don't have to go outside everyday to live a certain way, and I'm doing it independently. I'm able to raise my children instead of being outside pretending to be something I'm not and coming home unhappy. What's important to me is raising my children, picking them up from school, eating dinner with my woman, and if I am going to invest in something, I'm going to invest in somebody I love. I'll invest in my woman; I'll invest in my kids; and I'll invest in my real friends. It's my choice. That's what this book is about; it's about doing things independently if you have the confidence. Real independence is the freedom to choose your struggle, and understanding what freedom is and what real wealth is. I lead by example so I'm not going to tell you about this or that; I'm going to show you how I choose my struggle every time I start a new business. My life for the culture is like the movie: "The Truman Show." You'll get to see what it is to be an independent; you'll see what it is to grow a brand; and you'll see what it is to not be favored by the press and still have more than everyone else ten years later.

Since I didn't need them, you don't need them. Instead, invest in yourself, fuck them, don't be scared of them, and when you get in a room with them, question them to protect yourself, period. Again, in conclusion, a **Culture Vulture** can be black or white. It's the people who exploit other cultures and make money from them when they can't make money off of their own culture, not giving back, and robbing people like robbing a child because he doesn't know any better. The interesting thing is that the people who were in the game ten years ago could tell you exactly who robbed them, but they're still scared to do so. I've never feared them, which is why I'll never sit back and watch my culture get exploited. I'm going to warn my culture by any means necessary, and I think it's everyone's responsibility, but everyone isn't built for that. So, until then, I'll continue to play in my backyard, raise my children, play with my dogs, make my clothes, drink my liquor, and hang out with my friends and if you don't like it, turn the channel.

Damon Dash
G5 Headquarters
Las Vagas, NV
3:41pm

Damon Dash
PCH
Malibu, Ca
6:57pm

LIFE AFTER CORPORATE WEALTH

"My rule of thumb is to don't smoke until you make your first million."
- Damon Dash

When I was growing up, my only fear was losing my mother, so when she passed, I was devastated. From that moment on, I went into a fearless zone. I became unafraid to live life to the fullest, especially since I didn't have the security of my mother to fall back on if something went wrong. If I didn't have money, I always knew that my mother would take care of me, so not having that crutch to lean on was when I became a pure Cake-Aholic.

Everything that I am is because of my mother. Independence was very important to her; she never relied on anyone for anything. I've always seen my mother take nothing and turn it into something. She always made sure I saw the world, and because of her I went to private school, as well as boarding school. I never graduated, but I eventually got my G.E.D. I've always read a lot and stayed fluent in math with or without school. Reading is important, writing is important, and just being able to add and multiply is important.

To all of the dropouts that might be reading this book, getting your G.E.D. isn't a bad move. It's actually a good way to continue finishing anything that you've started, which is a major plus in accomplishing further goals. But, I also didn't go to school for fashion, making movies, or music. I've directed movies and I'm not gonna lie, at times, when I think about it, it's crazy for me to believe that I'm actually directing because I didn't go to film school. I'm not trying to push that education isn't important by saying all of this because my belief is that school plus street knowledge is the ideal way to come up, but for me, experience was always my best teacher. So, if you don't know what you wanna do I think it's best to go to school until you find out what it is you wanna become, and when you do find out what that is, my advice is that you have to go out and live it.

To me, none of this was brain surgery. I'm from 142nd street and Lennox. I've been getting money my whole life, which is what made me confident in business. When I was fifteen, I had rope chains, and a Max (Maxima). I have an air of arrogance because I've accomplished things on a street as well as business level that most people couldn't. It's not that they can't; a lot of people just don't have enough guts to go out and make moves that lead to success, and from my perspective that would be the only thing that's holding anyone back from accomplishing any dream.

My objective wasn't just to be a rich kid from Harlem, but to take over the world. I knew all of my life that I was going to be rich. I didn't know how I was going to make my money; I just knew there would be opportunities that I would capitalize on. What I started to do was draw my ideas out in storyboard form to help me visualize, and that was even before I understood the power of imagination. I definitely believe that if you can't visualize something, it won't become a reality for you. For me, I've always imagined my desires in full detail to keep me aligned with what I was working towards. So, I guess you can say that because I focused my attention on where I wanted to go, things began to happen, and from a scientific level, the universe responded to my movement.

Before Biggs, Jay Z, and myself created Roc-A-Fella records, we used to go out and look at real estate that, at the time, we knew we couldn't afford—houses, apartments, and other stuff. We did this just so we would be savvy in the market place when we finally could afford it. Since I've always had a strong belief in my abilities as a hustler, I honestly never believed that anything I ever went and looked at that I couldn't eventually afford it. Whether it was houses, cars, or jewelry, once I find out what something costs, I've always figured out a way to get it if I really wanted it. I'm a firm believer in calculated movement, so I never make moves without first doing my homework, which is research.

Research can stop you from becoming overwhelmed, which usually leads to giving up. This rule applies to everything. Research helps you to measure what it'll take to make things happen. Whether you're working a nine-to-five or hustling in the streets, it's important for everyone looking to come up to at least dedicate an hour a day towards advancement. Yeah, I know a lot people will think, "Well that's easy for him to say, he already has money." That's true, but the same way I came up would be the same way I would tell someone working a full time job to come up. That would be to make your goals a part time job that requires only an hour or more of concentration each day to turn your dreams into a full time lifestyle.

I call it "lifestyle" because I don't like to use the word "job." To me, it's not fun. The word job is one of the wackest words in the dictionary, and to have fun is the secret behind all of my success. I'm speaking from experience. This is why I only build businesses that I love. I love to play drinking games with my friends, so I went into the Vodka business. I love looking fresh to def, so I created Roca-Wear. And as you saw, I loved Hip Hop, so I went into business with my friends by creating Roc-A-Fella Records. The excitement of the journey is what I'm into and it's the reason I've always found my way back to success; I stay on the path of what I love to do.

What I did before I can't do now; that's an old business model. When I launched Roc-A-Fella records, I was in my twenties. Now I'm in my forties. I'm a totally different person now. When I was in my twenties, I wanted everybody to know I was rich. I was insecure. At this point in my life, I'm comfortable being behind the scenes, all cash and carry. People always ask me what happened between Jay Z and me as if there was some sort of beef that broke us apart. Before I would never answer that question to add interest to intrigue, but now it's time to come clean. All we did was create a company together. We sold it; he went corporate, and I decided to stay independent. There was no beef.

I'm proud of Jay Z's success as well as Kanye's success. Inside I feel like I had something to do with their success. I don't have anything but positive things to say because what Jay wanted to become, he became, and what Kanye wanted to become, he became. I have a love for doing business and seeing my old friends successful is a piece of my enthusiasm. I never wanted a boss, and if I did have a boss, he would have to pay me like I was a boss. So I had to create an opportunity for myself that would allow me to control my environment. That's why I choose independence.

Being a successful independent businessman, I'm usually asked how I turned Roc-A-Fella into a success. My response is that I made it a brand that stood for something. We were known for aspirational living, getting money, and having the best. Being that the brand defines the company, the minute that any one of those standards were compromised Roc-A-Fella went down because if you sell something to the consumer, it has to be real. If you're known for being a nerd and the consumer buys into it, the minute you're not a nerd, they may stop checking for you. If you're known for being thorough, the minute you're not thorough the consumers may turn their back on you because the psychology of the consumer is to buy into a brand's consistency. Just think about it for yourself: how many times have you went into a restaurant that you frequent only to find out they not only changed the menu but the flavor of the food. What does that do? It makes you search elsewhere to eat. It's the same thing in business. To upgrade is good as long as you're upgrading an existing brand for the better.

Your company is as good as the people you surround yourself with. Where I'm at right now in business I don't feel like the smartest person in the room, so I surround myself with capable people who have vision as well. When I had Roc-A-Fella Records, I used to get so frustrated with people who didn't get my vision, or those who were trying to exploit the culture of Hip Hop that I would find myself fighting and arguing for position all the time. But now, at this point in my life, I'm at peace. I only surround myself with like-minded individuals.

It's true that I love all types of money: I love the yen; I love the euro; I love the frank; pause, and I love the dollar. Since I love different types of currency, I have to be in different places to do business. At times, I do feel like I spread myself too thin, but it's what I've asked for. I made a decision to be a businessman so I have to live it to the fullest. My nature is optimistic. I can sell anything. I breathe, eat, and shit money. I know it sounds cocky, but it's real. It's that type of realness that a person has to have to in order to navigate their movement towards doing and accomplishing whatever they want. Period.

I remember when I first got into the music game; I would see cats popping champagne and I knew they didn't put in half the energy and time that I put in. From seeing that I knew I had to get this money. That's why I got my friends together and began doing business through our love of Hip Hop. My aim was and still is to build a team of friends and create wealth. My belief is that I have to be able kick it with you to do business with you. I couldn't imagine surrounding myself everyday with people I don't like. To me, at that point, creativity becomes limited.

As you've seen, when it comes to the press about Dame Dash, it's usually full of doubt. So, to me I have to be good at what I do. I'm a very competitive person. But, in the process of being competitive, I don't take anything for granted. I still appreciate the little things in life from a chauffeur opening a door to flying on a private jet, especially when it comes to my family. It doesn't really matter what the press and other people think about me. As long as my family is cool with me being who I am that's what's important to me. As long as I'm breathing, I'll always be independent and hungry for more. Which is why I'm still making moves today. I can't stop. What else can I say? I'm addicted to business. I love getting money.

Kenyatta Griggs
PCH
Malibu, CA
10:34pm

THE BIRTH OF CULTURE VULTURES

"All of us are self made. But only the successful will admit it."
- Earl Nightingale

As a barber on Crenshaw Boulevard in Los Angeles, I've always been interested in what it takes to become successful and maintain a certain lifestyle. So, through my clientele, I've done my own census over the span of twenty years. The conversations and data that I've collected over those years would make any clinical psychologist envious of the work I've done. What started out as light conversations over a haircut allowed me to enter the lifestyle of each client, low-key turned into an obsession which transformed me into a "Student of Nature." As I became Nature's student, I received infinite messages not only from people who were doing well, but also from people in all forms of life. From peeping game on how an ant gathers food for the winter to how a crack head chases his high by any means necessary, I gained knowledge. Regardless of what presents itself, I'm checking out the scene to learn something valuable in all situations. Word up!

So, "What does it take to become successful?" What's interesting is that one question always has different answers, but many find that success has everything to do with what side of the financial ladder a person is on. For instance, when I asked my homeboy, Tone, who happens to be a successful street pharmacist, he said, "On the real, my success comes from how hard I hustle, by staying on my grind, and never tricking my money on bullshit." Then when I asked my folks, Dr. D, who happens to be a medical doctor with his own successful herbal supplement company on the side he said, "My success has everything to do with how many people I help. I've learned that helping people is the one and only answer that defines true success." I agree; helping people, of course, is an obvious mission when it comes to the amount of money we expect to accumulate. But is that the one and only answer of what constitutes success? Think about it, first overlook the morality of Tone's illegal street hustle, and process that information without judgment for a second: isn't Tone in the service business as well? I mean the only difference is that Dr. D has a legal practice that serves patients in a hospital, and Tone has an illegal practice that serves fiends in the street. So, just service couldn't be the answer to continued success because just recently Tone got locked up on drug trafficking charges. There has to be more to coming up than providing a service. I later found out from studying a wide variety of people who have achieved success on different levels that there is a common component that lies in the hearts of the successful in comparison to the "minds" of the unsuccessful. The answer is love. A love for what they are channeling to the world. I say channeling because all creativity is God, and each individual is capable of being used to translate this unique creativity.

Midway into my career as a barber, I began to build a strong clientele of entrepreneurs including entertainers. Without name-dropping, I must say I've had one hell of a career working for people on stage, on screen, and executives behind the scenes. What I've witnessed was that whether someone was the star or the person behind the scenes, their success had everything to do with the amount of love they had for what they were doing. That being the case, one of my favorite clients and favorite people, Dame Dash became one of my main "Barber Client" case studies. I first started documenting Dame back in 2004 after I created an audio book called Think and Ballout where I recorded a twenty-minute interview with him called The Secret To Ballin. From there, I started recording and documenting everything going on with him over the next ten years. Every time I went to cut his hair, I was either jotting down notes, recording, or filming an interview with him. Even when he was back in New York, I would call him to check in, especially when I heard about news like him being broke, his divorce, and court battles with his son's mother. Besides loving the business he conducts, the one thing that I did gather from Dame was his reaction as well as his approach to "ups" as well as his "so-called downs." He remains above the pendulum swing of life by remaining happy no matter what's going on, so to me he always appeared to be one of my richest clients. If not financially, then it would have to be the richest in spirit, which at the end of the day happens to be the most important wealth anyway.

After years of documenting so much of Dame's life, The Hip Hop Motivation Team, including myself, decided to continue filming Dame. This time we edited the conversations into YouTube videos since we didn't have anything on our own YouTube channel or website. It just so happened that his ex-wife, Rachel Roy was in the news due to an altercation between Jay Z and Beyonce's sister, Solange. We got a lot of attention from our video where we asked Dame for his opinion on what happened, but mainly it was due to the various media outlets putting that video on their sites. At the time, we were using my boy Shonathen, who's the director of our film The Secret To Ballin, to capture the first interviews at Dame's crib in Malibu. My partner in Hip Hop Motivation, Carolyn, was at work during the time we had to capture that footage, so we did what we had to do. From there, Carolyn, my girl Michelle, who is on lighting and audio, and myself handled everything from that point on in order to put the videos up weekly. The music is the product of my other partner who lives in New York, John "Lil Sci" Robinson, and his brother, ID4Windz, who creates all the music that you hear during the interviews. Then you have the Hip Hop Motivation Logo and The Secret To Ballin billing block that was created by Kirk "K-Double" Webber. It has been viewed today over three million times according to YouTube's analytics, all thanks to the fans that support our Hip Hop Motivation movement.

I pray that this book will enlighten you, the reader, into tapping into your true independent potential. In spite of what you might have heard about yourself, each one of us was born a winner because out of the millions that competed marathon-style to reach our mother's egg, we were the ones that made it, which makes us natural born winners birthed unto a rich father with infinite lineage. I'm not talking about our physical father; I'm talking about the source that some of us call "The Heavenly Father." We're the spiritual descendants of the richest and most abundant force in the universe which makes it our birthright, as vessels of the most high, to "Know" if we seek and to "Teach" when we speak. This is why Hip Hop Motivation, as a whole, is a vessel that will continue to channel forth information that can possibly wake up the greatness that is within all of us. Don't sleep. Like light bulbs, we illuminate different degrees of power that's connected to the same generator of infinite power, and as you read this book, you will see that Damon Dash is also one example of God's expression whose opinions are both right and wrong, at the same time because there is no absolute right as there is no absolute wrong; being that truth and falsehood are mere degrees of the same source, which is God.

Each individual expression of God plays a dynamic role within the body of the universe, similar to the role that each organ plays inside the fine tuned engine of the human anatomy. So, even if you don't agree with what you read in this manuscript, it will at least open the door to a polarity of dialogue that can raise awareness in one way or another. The culture of Hip Hop is a spiritual tool that over the years has been used to uplift as well as confuse. It's a culture that has circulated love at times and sometimes hate, but my love for the culture is the spark that ignites this movement to help the people that, by design, were led to stay in the dark. So, from The Hip Hop Motivation Team including myself, we appreciate your purchase of this book and your continued support. God bless your movement.

SECTION 1
REASONABLE CLOUT

Biggs, Jay, Dame
New York, NY
2:59pm

REASONABLE DOUBT REFLECTION

The Hip Hop Motivation team and myself started off with the idea of doing more of a biography on Dame called Reasonable Clout. As we kept interviewing him to compile that book, we thought it would be a wise move to give the culture more than a braggadocios reflection of a man that has affected pop culture on so many levels with the artists and the movies he's submitted to the world stage. So, instead we decided to create an independent business memoiré on Dame, someone who's kept his integrity without selling out the culture through the corporate demands to kill his independence, which now spans over twenty years strong. The questions that started our collection of work for Reasonable Clout started with a series of interviews that we felt should focus more on his first major accomplishment in the music business, and of course that's creating a lane that put Jay Z in the game.

When we arrived at his house on Venice Beach we were greeted by a few friends of his, Dusko the Dog, and his girl slash business partner Raquel Horn. After we set up on the third floor of his luxury home, he came upstairs, sat on the couch ready, and laid the first stone of what is now known as

"Culture Vultures" the book. Without hesitation, I asked him what album or songs would best represent the beginning of his career in the music business? He paused for a second then broke it down.

The albums that reflected exactly what I was going through in the beginning of my career would have to be Reasonable Doubt, The Blueprint, and the BlakRoc album. The BlakRoc project was "ILL" because that solidified me on the Rock and Roll side. I caught that lick; I needed that feather in my cap bad, and The Black Keys gave me that. That made me legit in another way, like if my career consisted only of BlakRoc I would be good. The reasons for doing the BlakRoc album and the way that we did it was dope, at least for me; it was very gratifying. But, Reasonable Doubt, I would have to say, was a very authentic reflection of what was going on in our lives including our perspective of how we approached things. What's crazy is I still get asked all the time if I have any of the music that didn't make the final version of Reasonable Doubt. We made a lot of music, some real "ILL" shit. Clark Kent should have all the demos. The stuff that didn't get released was dope. I mean what else would you expect? It was Ski on production and Jay rapping. All that shit is on DAT's, but Clark should have them, that dude still got his Pelle's and all his sneakers from back in the day so he should have those Jay Z DAT's. All the demos were "ILL." We made a lot of demos. That's one thing—we made a lot of records. That shit wasn't given to us. We earned that spot; we took that shit. We wore it out and didn't stop for ten years straight, and the pivotal point in that ten was when we made the movie Streets Is Watching. We made Streets Is Watching because we clowned out in the Sunshine video, and people were laughing at us. On the real, that almost fucked our whole shit up. So, we had to double back, and do the B-sides, on some gangsta shit. Since Def Jam didn't want to be our partners in it, we did it ourselves, putting up our own money. It took back off, and of course Def Jam jumped right back on it. I was leaving Def Jam at the time by buying my way out of our partnership. A record company's strategy is to always keep you in debt.

I remember we would get in arguments when I would owe them three million, and I'd be like, "That's alright, I don't give a fuck. I'll get that three million back."

My thing was to have enough money to buy out whoever was putting up the money at any second. Like I've loaned people money to be my partner because I want them to do something that I don't want to do every day. I'll be like, "Let me put you in business. I need this partnership." All of my partnerships are strategic—if I have any. They were put in to do something that I'm not good at, or to do something I don't enjoy doing. You have to realize when you want your brand to make money, or when you want it to showcase coolness, certain partnership strategies can uplift the brand. Like, some brands I have are only there to showcase coolness like Poppington, and my art galleries. I'm not trying to make any money from an art gallery. At some point, I probably will, and I'll incubate some art, which takes a lot of patience, but for right now, the art galleries are there to showcase how cool I am. As you see, Hip Hop is into art now. I've been having art galleries all over the world for the last four or five years. I think it's a good thing; I like to sophisticate my culture. I feel like it's my job to implement a little taste here and there. My business model is to collect art when an artist is brand new. Like, to me if you buy an artist's work when he's full-blown, you're a Johnny because you're paying full price for it. It's better to discover an artist before you pay full price. You'll get it cheap and then when he blows up, something you paid a thousand dollars for is now worth maybe twenty million. I'm not a Johnny; I don't need to buy it after everybody else bought it says it's cool. I want to make it cool, so that takes longer, but I have galleries all over the world, but I don't do it for money. Anything that comes under the Poppington name, I don't do it for dough. I don't even want people to buy my clothes. In order for men to buy Poppington clothes, they have to buy a piece of art, and then you can spend some money on the brand because I really don't want to walk in a room and a dude has on the same clothes as me or he has my name on his body, but women they can all wear my stuff. I'm a definitely let that go. For the men, I have to give it to you, or you have to buy some art to pay these crazy prices for what I'm making out of my closet; again, if I don't make a dollar that's not what it's for. It's never about the money, ever. I don't do anything for money.

With Reasonable Doubt, we were monetizing our lifestyle; that's what was going on. We weren't compromising, we were just talking about what we were doing, and our perspective on life at the time, our mentality, and it just so happened there were people that had the same exact mentality, and that's why they could relate, and we were able to go on a stage and perform it all around the country, and people were able to see it, and know it's real, so they believed in it. That's what I'm saying: our foundation wasn't given to us. We did hand-to-hand all around the planet and never stopped. You just keep doing the same thing. The same circuit and it gets bigger and bigger and you just have to be consistent, and the work has to be consistent, and then you'll have fans. Everyone starts with none. That's how it happens with anything; you have to prove yourself as a brand. After ten years of doing anything consistently, you're gonna be the man, and if you don't stay consistent you're retarded, no disrespect.

Gems:

Nothing is given to you. You have to earn your spot through hard work.

All partnerships should be strategic. You will always need to network with people who are good at things that you're not good at.

When you start helping people achieve their dreams, you will manifest the things you've imagined coming true.

Value taste over the amount of money you can make from your brand. The coolness of your brand will outlive all get rich-quick brands.

Initially, in building a brand, it's never about the money you can make. For quick money, think profit, and for brand, longevity think quality.

In business, you shouldn't do anything just for money. Instead, sell a certain lifestyle and never compromise your brand by not keeping it real at all cost.

A brand's consistency provides consumer comfort. Consumer comfort is something that attracts fans to your work after you prove yourself as a brand over and over and over again.

If you keep working on your brand for five to ten years straight you will one day enjoy the fruits of your labor.

Pat Carney, Dan Auerbach, Damon Dash
Williamsburg, NY
3:47pm

Mos Def, Dan Auerbach
Williamsburg, NY
5:33pm

Q-Tip, Damon Dash
Williamsburg, NY
1:03pm

Dan Auerbach, RZA
Lower East Side, NY
10:39pm

Dame, Jay, Biggs
Johns Street Office
New York, NY
5:01pm

WE PLAYED OUR POSITION (ALL JAY HAD TO DO WAS RAP)

From my own observation, all of Dame's business ventures seemed to run smooth. But just like any entrepreneur, ups and downs are a normal part of the business. The only difference is that some people focus on the problem while others look beyond the problem for the solution. I asked him about some of the obstacles he faced while building his career.

One of the greatest rules that I live by is to never give power to anything outside of myself. I don't focus on obstacles, to me there's no such thing. I mean at twenty years old, what obstacle is there when you're living your dreams? I was so successful in my twenties that there could never be any obstacles. Like, just being able to pay my bills at that age was a big deal. There's no losing when you're trying to come up. At twenty-five, I was running a five hundred million dollar company and it's something that was independently funded. Even right now, there's no obstacle in what I'm doing. Business means problems; that's what business means. There is no business without problems. If there's a business without problems, it's not a business, and it's

definitely not a successful business.

A boss' job is to fix problems, and untie knots, while staying calm in pressure situations. To me that's the difference between a good boss and a bad boss. Then it's all about who works the hardest, who stays the coolest, and who can strategically fix any problem while making sure that the people around them are confident even when problems exist. Being a great boss is also connected to consistency and who makes the most profit. That also describes the best business.

Looking back at what allowed us to obtain major success at such a young age was the fact that we all had different roles where each one of us played our position well. I mean all Jay had to do is rap; that's all I needed him to do. When it came to drawing up plays and running the day to day at Roc-A-Fella that was my responsibility. All Biggs had to do was keep telling us about the "flyest" shit in the streets. He gave us that taste level, so we all played our position. It was my job to hustle hard and that's it, and to not let anybody in the room out hustle me. Period. I always killed the food I ate in front of my crew, so they could also learn how to eat the food they kill. My job was to lead by example. I'm never going to send somebody to do something that I wouldn't do myself. I'm frontline right with you and that's what it's supposed to be, that's that. In a funny way I guess I motivated them but where I'm at now I feel like if I gotta motivate you too much then I don't need to be dealing with you. If you're a partner I'll coach you and if that doesn't work I'll use my own scare tactics. I'm from the streets, where you make examples outta people. In the streets that's detrimental towards survival whether it be jail, getting robbed, or killed, when you come from hustling on the block you can't show any signs of weakness because if you do someone will run off with your work, so you gotta stay strong and handle things accordingly no matter what.

So, from that mentality into the business world I had to change my method of scare tactics by doing the next best thing by embarrassing the shit out of you by laughing them out. Which was really what most people are more afraid of when they deal with me. My method was never violence, or that I was going to come in kicking ass, it was that I was just going to laugh at you until you felt like shit, until you needed a therapist. I would laugh at them in front of whoever thought they were cool, and that's what people feared the most when it came to me. It wasn't anything about violence; it was only laughter. So, like I said, one of my main tactics is laughter, and then once in a while, when I start losing money, that's when I use the yelling tactic to instill fear, and that's usually a move I make when I can't fire you. Sometimes you have to scare people into doing the right thing especially when you're putting up the money or representing the people putting up the money, which is another place where all my over-compensating was coming from. Anytime you would see me yelling, I was yelling because I wasn't putting up the money. When you're putting up the money, you don't have to yell about anything. What you say goes because you put up the money. If someone tells me they don't wanna do it my way I politely tell them they're fired. That's it, and it's not even gonna fuck my day up, but if somebody else is in control, and I have to solicit it, and I have to convince them, and it's not even their money that definitely becomes aggravating, especially when that person never put up a dollar of his own money trying to tell me what to do, that's when the fear tactics come in.

The way I used to motivate people that weren't family was fear. Again fear of embarrassment, fear of me punking them, anything to get them to make the moves I needed them to make. That was how I got things done for many years. That style was also a good way to keep the other people that worked for me in line. I couldn't have the people that worked for me watch me being told what to do; a boss doesn't get told what to do. That doesn't happen in my world. A boss doesn't ask. A boss might tell you something out of courtesy, but a boss doesn't have to do anything. He's putting up the dough. Another thing that was always an issue when I had a corporate partner was that they were always trying to approach my staff or belittle me in front of my staff, and I thought that was foul, especially when it was coming from the people who weren't putting up the money, people that were over compensating because they could get fired, acting like they were cool because they had a job. But you can't be cool if you have a job. I don't think having the ability to be fired or laid off is cool. Like, anyone in my staff that works with me always has the ability of being my partner in some way. So it's not like they work for me. They have to pay their bills, and that gives them the opportunity to be creative, and also experience being a boss by monetizing what they do. At that point they get access to all of my resources, so it becomes about their effort or lack of, so I'm never going to just hire people and I'm their boss. We have to be partners in some capacity because I can't have people around me working for me, when I diss people that work for people all day. That would make my crew feel crazy, so they have to have the ability to be my partners in something, and every single person that works with me is my partner in some way shape or form, whether or not they're taking things to a monetizable level or not we have equally create and build something that we equally own together; that's the only way I do things. Like, I had a meeting with someone today, I'm not gonna say their name or who they work for, but they were telling me that they worked for a certain person for like eighteen years, and I was like, "Well, do you own a piece of the company?" And they said, "No." I was like, "Well I know they just sold their company. Did they give you a check when they sold the company?" And they said, "No." That's crazy because I've never sold a company and didn't break the staff off. That's never happened. Go talk to my staff or anyone that's ever worked with me. They'll tell you when I received checks after selling any of my companies I always spread it around; working without owning a piece of the company is nuts.

The sacrifices I had to make as a young entrepreneur, while building my salon, were real. At one point I stopped wasting money on sneakers, clubs, and the dating scene so I could invest every dime back into my shop, but once the money started coming in those were some of the best times of my life. My shoe game got real, and even my dating game was at an all time high. Dame further talked about his best experiences in the music business including the moment he knew things in business were getting real for himself, Jay, and Biggs.

In the beginning of Roc-A-Fella everything that happened was

Reasonable Clout

a good time: a first time in anything positive always feels good. The first time I got a record deal, that shit felt great because I was nineteen years old. The first time I had a record played on the radio was a big deal. Yo, when we won "Battle of the Beats" that was "ILL." The first time we did anything was good. When we used to do "Battle of the Beats," I would have an office full of people calling in. At the time I didn't look at that as cheating because I needed that win. Back then "Battle of the Beats" was a big deal. The first time Flex dropped bombs on our record was a big deal. The first time we heard our record in the tunnel was a big deal. The first time we went gold off a single was a big deal. The first time I sold the company, and got the extension, and then I stuck my middle finger up during the picture, and they were like, "We just cut you a big check, how can you do that?" and I was like, "First of all, you fucking work for Universal, I earned what I just got. You ain't cut nothing. That was based on a formula. You didn't even wanna cut that check." Back then they all felt good, including now, like being on Pitchfork for the first time felt good, and that really felt good because I didn't know what the fuck Pitchfork was until I was on it. Again the first time in anything positive always feels good.

Having a company that's one-hundred-percent independently funded, feels good, that feels really, really good. It feels good right now because I don't have to worry about anyone funding any one of my companies, not one of them, and I got a couple, and it feels really good to be able to survive without compromising my quality of living. But knowing that I'm going from being corporate to being one-hundred-percent independent, consciously making that choice that feels really good. Like, being a real boss, being a real man feels really good. Having balls feels good. Like, having them shits swinging, no disrespect. Having nuts feels good. I don't know how it feels to be nutless. Would you hand over your nuts for twenty million? I know I wouldn't. I've been seeing people give them up, pause, for way less. I used to be like, "Damn, this nigga just gave his nuts up for no reason." Pause." But, back to "First Times" I still pop bottles for everything I accomplish. Every first time is a bottle popping experience, especially now. I'm only looking for first times. I love first times. I love it.

Overall I feel great. I've helped people achieve exactly what I told them they were going to achieve. They're exactly what I told them they were going to be. I was right again. I feel good. I think it's great. I feel like it's a testament to what I do, especially when it comes to Jay and Kanye. That shit is the best feeling in the world because I know that the people I put in business ten years ago are still on top, and it's probably because I haven't been in business in a minute. When I feel like coming back to rap, I will, and it'll probably be someone that'll be on top ten/fifteen years after they started. I created their business models. I developed them. Always keep a good publicist on you, and keep being consistent. Work harder than everybody, be good at what you do, and be an individual. Period. Basically if you keep a full staff of publicists on you at all times you'll stay in the news.

Once seeing and now listening to his journey of how he reached success brings me back to the quote that says, "All of us are self-made. But only the successful will admit it." This means that success is something that's self-bestowed and not some mystery system that falls in the laps of the lazy observer. This is why I'm an absolute believer in consistent effort to achieve all things. Dame further explained why consistency is an important piece to staying on top.

Consistency is everything in business. That's how a brand is defined, and building a brand takes time. You have to keep making moves over, and over, and over again until people feel comfortable with buying your brand. All brands have to stand for something. People have to affiliate what you're selling with something cool. You're a barber; you know what consistency means in the barbershop. You can't give someone a good cut one time and a bad cut another time. When you cook, you can't be a good chef one day and not be good the next. Consistency is important in every aspect of this planet. In your relationships, your demeanor has to stay consistent for comfort. Even for a child, you have to be consistent; children need consistency to one day become consistent adults. Everyone needs consistency on certain levels. It's important to have that kind of balance no matter what. It's the foundation of a balanced life.

Gems:

There's no such thing as a business without problems. A business without problems doesn't exist.

A boss' job is to fix problems and to untie knots while staying calm in pressure situations. This is the difference between a bad business in comparison to a good business.

Successful people are people that work hard, remain calm while fixing problems, and look good while doing it.

A consistent business describes the best business.

A business is like a professional sports team: when each member of the team plays his position that team has a better chance of winning.

If you have to motivate your partners to participate in business then you need to move forward and stop dealing with those partners.

Any person that puts up the money never has to yell about anything. What you say goes when you put up the money.

You'll get a lot further when you carefully choose the right team of partners.

It's very important to keep your integrity in check at all cost.

Anyone can be famous with consistency and a good publicist on deck.

Consistency is the foundation of a balanced life.

Kenyatta Griggs, Damon Dash
Malibu, CA
1:06am

LEE DANIELS IS BEING FLAGRANT

If there's any dissatisfaction in my life I would say it would have to be the fact that I don't have an Oscar. I'm really tight about that. There are only two things that I'll feel a certain way about when I'm judged or scrutinized, and that's in making movies and cooking. That's where I'm insecure; I'm aware of it and that's the reason why I take charge and attack both of them. I'm practicing being completely artistic in my life right now. You have to remember I've made a lot of money off of other people. With Roc-A-Fella I made money off of Jay, Kanye, and the other artists that were with Roc-A-Fella. With Rachel Roy, I make money off her name. There's no Damon Dash clothing line. I'm never getting scrutinized in fashion because I'm not wearing it on my sleeves.

Now, when it comes to directing movies, from a creative perspective, that's what I consistently wanna do. That's why I released the short film Loisaidas on the Internet directed by me, Damon Dash, and now I just finished Too Honorable. If you don't

Honor up filming
Catskill, NY
2:28am

Honor up filming
Catskill, NY
1:17am

Honor up filming
Harlem, NY
9:14pm

Loisaidas filming
Lower East Side, NY
1:07pm

like it, I have to hear about it; if you do like it I have to hear that as well. I have to wear it. So, I'm going to keep making movies until I don't care what people think about them—at that point, I'll know that I'm good. Once I don't care about what people think is when I'll know because right now, I only care what people think when I'm not better than them at what I'm doing. But that's the reason why I have this sort of asshole demeanor; maybe, I have that demeanor because in my mind, I really don't think that anyone is better than me at anything, so in my life I approach everything that way. It's an arrogant thing, but it's worked for me, so unapologetically, it is what it is.

When it comes to directing movies, I'm humble; I can't front like I'm one hundred percent the best, but don't get me wrong, I know I'm better than a lot of people out there doing movies. I don't have a bad resume of films. I made Paid In Full, and I took Kevin Hart off stage and put him in his first movies. That's another thing—if the success of the people that I've helped drove me crazy, I'd be nuts because look at how many people I've done that for, even the people that acted like they forgot like Lee Daniels. For a minute I couldn't even watch his movie The Butler until we talked because he was being a little flagrant about taking care of his debt he owed me. No lie, his success used to mess with me until we got that situation sorted out. As long as he stays successful and makes money, my retribution is guaranteed. I gotta get that two million back. I have to get that back. It's crazy when I think about the amount of people who used the black card on me—and not that you have to because I'll do it anyway—but also the ones that do that, and don't reciprocate is what shocks me the most. It's just crazy how many people are conscious of how we don't stick together culturally as black people and kill their opportunity to follow through. Usually it's the same people that preach, "We need to stick together," when they need something that completely becomes the epitome of a "Culture Vulture," and that's really what's crazy to me. I don't know if it's some sort of blindness or what, but it's aggravating. It's like not being evolved. You have to be really insecure to play dirty when you know the rules of the game. I believe the more someone cheats, the more they must think they can't win. Like, if I cheat on a test, it's because I don't know the answers, right? So, if I'm going to cheat in business, or I'm going to cheat in anything, it has to mean that I don't think I can win honestly, or I don't believe in myself. Someone that completely believes in their own abilities could never move with dishonor and cheat. A real confident, arrogant person always plays fair because they don't have to cheat, "What do I have to cheat for?" I'm not giving anyone the pleasure to spot me 10. Think about it: if you're on a basketball court and somebody says, "I'll spot you 10," you're not going to be happy about that. You'll be like, "Naw, dog, stop that! Zip-Zip." A real competitor doesn't go for that. Even when I'm playing ping-pong and the person I'm playing is on the phone I'll be like, "Naw, stop the game. Don't play me!" I fully live by the honor code.

Gems:

It's very important to always keep your word.

Your word is your bond that binds you to responsibility.

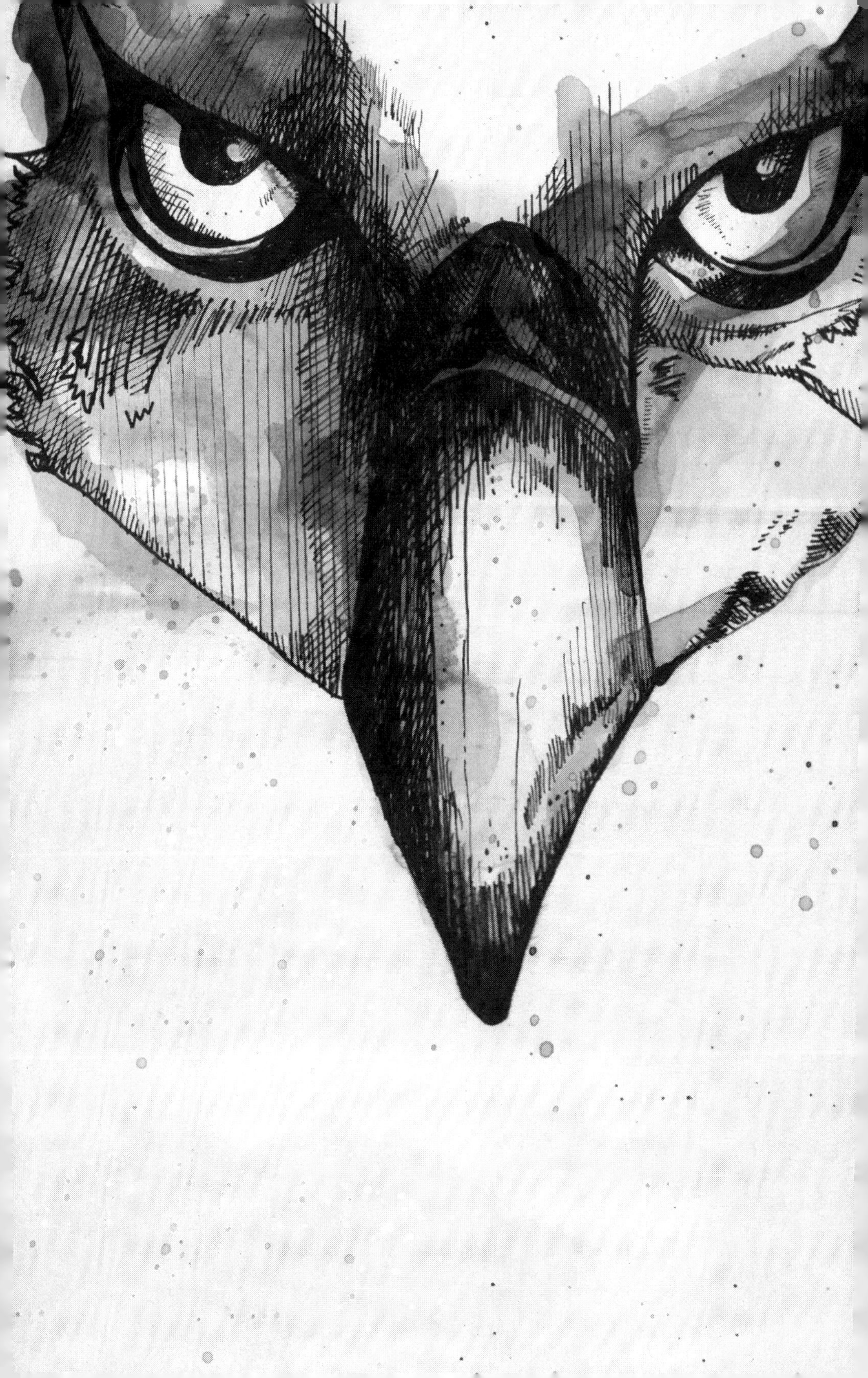

PEOPLE THAT CHEAT TO WIN

Being an independent businessman for over twenty years, I've had my share of ups and downs in business. After getting burned a few times in partnerships, I lived in fear for many years because I was always afraid of getting robbed by whomever I went into business with, even if that person hasn't done a thing for me to distrust them. My lack of business acumen always destroyed the potential of any partnership I had because no one can make moves under that type of pressure. That's like being married to someone that accuses you of every wrongdoing under the sun without any evidence that such accusations are true. That's wack!

As I began to work on my fears in business and start moving in faith, a network of people came into my life that I will continue to trust until shown otherwise. I Started completing more goals with partnerships built in faith than I did when I was moving in fear. But, keeping it real, what person can really trust anyone 100-percent? Especially in a world where everyone has a selfish agenda to use others for their own personal gain. The topic of trust is a word that always seems to amuse Dame.

In business, there is no trust. To be honest, you can't trust anyone in business. When it comes to business, people play business a different way—a lot of people approach it differently. Like, for me, I play fair. Period. I don't even consider it a win unless I do it in a way that's fair. So, it all depends on what you consider winning. Like, there's that weak person that just cheats. He doesn't even let you know what he's done to you to win. He doesn't even care that he didn't play honestly. It's a win to them, and they don't even care that no one knows that they did it. They cheat to win, and that's what they call a win in their terms. But you know, with me, I'm a person that if I'm not doing it honestly, if I'm not doing it on my own, then I don't consider it a win.

If I have to compromise anything that I live by, or any of my scruples, if I feel like I'm going against the grain at all for something that I believe in to make a dollar, then I lost completely. To me, that's a complete loss, but some people don't gauge it like that. Some people think perception is a win. Where people think you won or think you have more than you do, that's a win to them. If people believe I have more than I have, that's a win? To me it's a loss because you'll always have that false sense of self; you're always insecure, you always have to overcompensate. Actually, a lot of people's business model is to pretend they have more than they do, and they love it when people believe that they have more than they do. If you read something in the press, and then look under the hood, it's a completely different scenario. Some people do things for perception. I just don't consider that a win. I'm the kind of dude, like, if everybody's using steroids, I'm still going to have a desire to do it natural. I need to beat you naturally, no matter what. I have to give you a fair one. I'm about that. But again, it's just a different perspective. My approach has always been to just hustle harder than everyone. That's always been my approach on business. I'm always going to play fair no matter what. I don't believe in doing anything unless it's fair, like I believe there will always be karmic repercussions from doing things unfair. So what could appear to be a win, or something that appears to be fast money, I know in the long run I'm going to suffer for it, so I don't do it.

The way I see it is it's always a test. Anything quick is a test, but my mindset tells me I can still get it quick and I don't have to cheat, but if I have to cheat to get it fast, I don't want it. I'd rather wait. I've learned over the years that with anything you have to be patient. Not five months patient, but five years or more patient. Now, if you can be ten years patient, you can build an even stronger foundation that creates legacy. Empires were not built overnight. I always tell people that the Great Wall of China was a two thousand year old plan. Two thousand years. Think about how many lifetimes that is on one plan, getting people to move similarly with the same exact agenda for lifetimes, for generations. That's crazy. You have to be patient when you want to do something significant no matter what it is, and a lot of times that means not reaping the benefits of your goal immediately, and that's the test. But that's why in business, it's also good that you always have something coming in that's paying your bills, so that whatever you're creating has a chance to breathe. An income flowing in so you don't have to rush it. You don't have to push it to make money when it's not ready. Like, you kind of always have to have something solid that's paying your bills because even as an artist, to me, as a man, you still have the responsibility to take care of your woman and take care of your children, as well as take care of yourself, almost in that order. It's like children, your woman, and then yourself, but all of that you should be able to take care of. That's a real man, and as an artist you can't say, "Alright, well I'm not going to take care of my children, or take care of my woman, or even take care of myself to protect my artistry." Then that's not artistry to me. That's just being lazy. I think as an artist, you have to fight for that artistry. Like, you have to figure out how to pay your bills so that your artistry can breathe. That's what real men do to come up.

It's a plus as a man if you have a good woman in your life. They rock with you when they're happy. A woman loves when her man wins, especially when they're by your side. If they're not mad at you, there's nothing they won't do for you. This is why I usually have female energy around me because most men are insecure, and the more you help a man, the more he resents you in the long run. A man will always feel like they should be the one doing the helping. No real man likes another man to help them or take care of them, especially an insecure man. He really doesn't like that, but if he wasn't insecure he wouldn't need another man to take care of him in the first place. So, the more you rock with a dude, even your best friends, the bigger you get, there will still be some kind of a resentment there. It's always going to happen because that's the competitive nature of any man.

The way I see it, when a woman loves you, they feel like they've won also. Women are usually loyal when they rock with you, and they work really hard with passion. Like, I'm not saying women aren't insecure, but they're not insecure about the things that most men are insecure about. There's two different sets of insecurities. But just from what I understand about women, the more honest you are with them, regardless of what the blatant truth is, the more they're gonna rock with you. Period. As long as they know what's going on, and they're not deceived, and they sign on, they're going to rock with you and in business. But again, you can't trust anyone in business no matter what. But I feel like when it comes to feminine energy, it takes a lot more for a female to feel some kind of resentment towards you than it is for a male.

It takes very little for a male to resent you, but once you cross a woman then your ass is out. That's the dangerous part about dealing with women. There's nothing worse than an upset woman. So, when you do get into a relationship or a business relationship with women, as long as you play fair, I feel that you'll be treated fair as well. For instance, if you were once in a relationship then you're not in that relationship anymore, I feel like as long as you play fair with any woman, you're good money. But if you disrespect her, and she has the ability to hurt you, or make you feel any bit of the pain that you've made her feel, then you're going to get that, and you have to own it. But again, as a man you want to take care of your woman. Even if you teach her how to take care of herself, you'll still want to take care of her. When it comes to my daughters, I don't want them ever to be in a relationship because they fear their quality of living will change

Reasonable Clout

if they're not with that man on a financial level. I want them to be like, "Alright, I'm out," if they feel like they need to bounce. The man that they are with will know that they're only staying because they want to stay and it's love and it's not because of some financial benefit. I don't care what a woman says: when a dude has dough, it makes it a lot harder to walk away. I'm telling you, when he's paying for your quality of living, it's hard to be out. Even a heterosexual dude will stay in a situation where he's being disrespected because of a financial gain. It's just hard to walk away from something when you're dependent, especially on a financial level.

Never take pride in being dependent. I want my daughters to be able to take care of themselves. Whoever they choose to be with has to deserve the right to try and take care of them. From my standards, a man isn't good enough if he can't take care of them. I don't care. I don't think it's about money; it's just having the ability to do so because everyone has the ability to be a hunter, a hunter that eats the food they kill. It's just about how lazy you are. Period. It's all about your effort. Like, if a man wants to be with my daughters, he better fucking learn how to cook because I cook for my daughters even though I don't know how to cook that well. And every single thing that I've done so for my daughters, that's what a man better do for them as well. The way I take care of my daughters, a man better be able to take care of them and his daughters as well, the exact same way, even if they have the dough. Period. They'll look at any man that can't step up like a clown. They know not to bring no lames around me, not after I'm in these streets every single day making sure they go to the best private schools."

Culture Vultures

Gems:

To the extent that someone cheats to win shows the measure of how deep that person believes that they can't win.

The people that believe in themselves never cheat; they believe in their own abilities to win.

Real business is 100% faith.

Stay true to your morals and standards. Always build your business without compromise.

I'm the kind of dude, like, if everybody's using steroids, I'm still going to have a desire to do it natural. I need to beat you naturally, no matter what. I have to give you a fair one. I'm about that.

The key to success in any industry is to hustle hard and concentrate on the game you're playing.

There has never been an empire that was built overnight. The Great Wall of China was a two thousand year old plan. Two thousand years. Think about how many lifetimes that are on one plan, getting people to move similarly with the same exact agenda for lifetimes, for generations.

You have to be patient when you want to do something significant no matter what it is, and a lot of times that means not reaping the benefits of your goal immediately, and that's the test. But that's why in business it's also good that you always have something coming in that's paying your bills, so that whatever you're creating has a chance to breathe.

Any man that would like to add to his success should keep a good woman around, and any woman that wants to add to her success should keep a good man around as well. This is the true power of Yin and Yang.

SPIRITUAL BUSINESS

In the hair game, I have my own theory on what really brings clients into a salon besides great work. From studying the game, I found that the spirit of an individual's attitude is the leading force that attracts and allows for increase not only in the beauty industry, but all industries. The individual "I" nature of a human being either repels or attracts like or unlike events according to the nature of their attitude in the process of making moves. Within a group, as I've I studied in my salon, the feeling nature of attitudes that are on the same page are doubly more powerful when the individuals in an organization go beyond focusing on the way "I" feel to the way "We" feel dynamic. On the real, it's important for any manager to make sure his staff or independent proprietors are in tune with the fact that one's attitude towards yourself and others has everything to do with increase as well as decrease in all business.

During my first year as a salon owner, there was a situation that got real. One of my stylists named Keisha was causing havoc with a bad attitude, on top of stealing clients from her co-workers. I started my investigation after hiring a new beautician named Shay, who had only been in the shop for a few weeks prior, came and told me she was gonna have to leave because Keisha rudely grabs all the walk-in's even while she's working on a client. As soon as she told me that, I pushed the gas to arrive at a conclusion because three months before, a few of my other stylists said the same thing. A couple of them bounced after they complained about Keisha. Since she caused me to lose business and make everyone in the shop uneasy, I had to do something fast. After looking into what was really going on, I saw that Keisha was bumping her co-workers for walk-in's by acting familiar with every new customer that walked through the door, when in actuality, she didn't know them at all.

This type of con got exposed when she tried to steal Shay's cousin who she thought was a basic walk-in. When this happened, I immediately talked to Keisha to see what was going on with her movement in the salon, and of course, she denied what happened saying she thought Shay's cousin was one of her clients from back in the day, then she apologized for the mix-up in a sincere octave. So, I gave her a pass telling her to spread the wealth and chill on taking every walk in. This was all good until a few days later it happened again, this time while answering the phone. I didn't have a receptionist, so I would answer the phone when I was there or whoever could answer the phone did so. Some of the stylists, including clients, told me that whenever I wasn't at the shop, there was a lady that was answering the phone with an attitude, and as soon as she heard it was for a stylist in the salon besides herself, she would put the phone down without saying, "Hold on." When she did say, "Hold," she wouldn't tell the person it was for to pick up until after the client was on hold for five or more minutes.

To find out if what my staff was saying was true, I had my girl, my mom's, and my sister call in for random stylists that worked in the shop, to see what would happen. Just as I was told, Keisha was blocking people from receiving their clients. My sister said that when she called and asked for Shay, Keisha said she wasn't in and tried to bump Shay for her client referral when Shay was in the shop the whole time. It was U-Haul time. I politely called Keisha into my office and terminated her month-to-month lease. She begged me to give her another chance, but I had to do what was best for the shop. In my mind, I had to let her go in order to implement the spirit of doing good business. The dope thing about the spiritual standard of business is that it doesn't have a lot of complicated rules. It's simply defined by a word called "circulation," which means to give love is to receive the same in return and to give hate is to receive hate. After Keisha bounced, I scheduled a mandatory shop meeting where I talked about the spiritual law of circulation. Once I did this, we became the best salon on Crenshaw, and even a couple of the people that left came back because we all circulated respect for one another. Life is easier when you become a giver.

This chapter reinforces the importance of how showing love can destroy all forms of selfish behavior in everyday life as well as business. In this conversation, Dame knocked the ball way out of the park when he said, "There are very basic things that should be applied throughout ones life, like having respect, doing things fair, and continuously giving." I would have to say that that philosophy had a lot to do with the success I experienced in business for many years. In my salon, we respected each other; we treated each other fair; and we always circulated clients to those who were not working. On the real, I found that the true spirit of business is derived from the circulation of giving, which is what transformed the people in my salon from being "Cannibalistic Hustlers" into "Conscious Givers". Word up!

I once read that a man doesn't reach his spiritual peak until his forties, which is probably true. But I believe it depends on the type of people you have around you most of the time. I think it's about how aware you are of what a spiritual peak is also. I've been taught a lot. I've always been open to different things, and hearing different theories. I would search for certain answers at a very young age, and I haven't really heard too much that's been more impactful than the stuff that I heard at a young age. To me, it's very basic things that should be applied throughout life like having respect, doing things fair, and giving. Those are the rules I live by. That's all I know. When the best things are happening for me, when I'm my happiest, is when I'm able to project love. Like, when there's a woman in my life or when I'm just giving. I honestly believe that the reason why I've been extremely successful is also because I love my kids unconditionally. The more love you give, the more love you're open to receive. Just like the more negative energy you put out there, the more negative energy you're going to get back. Like when my kids are straight, and there's a woman in my life, usually that's when everything is good money for me.

Culture Vultures

The better I treat people that I love, that deserve it, the better my life becomes. That's it. It's very simple, and that's why you have to keep good people around you that you enjoy. It was funny because I switched my business model up, right? After my daughter, Tallulah, was born I began hiring lots of women and I told them that I was changing the way I do business. I said, "Number one, I'm a let y'all know everything that's going on in my business, then it'll be about spoiling," which is important because you can't yell at girls. You just can't yell at women. Every time I do yell or lose my temper, I feel guilty about it. I hate it. Where I am at this point in my life, I just can't talk to a woman a certain way. So that keeps me good. Plus, in front of my daughters, I would never yell; it's rare. Sometimes, if I have to, I'll lose it a little in front of Ava, like a couple times, but not really. I've never done that around Tallulah. She's not used to that. But, around Boogie, I used to flip the fuck out. Y'all saw backstage that really wouldn't have happened in front of Ava and Tallulah. Like, all I want them to see is flowers, roses, and good smells. I want life to be rosy. I want them on a beach. As a man that should be what you want for your little girls. I prefer things to be a lot different for my sons because I don't want them to be soft. Dusko is the toughest thing in their life, a hush puppy that barely bites his food. I don't want any Pit Bulls running around here, none of that tuff shit. Only soft shit around here. Big fluffy puppies—all that shit. That's the environment that I enjoy, and that was another reason why I had to get out of the music business because you had to be tough all the time.

 Today I choose my staff based on taste, talent, work ethic, and perspective. I need all of that. So when I interview or when the people I work with find more talent, they have to bring me a mixed tape because I need to know what music they're listening to because taste of music tells me a lot about a person. It really does. I have to know who their favorite designer is, what's the last book they read, and favorite artists. And it's funny because sometimes the answers are hilarious. They try, but you honestly have to have great taste. I look for all your senses to be activated. I need you to have good taste in music; I need you to have a good work ethic; I need you to be a good person; and I need you to have good taste in clothes. Basically you need to be savvy in more than just one thing. Everyone in my staff can do many things. There's not just one job that anyone does in my staff, and they all are very snobby, and they all have really good taste. Most of them smoke weed. They all like to laugh, and all of them are about independence. They all like aspiration, and none of them listen to the radio, none of them. Like, if I'm walking through and I'm seeing gossip sites on your screen, that's not what I need in my office. I'm always looking to see someone's source of information that's around me, and it better not be Bossip. Also what is their favorite magazine? Those are some of the questions I can ask. I need to know that.

It's the same thing when it comes to choosing women. I can know everything about a woman from her shoes. Period. So, it's the same thing in business. Like there's certain things that you know about a person from basic questions or basic things, and then I know enough, and then it's about work ethic, including communication, and what kind of problems they have, and if they can take pressure because I'm pressure. I'm looking for adventure. Like, I'm running around like a wild fucking animal everywhere, eating the food that I kill. That's what I preach, and I need a crew that wants to do that as well, and we do it around the world, pause. All I do is start companies from scratch. No matter what you've done in one thing, you still have to start from scratch in another. If you're doing things correct, if you're not partnered up with someone that's robbing you, if you're not the face of it, if you're not a mascot for it. But if you're doing it from the ground up, from the DNA of it all, it's a process. Just like every time you have a child, it doesn't matter how many kids you have, you still have to go through the same process. There has to be sex, there has to be forty weeks, and then there has to be a birth. It's never different; the same thing is true with business. There has to be some sex, the creative process, it has to be forty weeks of incubation, the developmental process, and there has to be a birth, which is any of the physical properties of business. Every time I have a company, I call it and treat it like one of my kids; my businesses are my children with full custody.

Damon, Lucky, Boogie, Ava, Tallulah
Carmel, NY
1:24pm

Gems:

Always find a way to give to those in need, whether it's your time or money.

Take pride in being a "Giver" more than a "Taker".

The greatest things happen when you circulate love.

Everything in the universe circulates including love. Understand that the more love you give, the more love you'll receive.

I give a lot of credit to my success because I take care of and love my children unconditionally.

When looking for teammates, pay attention to overall taste, talent, and work ethic.

The success of any venture is increased through the amount of love and care one puts into any venture.

The DNA of business is similar to creating a child: there has to be some sex (creating), there has to be forty weeks of incubation (development), and then there will be a birth (manifestation).

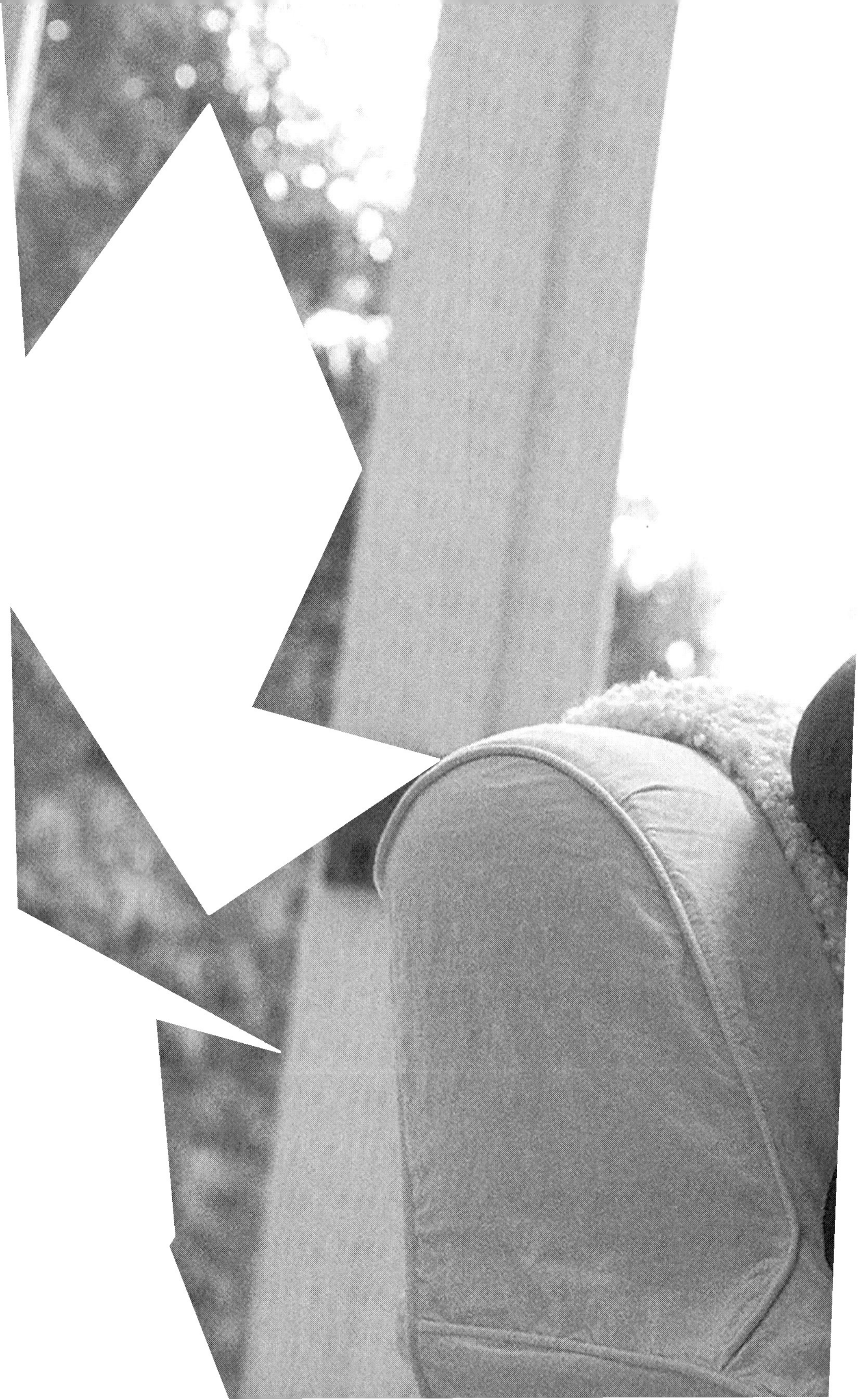

SECTION TWO
BUSINESS ELEVATOR

Damon Dash, Tiret Showroom
Fifth Ave, NYC
5:13pm

SUITABLE LAWSUIT

We arrived at Dame's crib in Malibu just as the sun was going down. We had to hurry up and get set up in order to catch Dame in his element because just beyond his balcony, his backyard was the ocean. Before we got into the official questions, he told us about how his company Rachel Roy won a lawsuit that day and that they were receiving some serious digits.

Well you can't breach contracts, no matter how much money you have, or how many lawyers you have. In front of the judge, you have to play fair. The system is actually very fair in that way. There's a due process that you know in the moment you may feel like you want instant gratification or instant justification. But it's a due process, and if you have enough patience for it, what's right usually works itself out. Regardless of what you may think, it really does work itself out. It doesn't even matter how you look, your gender, race, or whatever. The law is the law. And that's what's good about the law at times—it can protect you. When you're doing

things legal and correct, the laws can help you on all levels. A lot of people don't have the tolerance and nuts to see a lawsuit through. A lot of people are afraid to get in front of a judge. I don't know why. All you have to do is pay a lawyer a retainer, and when you win your case whoever you just beat has to pay your legal fees. If you're really confident enough, and you have a real serious case where someone's been treating you "unjustly," if that's even a word, then you'll win, and it's worth it. If you really believe it then you have to fight for what you believe in. But then if you let someone take you then that would be your fault; you can't get mad at anybody but yourself for allowing yourself to be a victim. It's like if somebody tries to hunt you down and you don't fight back then you're going to get ate because everyone in business is a wolf. Period.

It doesn't matter what type of nice guy they are or how they dress, people have different and negative ways of doing it. Nerds are usually sneakier about it, but being that I'm not a nerd, my business model is transparent. I'm always thinking in the future. See, that's the difference between me and everyone else. I've noticed that that's why I'm always arguing with people because of the stuff that I want them to pay attention to—they be like it's not going to happen for a year. They only want to be reactive, but I'm not a reactive player. I control my own destiny. I don't just deal with what's given to me and react to it. I paint the picture, and then I make it happen. I write the script; I have to be strategic; I have to take time to talk; I have to take time to think, and I have to always remember that. There's always going to be some kind of doubt, but I don't have any doubt because I know I'm right. That's how I feel. Now that things are moving faster due to technology and the Internet, you can do anything from anywhere, even on a beach. Look at me, I have everything running. As long as I have my iPad and my iPhone, I'm rocking and rolling, I'm good. Just recently, I learned that e-mails are actually a better way to communicate when it comes to business. In the beginning, I always said I hated e-mails, but I like to talk, so now I talk via e-mail because I find that people can't hear my tone. People can no longer resent the way I might say something because it's clear and they can read what I'm saying. Plus, it's legal. So now when I send an order no one can say I'm saying crazy shit just because I'm being direct. I've also noticed that people take offense to directions, but if you're administrative you can organize the directions with a certain tone. I really don't mind if a creative reacts based on emotion, but when your job is business you're not supposed to have emotions. You're supposed to be ice cold. Think about it, it's business. But sometimes, I find that business people tend to react to things like the creative, and then I start losing respect for them as business people. There is no emotion in business; there is only emotion in creativeness. In business, there should be passion. Emotion and passion are two different things. In business, you're supposed to respond, not react to things. It's not a good idea to react to events based on how uncomfortable you feel. In business, you can't do that. You don't want to make decisions during irrational moments. Period.

Gems:

The law can actually help you when you run your operation legally and correct.

Going to court is a normal and healthy part of business.

In business, as in life, you are the controller of your own destiny. You have the power to write as well as re-write your own script.

If you're confident about your case, pay a lawyer a retainer, and whomever you beat will have to pay your legal fees.

A good boss isn't reactive. A real boss takes time to logically think things out before making decisions.

Since people react negatively to directions that are given in a certain tone, I've learned to rely more on emails and text messages when I'm being administrative.

In business, you're supposed to respond, and never react to things.

SECURE BUSINESS INSECURITY

About five years ago, Dame told me what his life was going to look like when his businesses finally took off. I never doubted his focus to come up, but it did concern me that he was viewed through the negative lens of the press. He continued to make his moves, never responding to the streets or the headline story that he was broke. When I would catch up with him in LA, I would ask him about all the crazy stuff the media was saying that was making people's perception of him change, and he didn't have a response. He said he was only focused on "Hustling for his last name" by creating ways to make sure that the Rachel Roy Company, as well as his other businesses, would become relevant in the next five years. As you see, he's turned Rachel Roy into a fifty million dollar company that has dressed not only some of your favorite actresses for the Oscars, but has also designed clothing for the First Lady, Michelle Obama.

Don't sleep; it's an absolute fact that the confidence you have in yourself is the beginning step in achieving greatness in all things. When I asked him what was up with all this "Dame's Broke Talk" in the press, he low key shrugged and said, **"I'll be back outside. Watch what**

happens in the next five years." Which allowed me to see that one of his keys to coming up was to only focus on the bigger plays at hand instead of focusing on the negative bullshit delivered through the media. So, now fast forward into the future, five years later at Dame's new crib in Malibu, overlooking the ocean, where he's talking to me about most people's business insecurities.

When people over-project, it's overcompensation for insecurity. So, as soon as I see somebody overreact when I'm direct about something or trip off of a question that I have, I know that they're not prepared mentally. They become insecure about the answer, so they make beef, or they just begin overreacting, which is something that I've noticed. Overreaction is because of lack of confidence; over-projection is because of insecurity. Like, if somebody's yelling and they're trying to tell you they're tough, they're usually not tough. The loudest nigga in the room is usually the softest. Period. I have a dog that I walk everyday, and I see how he carries himself around other dogs. When dogs are scared, they bark, and when dogs are confident, they don't say anything. But when it's time to wreck shop, they wreck shop. You'll hear him growl, but they don't bark when it's really time to get down. Dogs growl while they're attacking you. They don't bark to get you away from them when it's time to do damage. They want to fight. A real killer wants to fight; he wants you to think he doesn't want it. He don't want you to know where it's coming from. So, all that over-projection always means fear, which is why if I send an order to somebody, and I'm direct, and they start bugging, that's when I know that they don't have an answer for me. I can also tell if they didn't do right by me. I know that they're not prepared. Plus I'm not trying to hear all that emotion in business, especially if I'm paying you. I don't mean to be an asshole about it, but I don't know, man. Every time I'm a nice guy I don't make history. It's weird, I don't know, what the fuck... I don't know, my way can't be the wrong way.

It seems like the independent makes money the artist makes, and it tends to touch pop culture on every level. It's hard not to be confident when you put comedy in business. The biggest black male in comedy now is Kevin Hart. I know that I took him off a stage and put him in his first movies. I know I did that. I know what I've done for Jay Z and Kanye. Not one and two, but one, two, and three. Like, it's so many that I put in business, that affect pop culture, even on a fashion level. Rachel Roy is probably the biggest American designer of her generation. I know all of this, so it's hard not to be confident in my ability as an independent.

If I'm good in fashion, good in music, and good in comedy, what does that tell you? Even Lee Daniels, even though he owes me two million dollars, I picked that. I put him in business. So, if everyone that I've put in business is doing well then I must know something. As you see, they've all reaped the benefits of my advice. Some of them haven't done right by me, but it's all gravy; it's all good. And even in art, three months ago I was like, "Yo, this dude named Brian (BK), he's the next big thing. I suggest you buy some of his art." Three months later, they crown him the new "King of Art" in New York. So, I don't know what that is. It's hard for me to take advice from someone who hasn't done anything or that hasn't put up the money. How could I not be arrogant when I'm telling them what to do and they're questioning my business intelligence? In business you have to listen to somebody and I consider myself somewhat of an O.G., which means you should listen blindly until I make a mistake—until I don't affect pop culture. Right now, I'm just starting. I'm independent now. I had a five-year plan, and as Kenyatta sat there, I told him all the stuff then that's happening now. He saw everything that was going on, and while he was cutting my hair, I was like "Watch, watch what's about to happen. Give me five years, and then watch what happens. I play chess…"

Brian Kirhagis, Fumero, Damon, John
Poppingotn Gallery, LES, NYC
7:22pm

Gems:

Over-projection is a form of insecurity, and overreaction comes from a lack of confidence.

When dogs are scared, they bark, and when dogs are confident, they don't say anything. This truth is the same in dogs as it is in all human beings.

You have to be upfront and direct to make history in all industries.

Keeping it real is the foundation on which success is built.

Hong Kong Family
Sham Shui Po, Kowloon
4:17pm

BUSINESS OBJECTIVE

Right now, I'm focused on being an artist. I want to be judged as an artist. I wanna put it all on the line. I wanna make money off of me for a change. I've always made money off of people my whole life. It's too easy, which is easy because I'm a businessman, everybody knows that. So now the challenge for me is to be an artist because I like new experiences, like a new woman, like how that's supposed to be. Nothing's better than experiencing something for the first time, like the first time you go to a club, the first time you get a check from a company, or the first time you get a record on the radio. Nothing's better than that. So, right now it's going to be nothing better than the first time—I'm respected as a creator when I can just direct, where I can lead with emotion and not have to be a gangster. I can't wait for that, and that's what I've been doing for the last five years, making it where I can do that. And the only way to do that is to put up your own money because no one is giving me anything. Nobody's giving me nothing. I'm not expecting noth-

Culture Vultures

ing. I don't want nothing. I'm a grown man. I don't lead with emotion. I have a tolerance for women, 'cause they have vaginas and they don't have testicles, pause, or any testosterone. And I have no compassion for a man that acts like he has no nuts, that reacts like he has a vagina.

I'm a man; I know what's hanging. I know how you're supposed to react as a man. So, with men, there's no excuse in reacting with emotion. Men are supposed to be men. Your job as a man is to take care of yourself, your kids, and family. Your job as a man is to take care of other people other than yourself. If you're just worried about yourself, and you complaining about it, then I see a vagina, and I have no time for a man with a vagina, at all, not even a little tolerance. Women, I forgive them all day. I don't know what it feels like not to have nuts, but I got nuts, pause.

Gems:

Nothing is better than experiencing something positive for the first time, so don't be afraid to initiate your life goals.

A man that doesn't take care of his responsibilities (family) has a vagina. Every man's job is to take care of people other than himself.

Damon Dash
Forbidden City Bejing, China
4:02pm

POHO 66 Gallery opening
Hong Kong, China
9:16pm

Raquel M. Horn
POHO 66 Gallery opening
Hong Kong, China
11:58pm

POHO 66 Gallery opening
Hong Kong, China
9:22pm

Charlotte Pecot, Ava, Damon & Guests
POHO 66 Gallery opening
Hong Kong, China
11:45pm

Boogie & DJ Wordy
POHO 66 Gallery opening
Hong Kong, China
12:03am

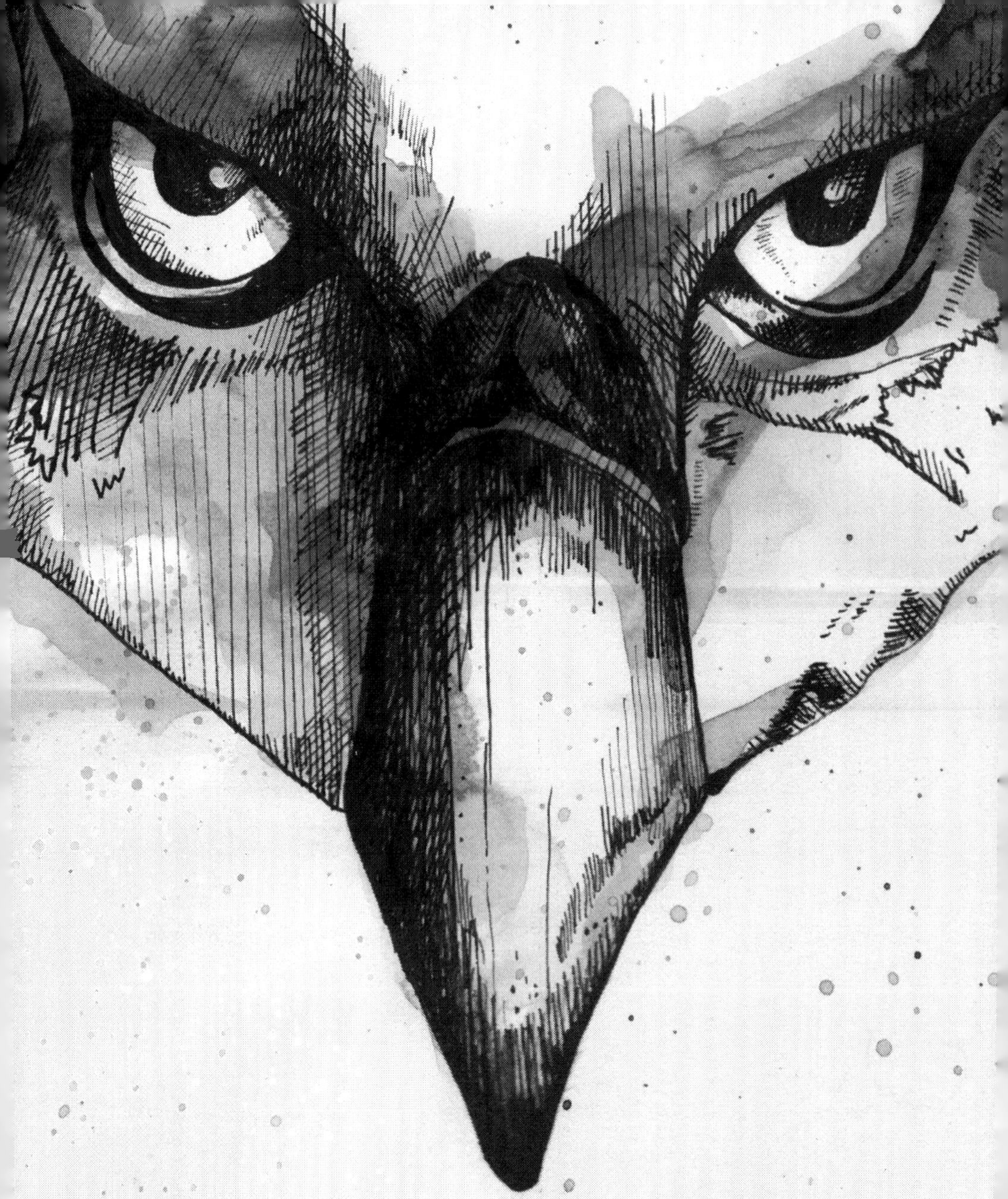

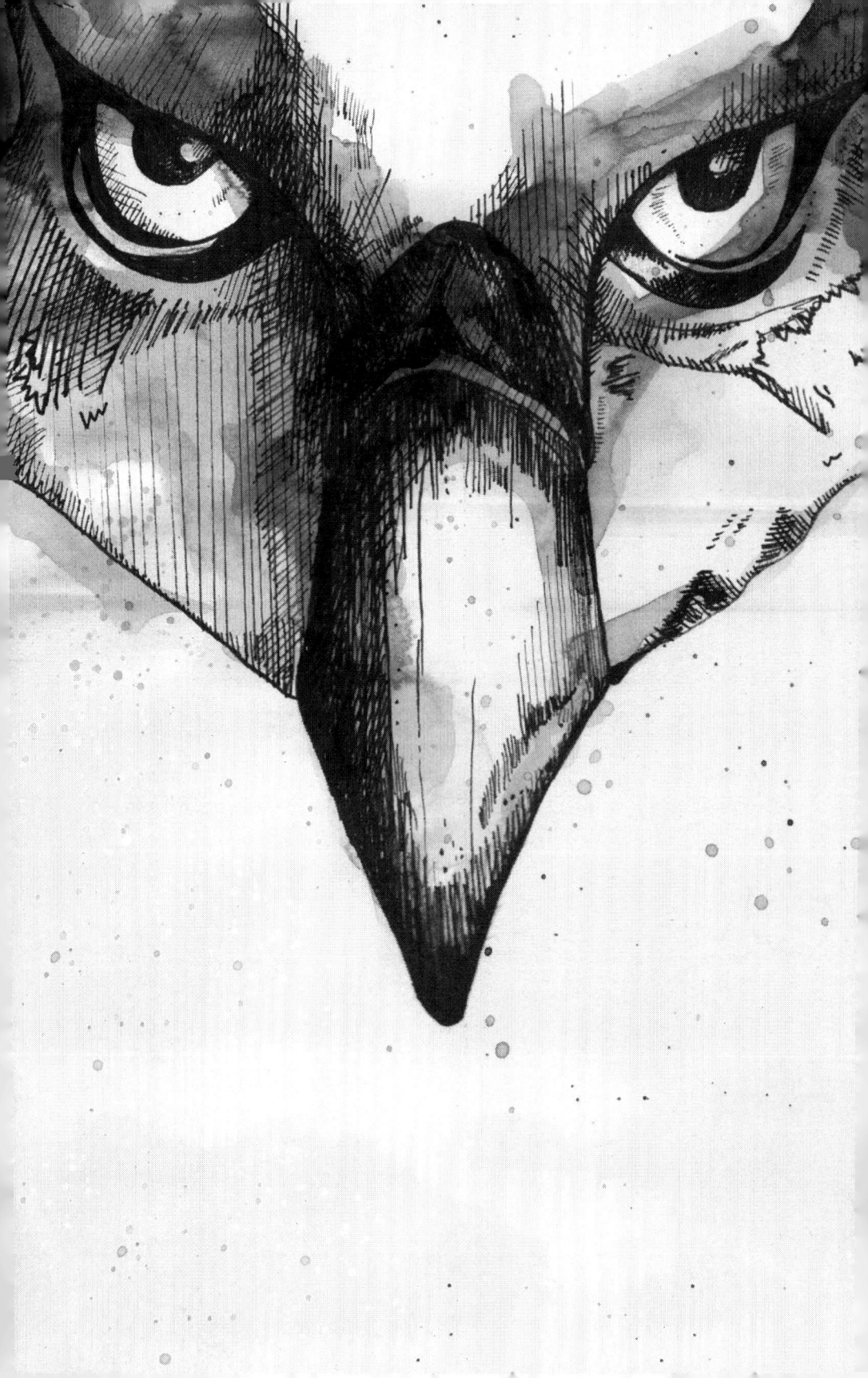

CULTURE PARASITE (NO BUENO, NO MAS)

In this section, Dame talked about Lyor Cohen's 360 deal and gave his opinion on why it isn't cool to do business with any executive that will rob their artist, especially Lyor. Keep in mind, Lyor is the guy that Dame said put the battery in Jay Z's back that led to the divide and conquer negotiation that divided the dynasty of Roc-A-Fella Records.

Lyor Cohen invented the "360 Deal." He invented the "Rob The Artist Deal," which allowed the creative corporate to get from one level to the next. Then when he gets fired or he retires, or whatever happened over there, all of a sudden now he's "All Independent"? But when I was independent five years ago, everybody said I was nuts. He was the main guy telling people, "Don't listen to Dame." He didn't think I was hearing about everything he was telling people. That's why I get at him openly. He's a "Culture Robber." That's whom I'm referring to when I say that. Lyor is corny; he's wack juice and whoever fools with him looks weak. So I suggest you don't mess with him. I wouldn't.

I would never mess with Lyor. If I messed with him, it would make me look like I don't have a backbone because I know he doesn't care about the culture. It's all about the money with him. Ask yourself a question: "Why is it that a man that robs our culture can't get money in his own culture?" That's what I don't understand, and I'm not scared of him. I think he's a joke. I want the world to know that he's, "No mas; he's no bueno." My advice to everyone is to stay clear of Lyor. He will rob you; he will ruin you for money and when you're with him, you look like a slave because that's how he looks at you. Trust me on that.

Gems:

Make sure you research the past and present resume of the people you plan on doing business with. The one character quality they should have above all is that they care more about the well being of other people more than making a check.

Stay away from all 360 deals!!!

Business Elevator

Recording Culture Vultures
Damon
Bel-Air, CA
5:17pm

Recording Culture Vultures
Kenyatta
Bel-Air, CA
5:17pm

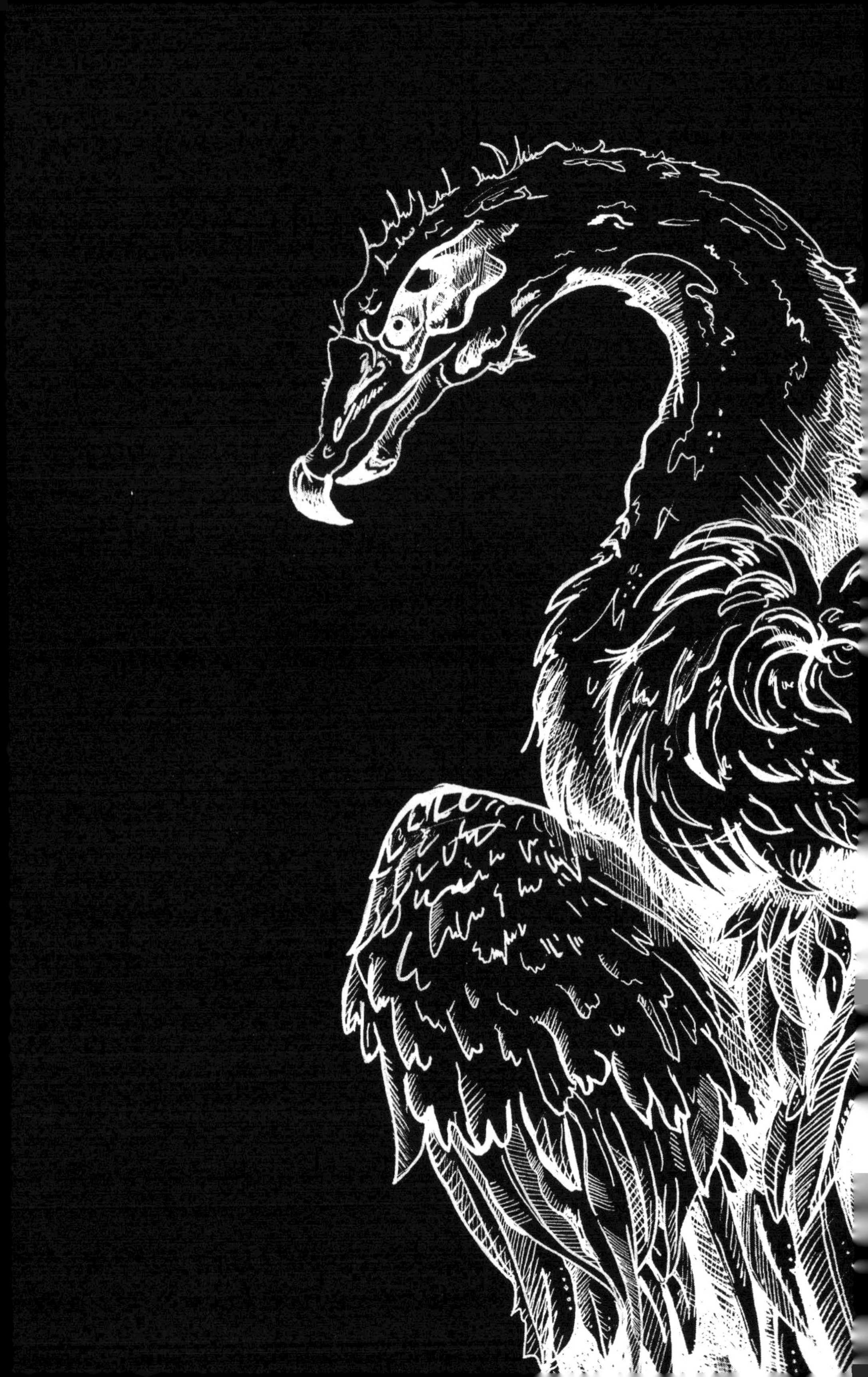

ELEVATOR INCIDENT (JAY-Z & SOLANGE)

When the footage of Jay Z getting kicked by Solange in an elevator in front of Beyonce hit the streets, everybody had jokes. That story was all over the web trending on every media and blog site there was. People were posting some of the funniest memes I had ever seen on both Instagram and Facebook, like the picture of Jay dressed like Sophia from The Color Purple that read, "You told Solange to beat me?"

The whole day in the shop everybody was clowning, but we were all clueless with one unanswered question: "Why did Solange wild out on Jay Z like that?" One-half of the people in the shop said it had to have something to do with Jay putting hands on Beyonce because no one is going to go crazy like that over their sister unless it was a domestic situation. The other half said that he must've got caught cheating because Beyonce didn't stop Solange from going off on Jay. Plus, she seemed like she was cool with what was happening. Then, to top it all off, word on the street was that Solange went off on Jay because he was getting at Dame's ex-wife, Rachel Roy which, as some say, led to the song *Lemonade*.

I had to cut Dame's hair in a few days, so I couldn't wait to hear his opinion on what he thought about everything that happened at the Met Gala that night, including the rumors of Jay getting at Rachel. The next day, I linked with him at his house to cut him up, and after I finished, he told us to roll the cameras so he could talk about "The Elevator Mystery".

When I saw the footage, I was laughing. I thought that shit was funny. I mean, I wouldn't have handled it like that. But I just thought it was funny because Jay's the kind of guy that you don't see moving like that. Anything that doesn't look cool in that type of situation is always gonna be kicks. Even back in the day, nobody would tease Jay but me for some reason. This is just the first time I saw people freely expressing themselves about Jay. What I'm really happy about is that when they were bombing on me and saying that I was broke, and all that, that Instagram didn't exist because I'm sure people would've been having mad funny jokes, but I would've been getting back at them. I like to snap. I don't think he should be mad about what happened. I think he should be laughing because that shit was funny. Everybody fights. Girls done spit on me before, but I'm a little more assertive like, "Yo, You better chill out!"

Real talk, I felt like Jay Z handled that situation the right way by not reacting aggressively, but it was funny to see him try and grab Solange's leg as she kept kicking him. He laughed when I asked him if he would have grabbed her leg like that.

Nah, that shit was funny. But Jay has to worry about perception because corporately, people pay him, so he really has to play that game. I thought what was ironic about it was that people got to see how he plays shit off, and how something crazy can happen then four seconds later, when it's cameras on, they act like nothing's going on. I thought it was interesting to see that and how good he is at it, but then it just kind of exposed them. Like, how do you trust anything moving forward? But again, he has to worry about what people think because if people don't like what he's doing then he won't get that corporate check. I'm not corporate, so we have completely different mentalities.

Like, if people seen a girl flip out on me like that it wouldn't have been a big deal. I would've been laughing. I would of come out the elevator fronting with the cameras like, "You see what this bitch just did to me!" And people would've been laughing because I don't care. I think if he cares then he's probably embarrassed, and if he doesn't care he should be enjoying it. Me, I wouldn't care.

I know how it feels to get bombed on in the newspapers. The media bombed on me for five years straight. I just laughed at it, and you saw how I held it down. So, being that I went through it, I could say what I'm saying, and Jay likes to play. He snaps. Last time I saw him backstage at his concert in LA, I was like, "Yo, what was all that 'Dame made millions' shit?" And he was like, "Oh, I was fronting on you." I was like, "Oh, we playing like that, bet! As long as you don't get offended when I play when I'm good and you're not." So, I think he's built better; he should be built stronger than that. I think he'll be all right, but it is funny, it's kicks. I love it! It's fucking hilarious. I like jokes. I like to laugh. I don't care. I feel like it's nothing. Nobody died, no abuse really happened. The shit was just funny. That wasn't about nothing. If he's worried about that then that's on him. I wouldn't be, that ain't about nothing. He looked a little funny, but who cares? A lot of people are laughing though. All the press I ever had rolled up into one is not as funny as this shit right here. Because you know Jay don't be yelling like that. He was probably like, "Oh stop, stop." Yeah, that's what I mean—it's kicks.

Like, if he still hung out with us, we would've been roasting him. We would've been roasting him and if he got mad about it then we would've been laughing even harder because that's how we get down. I don't think his circle is like that now. I know the people he hangs around, and I know they probably giggling behind his back, but they not giggling in front of him, and if they are then that's dope. I hope they are laughing at it, but if no one's laughing then he needs to look at his crew like, "You're not laughing at me because that shit was funny." Like one time we were in San Francisco and, like, a bird, outta nowhere, just smacked Jay in the face. That shit was funny as hell. I still laugh

about that because it was just an uncool moment. He just doesn't have too many uncool moments. So it's just fun when nobody's trying to laugh, which makes it funny. I was on the floor for like three days until he was actually mad because I'd be laughing, man. I don't care.

That shit was the funniest thing I had ever seen. Yo, we were going into a "Jack in the Crack" across the street from the hotel, and out of nowhere a bird just hit this nigga in the face. Yo, I was crying. I was laughing so hard man, like that's what I'm saying, that's what we do, we snap. So, if nothing bad happened, yeah, we gone laugh man, like that wasn't about nothing. He should enjoy that. I wouldn't be playing none of that off. I'd be like, "Whatever." Now if he was trying to holler at my ex-wife, though, that's kind of fucked up. Nah, I don't think he was doing that. That would be bad. That would be dark. That means he really has some resentment towards me, but I would hope that wouldn't be the case.

We asked him if he thought it would've hurt Jay's brand if he were any more aggressive with her.

Nah, I don't think so, as long as he didn't hurt her. If he looked cooler about it, it would've been better for him. To me, there's a lot of cool ways to hem a girl up without hurting her, and as a man, we should all know that. Like, we've all been to that place with our girls, where she's in your face, smacking you around, or spitting on you. I've gone through all of that, but I be like, "Yo, you better chill out."

Gems:

The key to overcoming many negative situations is to see the humor in it as much as possible.

Business Elevator

Ava, Solange, Atrak
coachella music festival
5:52pm

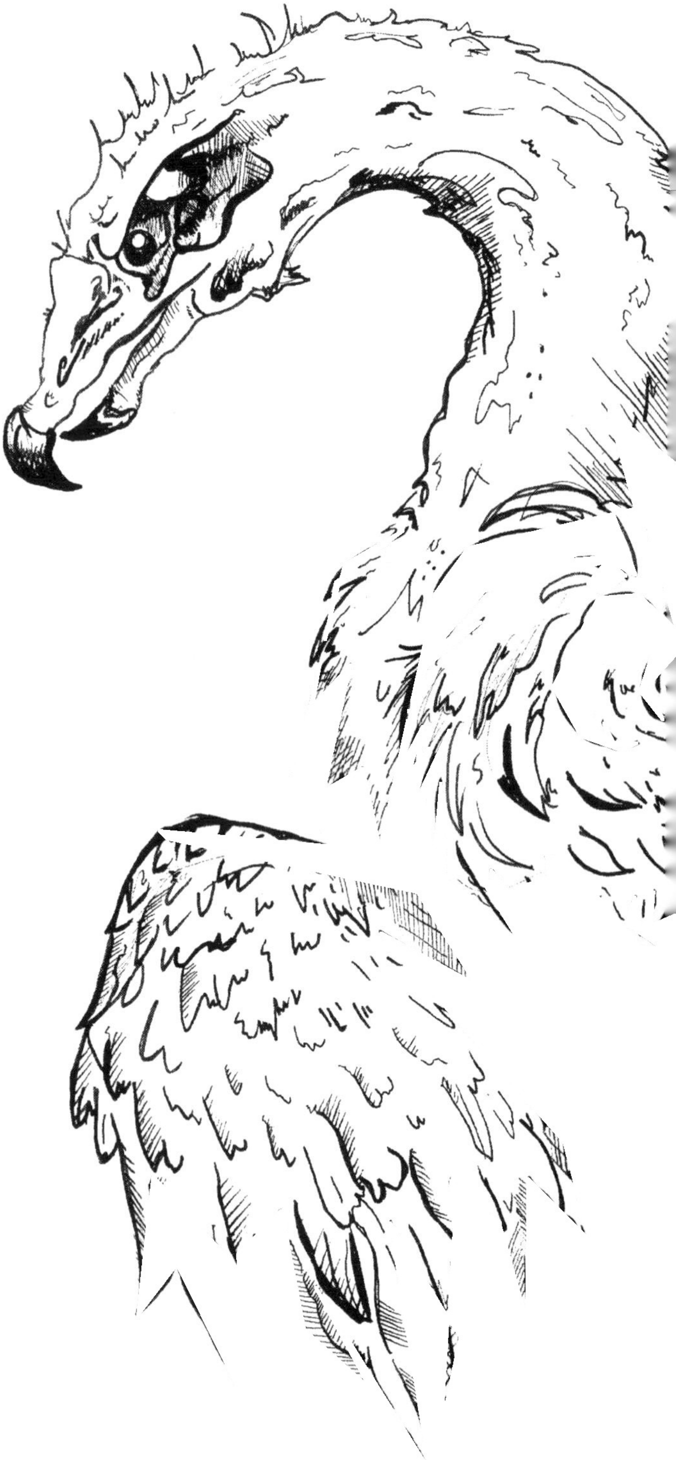

CLOSET RACISM (DONALD STERLING)

What was dope about this section of interviews wasn't only the Jay Z and Solange elevator incident, but also the story about Donald Sterling's racist remarks pumping throughout the media that were recorded by his mistress, including Sterling's response to Magic Johnson. Sterling said, "Black people never stick together," and he also added that he's done more for "The Blacks" than Magic has ever done. From my point of view, during the aftermath, even though it was the playoffs, I felt like the Clippers organization, its players, and its coaches looked wack as hell when they continued to play for a racist owner even after he acknowledged his comments, and by the way they still got eliminated. It's wack that they didn't send a bold message to not only Donald Sterling but all the closet racists of the world, but as we all know, everyone can't be a revolutionary. Shout out to all the freedom fighters that fought for our rights to be accepted as equal human beings. Word Up!

The people that choose to work for that racist should've exposed him. So, everybody who knew he was a racist shouldn't have been stopped from making money with him. Whoever was working for

that racist should've walked out on him. But what he said was in his house; that's his house. He can have an opinion. We don't have to like his opinion, but I don't have to fuck with him. I can just think he's a moron and keep it moving. I do think that since he has been exposed, he should pay the consequences of his actions. To me, that's not good money, but he did say what he was saying in his own crib. He got violated. You can think whatever you want in your own house.

I think he should lose ownership of his team in the NBA. But, fuck him, I don't care about another man's opinion at all. It doesn't bother me what another man thinks about me or my race. It doesn't make or break me. I could care less what other men are thinking. I don't give a fuck what another man is thinking because of the fact that I'm a man, and because of the fact that I think, as all men should, that they're the best men that ever did it. I don't expect any man to say anything good about me, especially in front of a woman. I expect them to hate all day. I'm used to that, like a dude saying, "Don't let Dame in the building; he's gonna take all my chicks." Maybe it's because I'm black, maybe it's because of the swag, or maybe because the swag came from being black. But yeah, I've been known to pick a couple of pockets, so I understand his frustration. I've been so-called blackballed before as you've heard, and usually the places that people say I can't go, I wasn't going anyway. It was corny.

Gems:

Racism is a corny excuse for a lack of self-confidence.

All racists are highly insecure individuals.

Cam'Ron, Damon, Murda Mook, Smoke Dza
Honor Up BTS, Long Island , NY
3:39pm

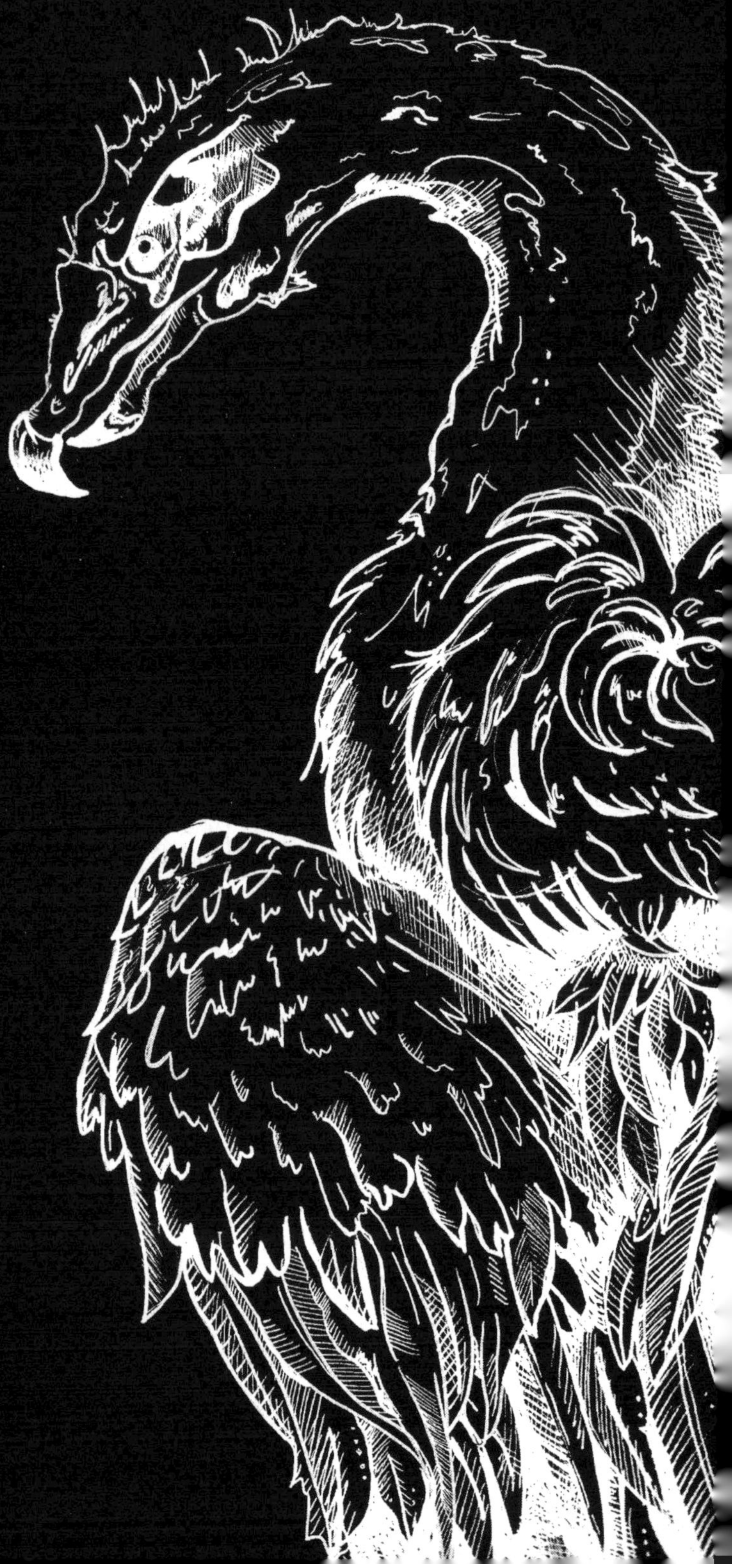

BLACK BUSINESS DYSFUNCTION

This segment was a continuation of the Donald Sterling situation. It turned into a conversation about how black people have a hard time sticking together. I believe that black people's fear of doing business with one another is a systematic psychological trick orchestrated by the unseen hands of the media that has force fed all people to believe that black people are not to be trusted. The media also targets Hip Hop as the cause for black people's problems, which is absolutely not true, especially when seventy-five percent of Hip Hop's following is a white audience. It's funny when people say that Hip Hop produces violence because I remember one time Dame said, "What about back in the day when killers were listening to Frank Sinatra or Marvin Gaye".

In regards to black people, a lot of us have drank the wack juice and have been brainwashed into staying away from uplifting our own people by performing group economics as other races of people have done with their own people. Do your research; in the past, when black people have stuck together, other races became fearful and made moves to pull us apart, brown paper bag style. The reason other races became overwhelmed with fear is because when something like that happens, you'll begin to see the strategic systematic power of psychological slavery come to an end.

When I asked Dame what he felt about Donald Sterling's comments about Magic Johnson not helping black people, further insinuating that black people don't help other black people, from his own experience his reply was straight to the point.

Black people never help each other out. We never stick together. We are the most retarded culture in the world for that. I always say that. For some reason, when black people get something they think that they can't share with other black people 'cause that other black person is going to take it from them, especially the people that have a boss. Culturally because we were slaves, I guess, we feel that we need another culture to validate us, and get us from one level to the next. But it's to be expected—it's human. We just got a black President in there eight years ago, so things are just changing. At this time in history, black people are sticking together a lot more than I've ever seen and I'm proud of that. But yeah, the old black man felt they had to shit on each other to survive. It was a survival tactic. To me, it's not excusable, but I understand it. But yet we can't act like we stick together 'cause we don't. For proof, we could look at how we always get separated, and it's always someone from another culture who separates us. I can personally tell you that. Yeah, no we don't stick together. We be clowning like that, but I'm a black man and I can say that. I've been trying to change that forever.

Trust me, you don't think back in the day I wasn't like, "Yo, let's get Roc-A-Fella, Bad Boy, Def Jam, Wu Tang, and let's stick together and say fuck everybody." But nobody wanted to do that. You know how many black people I tried to put together to make movies? And it would always be that one group—or because of someone like Steve Stoute—or somebody that's a culture robber who doesn't care about his culture who would break that up. What's crazy is when other black people break up other black people from sticking together because it will kill

their little check or because they got a connection with white people. Yeah, Steve Stoute, that's what he does. He would always break us up so he could bring us to corporate to get robbed. A guy like Steve Stoute will always take the people who are protecting the creative and eliminate them so he can rob the creative, just so he can get his money, even if it kills that black man or that person's brand. That's what he did with Mary J. Blige, and how I was against him putting Jay's whole name on a forty-dollar sneaker, just so they could get a check. Or how he had Jay doing a Budweiser campaign with a Confederate flag for a check. That's not good for your brand. I wouldn't do it like that. That's his approach. I don't like that dude because he doesn't care about his culture. He's also a liar, and I watched him tell me all of LL Cool J's business and Nas' business when they weren't doing well. So I never trusted him, and I also watched Biggie Smalls' crew put lipstick and a wig on him when he fell asleep. That's how I first saw him. So, I couldn't respect him from that day. He also tried to rob us for DJ Clue and I had to run up in his office, and tell him, "Cool your jets." He's a guy you gotta regulate. He's a sneaky guy; he's a nerd, a Culture Vulture.

Gems:

The key to breaking the psychological chains of systematic self-hate starts with loving yourself. Hate reflects Hate and Love reflects Love.

Having faith is more powerful than having trust. True faith is believing in something greater than yourself.

Other cultures have relied on the strategy of Group Economics to become a source of economic power in America. African Americans must start studying other cultures' rise to economic power and participate in forming chapters of Group Economics in their community.

Dinner with Rza
Los Angeles, CA
7:18pm

Carolyn, Kenyatta, Kenyatta II, MIchelle
Los Angeles, CA
3:47pm

SECTION THREE:
RADIOACTIVITY

Combat Jack, Premium Pete, Damon Dash
New York, NY
12:54pm

FUNKMASTER FLEX RESPONSE (BEING BLACKBALLED)

While I was working on the list of topics for the third section of this book, Dame posted a picture on his Duskopoppington Instagram page of a guy named Joe IE, CEO of Interscope Records, calling him as Dame calls it a "Culture Vulture." After reading his post, I called him to see what that was all about, and he said he got at him because he personally saw Joe IE start a war between two creative people for his own benefit. He said, "That's what Culture Vultures always do: divide and conquer. They could care less if somebody dies or gets hurt as long as they make money off of it."

On the same day, radio personality, Funkmaster Flex, got at Dame on his own Instagram page saying he was going to air Dame out live on the Hot 97 because Joe IE was his boy. Then on Dame's page, he posted a picture of Funkmaster Flex stating that Flex was getting involved in something he knew nothing about, and that they should talk face to face since both of them are men in their forties. So, I downloaded an app to hear what Flex had to say about Dame.

Culture Vultures

After dropping his signature bomb, Flex began his rant telling Dame, "Go sell clothes and slippers! You been Blackballed from the game!" Flex further tried to make Dame look like some type of fanatical racist because of the "Culture Vulture" title he was using to describe anyone in Hip Hop of another Culture he felt was enslaving people through 360 deals. I've had many conversations with Dame about what the culture of Hip Hop is all about and he knows, as well as I do, that Hip Hop is a culture that was created by black people, but is participated in by different people from all walks of life. To me, Hip Hop is Dr. King's "I Have a Dream" speech where all races of people come together to create in peace.

After the Flex rant, I went to his spot to see what he thought, and all he said while laughing was, "All that screaming was crazy. It was just a lot of over-projection for nothing. I just didn't like that he called me a punk. It was great publicity, though. I need to get some slippers made ASAP." He told me we should film his response to Funkmaster Flex. When we pushed record, Dame had a lot to say.

Let me explain this to you. The word "blackballed" means that I wouldn't have the ability to be hired by anybody, right? To be blackballed means no one is going to hire that guy. Can anybody hire me? So how can I be blackballed from something I don't want to do? What does that mean? How can I be blackballed by anyone? Now, of course, Flex is a guy that has a "job", and he's probably heard someone say, "No one will ever hire Dame." So yeah, that could mean being blackballed in his mind, but to someone whose independent would probably be like, "Yeah, you're right, no one could ever hire Dame." See, for me, there's not enough money in the world for me to work for a Lyor Cohen, or any one of those lames. Why would I let a nerd tell me what to do? Or why would I put myself in a position to act extra nice to a nerd in front of my woman just so I can get a check? Shit, I believe if my woman is with me because of status or a certain opportunity that someone else is providing then she will more than likely, start liking that guy also. Which means you're going to be tempted to do fucked up shit to make money because your girl is only with you because you have money, or because you're hot at that moment.

I'm not worried about none of that. Being blackballed has never been a concern of mine. The music business is too small for me. There's no money in selling records anymore. The only money is in the artist selling merchandise and making money on their show. So, in order to make money off of an artist, that means you have to rob that artist. Unless I'm the artist, I can't really be in the music business. I'm not into taking money off of artists. I don't want to be resented by my artists because I'm only making money off their efforts. I'm not into that. So there's absolutely no blackballing me.

The question I have is: what job am I blackballed from? Explain to me what I'm blackballed from. Like, who could blackball me? Who would have the power to blackball me, and what person could tell me "no"? What person would I be asking to give me something? I might speak on how we could work together, but no one can hire me. I've been putting records out independently forever. What was I blackballed from? People either say I'm blackballed or robbing somebody, but it's usually the perspective of someone with a job, someone who is feeling insecure about the fact they're being told what to do. They're grown, but they're not growing. How are you grown and not growing at the same time? You tell people you're grown in your house, but when you leave the house, you're not grown. You're only grown in your house. As soon as you walk outside, you're not a boss anymore you have to answer to someone.

To an independent, the act of so-called being blackballed doesn't exist. It's like The Loch Ness Monster. In today's market, being blackballed is a fantasy. That's something someone in the corporate world is saying to put fear in the hearts of someone. People will make up anything to give something outside of themselves power. I love it. What they're actually trying to do is dumb down my lifestyle. Flex saying anything in defense of Joe IE is wack. The target of my comments was from one executive to another. When he was screaming he said he was reading off of a paper; he was reading a list of stuff. I could tell he had no passion for what he was saying; it sounded like he was doing something he was told to do—that he really didn't wanna to do.

See that's what happens when you have a boss.

I know how it is. I, personally, had Lyor try to put a battery in my back, to go fight for him, and I'd be like, "Come on, man, get outta here. I'm not fighting for you. Are you fighting for me?" That's what I used to tell him. It's crazy because the first thing he tried to do when we got to Def Jam was put me against a lightweight. So, I had to personally check him off the top. I don't even remember what it was, but whatever it was it was nothing. Lyor was always scared. I remember one time he was like, "Yo, Dame, you gotta go with me to meet Dee and Waah," who owned Ruff Ryders. Even when he first went to see DMX, I had to go in there with him to protect him and hold his hand. He couldn't just go up to Yonkers like that. He was scared to death. He didn't know Dee and Waah like that. He would use black people to protect him, just like Joey IE using Flex to protect him. Now that their money is short and they don't have enough to get somebody to protect them, they're really shook up. They can't pay anybody to do their dirty work or give anyone a deal. They don't have the ability to help anyone like they used to, so no one's willing to help them because there's no gain like back in the day. If he had the ability to help, I'm sure somebody with more power would've stood up. I guess Lyor doesn't even have Flex's money. It's all they could afford right now, Flex money. Whatever Flex money is…I mean that's who they have speaking for them, Flex. That's what they can afford. It's whatever that amount of money represents all that screaming and hollering. Whatever that was.

Gems:

The act of being blackballed is only real to people who can be hired.

The word blackballed is the Loch Ness Monster to an independent; it doesn't exist.

Concentration is a skill that must be developed in order to continue making moves during times of adversity.

Remember, it's not important what "they" think about you, it's what you think about yourself that's important.

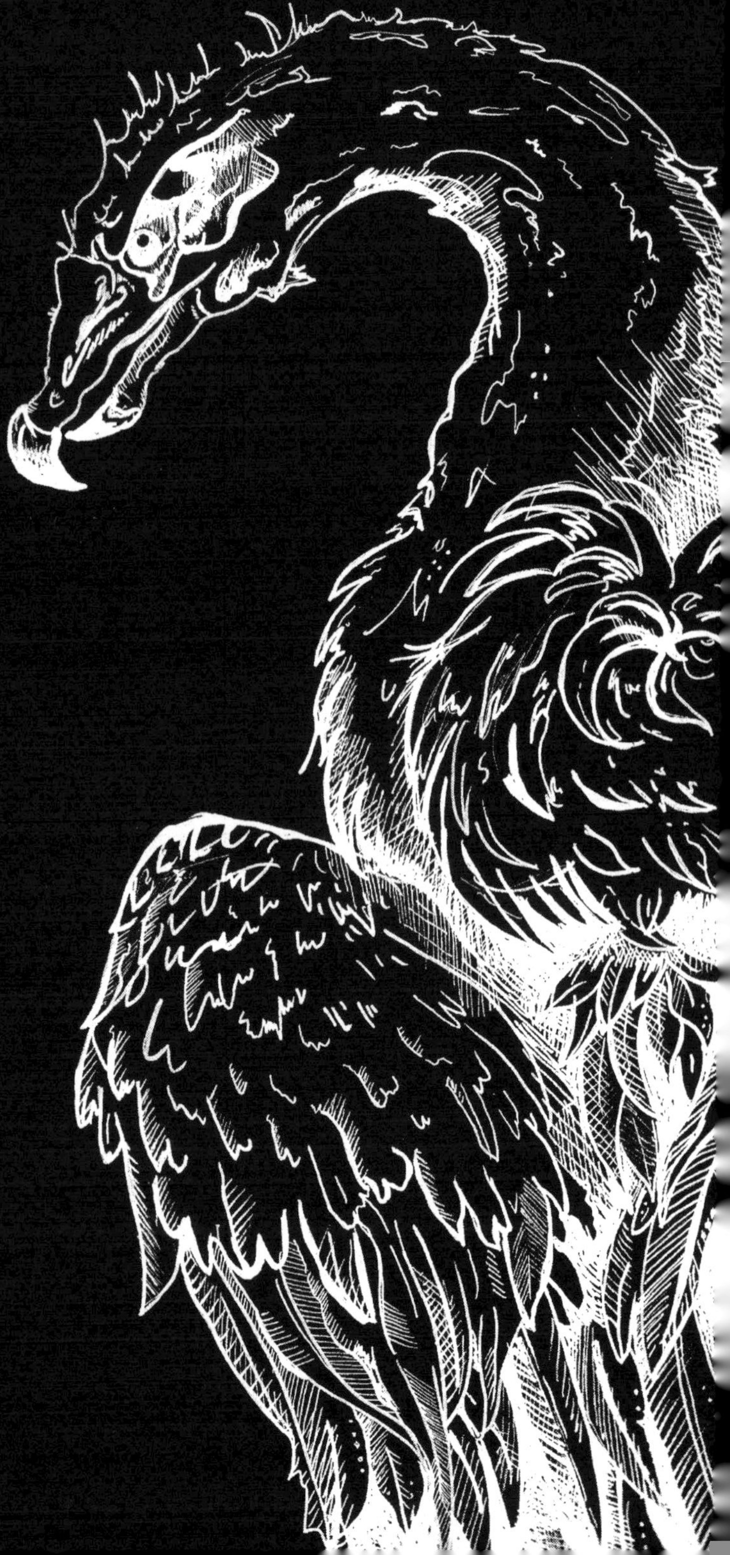

CALLS OUT EBRO OF HOT 97

Generally speaking, I wouldn't tell you to document this, but because of Flex at Hot 97, and now Ebro, who just texted me and asked me to come on his show, and I was like, "I'll come on your show, but just make sure Flex is there so we can have a conversation." I really don't understand why they're so afraid of just having a conversation with me. I don't see why I don't deserve a conversation after all the yelling Flex was doing. Think about it: he's on the radio; he has a mic; he's yelling; he's screaming, and that's fine, but I don't think that's the way men our age should talk to each other. Plus we should lead by example and show the culture better, especially because we're older we should conduct ourselves a certain way. I don't think Flex is used to someone talking back to him because he controls such a powerful slot on the radio. See, he can say what he wants and he's not used to somebody speaking back. I don't understand why he's so hype about the fact that I asked for a conversation.

The reason why Flex has been airing out his perception of my businesses is because of another man. Which is questionable to me off the top, but then he just continues to keep talking, and it's just like alright well, let's talk then; I'm all for it. Why keep yelling? That's not the way people communicate. But there's really a message here. I also just don't understand the concept of other men counting other men's pockets. It's weird to me because you can't do that in real business, or even where I'm from in the street. That just doesn't add up to me. It's like if I'm rolling dice with someone, and somebody that's not in the game is speaking on the dice, or asking me why I'm rolling it, or why I'm doing it, and they don't have money on the table, we have nothing to talk about. That could usually get you decked in the streets.

So, Ebro texted me and asked me to come on his show, and I was like cool, but let Flex come, pause. I guess he didn't want Flex to be in the same room with me. There's no violence that's about to happen, and then he started to Twitter out, "I'm talking to Dame." And when we went back and forth his perspective blew my mind. I have no problem talking to Ebro, but he says things and speaks things that aren't factual, and he's discrediting people, and that's not fair to make an honorable man look dishonorable on any level, especially when it's none of your business. I feel like since Ebro thinks he's articulate and that he's smart, why not have a conversation with another articulate and smart person. This is a publicity stunt. I definitely wanna bring attention to everything I'm doing, and I wanna use all the people who are violating and exploiting our culture to do so, the same way they exploit us.

I don't understand how Joe IE doesn't feel like he should have to speak, or what he's afraid of, or what his publicity department over at Interscope is telling him, but I don't see how he could be a boss and tell people what to do with any kind of authority. And he's not leading his team like a strong leader. He won't even fight for himself, so how could he expect people to fight for his company? Think about it, he won't fight for himself. I don't see how he can face the people he works with, and if that's the case then he's not there to do any job, he's just there as a position. I don't even understand why he would have the title "President of Urban." That's disrespectful. I'm curious to know why. What did he do to become the "President of Urban"? What does that even mean? So, I just wanna ask, with no disrespect because I'm curious. I mean who knows? He might shed light on something I don't know, or bring forth a different perspective that I haven't seen. In his response, he might be dead right and I'm willing to accept being wrong publically, but I do have questions, and I think these questions come from a lot people as well but they're not in a position like I am to ask. I think it's entertaining and cool that you'll be able to see it on my own independent television network, and if I'm going to do press and promote it, why not do it in this way? Why wouldn't he want to help me promote myself as another black man who works for somebody else and doesn't own anything? Which is absolutely no parts of what he's protecting. So, Ebro, I'm calling you out too. You say you're articulate; you have an executive job; plus you're an entertainer, you asked me to come on your show, and I'm asking you why you won't come on mine. No beef. Let's just keep it smart.

What's crazy is I can't really have a conversation with Flex about anything because he has a job and I don't. So, his perspective—that I should appreciate what someone else, from his perspective, gave me—is a different language to me. Like, I can't speak that language. I don't even like to spend too much time on one particular person. He's in my rear view already, pause. It feels like I'm in The *Twilight Zone*. The things they're doing publically is kind of embarrassing. I know their families are asking them, "What are you doing?" and "Why are you yelling?" "Why don't you just talk regular, without the bombs and all that?" But the good thing is there's always a platform, like Dame Dash TV. I'm not on the radio every day, but every time someone says something that can evoke attention to the cause, I can get right there and speak back.

So, Ebro, I think you're scared, man. I think you're scared of me, and I'm talking about on an intellectual level. Why are you scared? What are you scared of? I'm sure you talk a very big game in front of people who don't really understand exactly what's going on, and I don't see how you, as a person in the radio industry, could intelligently speak on someone else's business in another industry. I think we should lead by example and promote something positive, as opposed to always promoting a negative in Hip Hop and making money from it, especially for someone who has no respect for Hip Hop, and you don't own any part of it. Why are you scared? Don't be scared. Think about it: you're scared in front of everybody, all your girls, and everyone who loves you. They're watching me call you out, on an intellectual level of course. It wont be anything violent, or anything ignorant, just a debate for the better good of the culture. Let's lead by example. A lot of people are watching, so let's talk it out. Everyone's entitled to an opinion. I'm not mad at anybody at all. He wants to interview everybody all day and make money from it. So why don't we interview him sometime to see where he's at with it? As opposed to him being a spectator and a fan and always judging the game, he should suit up and come out and play.

Gems:

A debate should never lead to violence or anything ignorant. Everyone is entitled to his own opinion.

After any debate, lead by example and peacefully agree to disagree.

"Don't allow someone's opinion of you to become your own reality."
--Les Brown

Moving to LA
Teterburo, NJ
10:11pm

Moving to LA
Burbank, CA
12:16am

Damon Dash
Malibu, CA
2:11pm

IS DAME BROKE?

One of my clients showed me a funny Instagram post of Dame unshaven with a crazy expression on the front page of a New York newspaper in bold text that read, "I'm Broke." When anything hit the pavement about Dame or anything associated with Jay Z, it was typical in the shop for folks to throw shade on his movement any way they could, especially because I've been cutting him for over thirteen years. On the real, I laughed my ass off as soon as I saw that picture, not only because it was a wack picture of my boy—looking like he was begging for food—but because I had to go and cut him up at his house in Malibu later on that night. While the clowning was going on, I didn't say a word. I just chilled and listened to all the insults of why Dame fell off.

As usual, I gathered the Hip Hop Motivation team together to capture the talk. While my team set up, I showed Dame the article of him saying he was broke and looking homeless. He laughed like it was the funniest thing he had ever seen. I definitely thought he was gonna trip a little bit, but all he said was, **"Damn, they could have at least used a better picture of me. They caught me out walking Dusko without a shave!"** He shrugged it off and gave his opinion.

First of all, how can I be broke when I have all these companies including Rachel Roy? And second of all, why in the hell are people talking about another man's pockets? That's a general problem in the black community, being too worried about other men's pockets. If that's all black people are talking about—someone's pockets—then that's the death of black people. A man that's worried about another man's pockets has just been emasculated. You're not a man anymore when you talk about another man's pockets. Like, you could be a tough guy and all that other shit and then you talk about another dude's pockets. At that moment, you've just lost your manhood. Worrying about another man's pockets is not reflective of a real man's perspective. Real men do not give a fuck about how much another man has. It's incomprehensible for me to hear another dude talk about another dude's pockets and argue about that... That's crazy to have another man's pockets on your mind. "Pockets on the mind" is crazy! A dude with "pockets on the mind..."

Any man that talks about another man's pockets should right then and there be eliminated out of your circle because they're worried about another nigga. That should be a flag. "Pockets on your mind!" Get outta here." That means that he's disguising something he is because that is a sign of weakness. That goes for anybody, I don't care who it is. Anyone that talks about another man's pockets is emasculated. "Pockets on your mind... I mean I don't even know how many times I've had to say, "I don't care how much money I got. Don't worry about my pockets."

And another thing, just so everybody knows since I'm never going to hold a dollar because I flip, I'm always broke. I'm always going to put it back into the streets. I'm always going to buy shit and flip. I'm going to have companies; I'm going to have buildings; I'm going to have art, but money...No, I'm not holding that. Are they worried about am I liquid or are they worried about what I'm worth? If so, naw, I'm cracked.

I always say that, but ask someone else with money how much

money they have and they're gonna probably say the same shit. You're never supposed to ever say you have money anyway. What happens when you have money? You have to give it away, you gonna get robbed for it, or somebody gonna try and take it from you. Anyway, someone who says they have money usually doesn't. The people that have money usually don't speak on their money. Come on, you think the people that have money want everybody talking about their money? So, what do you think about the people that keep saying that they have money? Why do they keep saying that they have money if they really do have money? You know why? Because without money, they wouldn't be able to get girls; they can't get in the club. They get bottle service. It scares them when they don't have money because they don't have power, especially for a nerd.

I've been flipping money every since I was sixteen when I bought my first couple of grams. I got the money back, and then I bought double of what I had before I paid my expenses, and paid the people that sold for me. Not that that's the most positive thing in the world, but it's the truth. I found out the effects of flipping money early as a teenager. I already knew what was up by the time I became an adult. On the real, I found out that the drug game was the same as the corporate game. It's the same thing; you have to pay people; you have to put money back in; and you have to re-up. It's the same shit. It's all the same, there's nothing different. Only thing that's different is that it's illegal and guns are involved. In corporate, independence, and in the street, you have to constantly buy more goods to supply your demand.

A real hustler doesn't want anything on consignment unless it's ridiculous because most hustlers want to pay for what they want. Every now and then you might take a plus-one. It's yours. It's profit! As soon as I get it, I put it back into my companies. I never hold liquid; I would never in my life hold money. I buy shit. I buy more work, and I flip it. Whoever says I'm broke, they don't understand business, so that should tell you right there. If I wanted to hold money and play it safe, I'd take a job. As an independent, the government wants you to put money back into

Damon Dash & Dusko Poppington
Thompkins Square, East Village NYC
11:09am

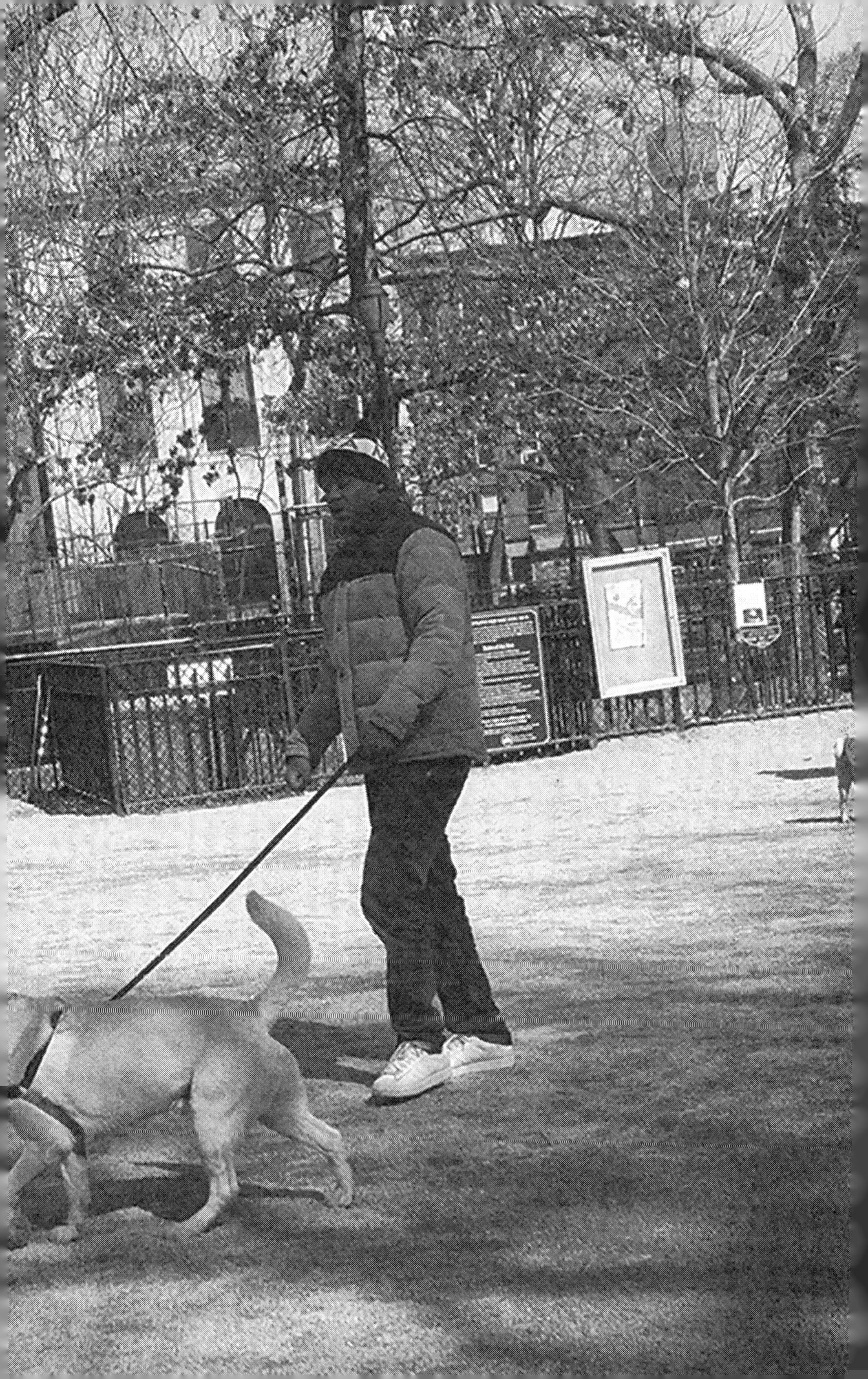

Culture Vultures

your businesses. Actually, what the government does is give you capital gains taxes, which is less, and they try to incentivize you to put it back in. I love it. That's why the taxes don't get paid, 'cause they're always going back into the company. There's no profit; it goes back into the company. What's the explanation? How can I be broke if I own Rachel Roy? What's the explanation for that? Am I supposed to have women's clothes everywhere I go? It's called Rachel Roy. What the fuck am I supposed to do with that?

I guess they think I'm supposed to sell my celebrity just because I'm black. That's some racist shit. So everybody that's black with their own company has to be out in front of the camera for their company? It's ridiculous. You know why? Because they think black people only have the ability to sell their celebrity. They don't think they can sell their skills, and lifestyle. Any black person could be rich without celebrity. I'm not in music anymore, but even with music, you don't usually know who the CEO is or the A&R. You don't usually know who they are. You don't see them. It's a curse; the swag could sometimes be a curse that deflects expectations.

Really, the people that are saying I'm broke have to be nerds. If you're a corporate nerd, your girl knows it, and she's only with you because you're making her life better, and the minute that's gone, she's gone. That's usually the only reason any girl will mess with a nerd. That's the pedigree of that girl: security. Just like the nerd has a job for security, to the girl, the nerd is her job, he's a Johnny. Like, if you're corporate to your wife, you're just a customer; you're a Johnny. She'll let you go broke, she's gone to another Johnny, another customer. So how can a girl be loyal to a Johnny? He's a Johnny; it's a chain of "Johnnys in the world." She's watching you be told what to do by another man; she don't respect you. She says she does, but that's contingent on if you keep paying her, then she'll continue to respect you. See a nerd has to hold on to every single dollar to feel secure, or it's a wrap. I don't live by those rules, I'm a hustler…

Gems:

A man who is worried about another man's pockets is a man who has just been emasculated.

A person who is paying too much attention to what other people are doing is an indicator of an individual's lack of concentration on his own goals.

A man with pockets on the mind should be a sign for a woman to get away from that man because his lack of focus on himself will stunt his own growth or coming up.

Flipping money is better than sitting on money. Circulate your money back into your business and watch it grow.

The government actually incentivizes people to put money back into their businesses by giving them capital gains taxes, which is less than annual exemptions.

Damon, Lucky, Boogie, Tallulah, Ava
Montauk, Long Island
3:19pm

DEFINITION OF A MAN

The one thing that I've always admired about the homie Dame is his approach to fatherhood. It's not often you see men in love with their children enough to do anything to make sure that they experience the best things that life has to offer, even if that means securing the mothers of his children beyond so-called child support. I relate to that philosophy because I'm also a man who loves his children beyond the call of child support payments. Through building with Dame over the years, it has helped me to step my game up when it came to my children's mother after a conflict I caused that I had to live with.

The conflict I caused came about when I got caught cheating. I talked to Dame about what I was going through with my daughter's mother, who was using my seed as a way to inflict pain. It worked because every time I talked to her, I found myself arguing and saying things that were totally out of my character. He said, "It happens. Sure, she's showing you a different degree of feelings than you're used to seeing. What do you expect? You got caught up. But don't be mad at her, forgive her. She's reacting off of emotions that, at this time, she doesn't have the power to control."

From what I experienced with her down the line, he was right. Just like hot and cold, love and hate are different degrees of the same thing. I had to fall back and reevaluate my negative input, which was fronting like I was loyal when I should have just kept it real from the gate—I wasn't ready to settle down. But when the shit hit the fan, I started overreacting to all the negative moves she started making when all along, I was the culprit in what was happening. I realized that I was lowering my stock in the game by violating the natural law of her right to make a choice if she wanted to be a part of the rotation I had going on. I wasn't the valuable man I needed to be in order to get the respect I always got; but instead, I reacted emotionally to all of her games by staying away while I was still sending support. But that was wack; not only did I miss my daughter, she missed her father.

It was written that Adam fell short in the Garden of Eden because he allowed Eve to steer him into disobeying God. When I stopped reacting to her emotions and stayed focused on playing my position as a father, things began to flower into a new relationship of peace. She could see that no matter what game she played, I valued myself enough as a man to continue being a father to my child. After this evaluation, my philosophy became: "No woman had to be a certain type of woman in order for me to be a man. I will always remain a man regardless of her actions." This one goes out to all of the fellas going through Baby Momma drama. As a man, you have to remain calm, play fair, and take your wounds. Keep in mind if she sees you reacting like her, she will absolutely never respect you. Why? Because you're acting one-hundred-percent just like what she is, a woman. Word up!

Now, before we went into the definition of manhood, I told him that it seems like the average person would be shook to leave behind their so-called corporate security to approach the freedom of an independent mindset because independence is an all-in bet.

Most people are scared to death to leave corporate for independence because initially you have to put up your own money; that's the real reason. People don't even understand putting up their own dough. It's not fathomable to some people.

Radioactivity

If you ask anybody that's a true entrepreneur who's put up their own money, that's normal for them. Kenyatta can think that way; he has his own shop and he can get up whenever he feels like it. That's what I was telling my son, Lucky, the other day. I woke up, got on the phone, and then I was messing around on Instagram. Then I was like, "See, Lucky, when you're a boss you can go to work whenever you feel like it, but when you do go to work, you have to work."

The only way you can get up and go to the office at 1:00 pm is if you're the boss, but the only way that's embraced is if everyone's eating and everyone's doing well. I'm very responsible, but on my own terms. See, when you're a boss, you can be responsible on your terms. A boss gonna tell you how to be responsible on his terms, and a man shouldn't be told how to be responsible on another man's terms. That's just how I see it. I think we have to understand what it is to be a man. Culturally, I don't think we know exactly what that means. A man's job is to take care of his family and to take care of other people before he takes care of himself, and to do anything it takes to make that happen. That's a man's job. That's the reason why God gave us nuts. He didn't give women nuts because they're not meant to fight; they're not supposed to do that. They're supposed to have children, and they should be taken care of whether they have the ability to take care of themselves or not. Even if my girl is rich, I'm still taking care of her because that's what I'm supposed to do as a man. Why? Because I want my daughter to see that and want that kind of man.

As you see, I have supported anything Rachel has done one-hundred-percent because I want my daughters to see how independent and powerful their mother is—I want them to be independent, powerful women. I used to enjoy being a slave for Rachel in front of my daughters because I wanted them to be accustomed to a man that enjoys being a slave for them as well. I want my daughters to be used to a man doing every single thing for them. I want them to have a slave without compromise. So, I have to be that example, but that only goes to a certain level. I'm like her assistant, and I want her to feel that a man should be like that. I teach my sons that their mothers are the only women that should spoil them, and don't get used to that. Use that as an example on how to spoil other women. I tell them to practice taking care of their sisters. That's why Boogie doesn't wanna take money from me, 'cause he doesn't like the way it feels, pause. He'll be like, "Naw." I remember one time his sneakers were a little dirty and I was like, "Yo, are you doing that because it's a look?" He was like, "Naw, Dad, I have to pay rent." I was like, "Come on, man, let's go sneaker shopping. What's wrong with you?" I love that shit about Boogie. Yo, I love that my son bought these sneakers on my feet. I've been stepping up my sneaker game lately. I didn't realize they cost so much because I'm buying them shits now.

Gems:

A real man hustles for his last name, not his first name.

A man's job is to take care of his family and to do anything it takes to make that happen.

Men should especially show their daughters as well as their sons what a good man is supposed to be, and women should always show their sons and daughters what a good woman is supposed to be.

Remember, children don't listen to what you say as much as they pay attention to what you do. So always lead by example.

Kenyatta and Kenayatta II
Los Angeles, CA
6:12pm

Kalei Moon, Kamaile Star,
Kenyatta II, Kenyatta, Karma Sky
Los Angeles, CA
7:17pm

Kenyatta, & Krisna Love
Los Angeles, CA
6:32pm

Kenyatta, Kamaile Star, Khari SUN
Los Angeles, CA
4:02pm

Lucky & Dusko Poppington
Lower East Side, NYC
1:01pm

RULES TO THE GAME

It was Dame's birthday when I did this interview. Raquel hired a personal chef named Kayla to hook Dame up with some of his favorite dishes. He had everything from ox tails, grilled chicken in some sort of green pesto sauce, an alfredo dish that was off the hook, super bomb grilled vegetables, and to top it off, fried Oreos. After we all ate, the "itis" took over and everyone was in full lounge-mode. It was also after 1:00 a.m. That's why, during the interview, Dame was laid back chillin'.

This interview came from a conversation I had with one of my clients, Rodney, who earlier that day fell out with one of his childhood friends over a business partnership that went sour. It got him caught up in a tax situation that led to him getting audited because his boy tried to sanitize street money through their company without telling Rodney what was going on. The cold thing about it was that Rodney's money was legit cash that he stacked from his paychecks before he got laid off. So this chapter is for the homie, Rodney, and anyone else who is looking to go into business with friends, or the people going through tax problems. I hope this chapter helps you in making sense of the situation you're going through. God Bless Your Movement.

Rule #1 - Doing Business With Friends

It depends on the position you're in. Like, if my bills depend on a certain business more than likely I'm not going to do business with my friends. Only because I can't really fire them, and if I hire somebody I want them to do something that they're good at. I'm not just trying to give somebody an opportunity to get a job and get a check, or pay them to do something that they're just learning to do. It's not beneficial to the overall big picture. Then, also friends sometimes tend to get or become entitled because of the friendship. Like because of the work they put in with you on a personal level, they feel like they deserve a certain amount of room for error on a business level. It's just hard. But if you're doing something you're not depending on to pay your bills, then doing business with your friends is dope. The best way to work with friends is when you can do something for passion or for fun. Like, sometimes I do business with my friends, but it's not with any anticipation of making any money. The way I look at it is like loaning your friends money: "You know you ain't getting that shit back." Doing business with friends is like that.

Rule #2 - How Much Money Should I Flip?

It depends on how much business you want to do. For myself, I just wanna do so much business that every dollar goes back into the streets. I just pay my bills, and if I'm going to buy something, I'll buy it. But I'm generally trying to independently finance all the things that inspire me without compromise. So every time I get a dollar, in my mind, I already know I'm not holding any money. I'm so in-tune that I already know how I'm spending my first billion. I'm a buy a football team. I have no intention on holding any money, and the only way to get to a billion is to keep putting money back into your companies and keep flipping. I'll be flipping my whole life because that's just my game. As long as I got cash flow, I'm cool, but I don't really believe in holding money. I think that's for suckers.

Rule #3 - What Should I Know About Independent Business?

I mean you have to understand that you have to lose money for a little bit and be uncomfortable in the process. As long as you're independent and there's a demand to buy your product, you're always going to be broke because you always have to keep buying inventory, as long as somebody's ordering and the orders get bigger. Like if you sell a million dollars worth of stuff and you got a two million dollar order, you will have to raise the money to facilitate that order. So, the bigger the company gets, the more you have to spend to supply the demand. The process is that you have to collect money to make more stuff, and sometimes people don't pay on time. So, at times, it'll feel as if it's almost damn near impossible to grow and stay independent. You'll never make money and hold it. You always have to put back into your company. The first step is that you have to understand how you're really making your money, and how much tolerance you have for loss, and for building a brand. If you can sustain, you can get to a level where you can license your brand out or make money doing other ancillary things. Like, one thing that happens when the brand becomes a commercial is all the other little things make money based on that commercial, but it almost always takes five or more years to build that commercial. So you have to be able to sustain that loss on a lot of levels. The flip depends on how fast you want to come up and make money. Keep in mind that while you're investing in one thing, something else should be paying the bills. To some people, it becomes difficult to kick-start their businesses because of bad planning and a lack of patience. For all of us in business, there has to be something paying the bills while we build our brands.

Rule #4 - The Facts About Taxes

First of all, stay calm. Like, If the IRS starts coming through and you ain't got nothing to hide, just be cool. The government is really not trying to put you out of business; they're just trying to finance the country and the people finance the country. But generally speaking, if you have to go through an audit, go through the audit. And if you're not making any money, it doesn't make sense to pay your taxes, 'cause all they could take is your profit. If you keep investing money into your business, what are they going to take? So, you settle your taxes when you got the money to give them, when you have expendable income. Other than that, just hold your head and be calm.

What's common is that most people panic when it comes to taxes. If you're just flat out not paying your taxes, yeah, that's a real issue. But if you're putting it into your business, the government generally is a bit more tolerant because they know shit happens in business. Like, to be honest, on the low, my biggest ally has been the government because them auditing my books showed me exactly who has been robbing me, and they're also aware of who's been robbing me. They know that I've been getting robbed and that I'm a good dude. If the IRS gets at you and they want to investigate your situation, just have patience and stay calm. You have to be resilient; that's just part of the game.

Misunderstandings happen. But now, if you're intentionally breaking the law, yeah, you deserve what you get. But if that shit happens, and it just came upon you just because of negligence and a lack of knowing something because it's your first time doing it, you'll feel anxiety 'cause you don't know what's going on. You're in the dark, but just stay cool and it will work itself out. Just be cool, get a good accountant, and just settle your tax situation. It's not a big deal.

Gems:

The key to doing business with friends is to stay away from the anticipation of making any money.

I've never believed in holding money. I think holding money is for suckers.

While building any independent company, it's important to have something paying the bills so that over time, your venture will have the room it needs to grow.

What's common is that most people panic when it comes to taxes. If you're just flat out not paying your taxes, yeah, that's a real issue. But if you're putting money back it into your business, the government generally is a bit more tolerant because they know shit happens in business.

Ava, Damon, Gov. & Tallulah
Los Angeles, CA
3:57pm

SECTION 4
INDEPENDENT CHEESE WITH CORPORATE CRACKERS

Redman
PCH - Malibu, CA
11:27pm

CRACKERS WITH CHEESE (THE CHALLENGES OF INDEPENDENCE)

Before we started filming the "Crackers With Cheese" segment, Redman and I got a little hungry. So, Dame went to the fridge to see what he could come up with. He pulled out a white brick of cheese that looked like a key. He opened the plastic, placed the brick on a cutting board, slid a knife gently into the rind, laid a stack of white crackers in front of it like falling dominoes, and put a container of cranberries next to it like, "Voila!" Yo, that platter was similar to a layout you might see a caterer throw together.

As soon as he dropped it on the table, we ran through that platter like we just came off of a fast. We ate all of Dame's crackers and damn near all the cheese, slicing big and dropping crumbs. It got so crazy Red even dropped one on the ground, picked it up, ate it, and then looked in the camera like, "What?" The munchies were in full effect. I don't smoke, so I guess it was the contact. But anyway, it was all good because what a lot of people don't know is that Dame is a real hospitable dude. On the real, he's one of the most giving people I have ever meet, so I know he wasn't tripping. Don't sleep, this chapter you're about to read is in full—minus the crunching. Check it out.

I asked Redman what's the one thing he's realized, so far, about being independent after being a signed artist for over twenty years. Red thought about it for a moment and said, "That it's definitely a lot harder, a harder challenge trying to do the business and being an artist at the same time from my perspective."

Dame asked Red if he does all of the business himself. Red responded, "Well, naw, but I do play a big role in my business. But I do know, from hearing you back in the day about trying to own your own shit, that's the movement I'm trying to do now. It's just trying to be at a pace where I can own my own shit. I ain't signed nothing yet. Me and Meth haven't signed anything yet." Dame asked him if they were coming back out as a group, and Red said they might sign a group deal with somebody because they have an album they are working on while also looking to sign solo deals. At that moment, Dame went into the nature of doing independent business.

At the end of the day, you make most of your money from your shows. So, all you have to do is put out a record, make the event, and then tour it. You create on an indie level. It's not about radio, it's not about anything, but really your performance, the environment you create, and then how many people will come and watch you perform. So, you already have a foundation; you already have a brand; you have a core demographic; people fuck with you, and you're on some legend shit right now. You're gonna make the 'Hall of Fame' thing. You should. So all you gotta do is put out a record and you're going to make money selling merchandise and of course selling your show. So, as long as you got somebody to run your merch and make your clothes, which is easy, you can just put out a digital project. As you know, nowadays you can put everything out on your own. But it doesn't have to be digital. Like, you can do the CD thing for perception plus digitally, but, like, at this point you can make money, selling vinyl. It's like art. That's the original way; it will always exist.

Red then asked Dame what he thought about digital distribution and the role it's playing in the music as well as movie industries.

I think it's dope because you don't have to buy inventory anymore. So, you cut the middleman shit out and have a direct consumer relationship. It's easy. You don't have to pay a middleman because the Internet made everything fair. Nowadays you don't need to talk to anyone to be seen.

It's a completely even playing field. There were so many people making money as middlemen before, and now they out of business, and they have to find a different hustle. People getting money just because they knew people, or they could get things paid for through corporate so that they could get seen through a spot, a slot, or certain television platforms. See, back in the day, you had to pay two hundred thousand dollars for a video, three hundred thousand 'cause it was so much competition for those slots. There wasn't an Internet, so you had to be with a label to even be considered or taken seriously on those major platforms. But it's not like that anymore. You can make a video for five racks, one rack, really any rack as long as it's dope. Back then there were no digital cameras. It was film, so you had to pay for film first in order to shoot. We used to be like, 'Damn, we gotta get a sixteen-millimeter camera.' Back then you had to be conscious of your takes, but now you could take as many takes as you want. It's too easy right now. Everything that you had to pay for before doesn't have to be paid for now.

So if you look at everything you had to pay for before, what you needed a label to pay for, it's now all eliminated. So really, what do you need a label for? But, you will need a team; you can't do anything on your own. But you got a pretty solid team. That shit ain't hard. Some people are afraid of the unknown, that's understandable because you haven't done it before. It's like that. Like death, you don't know what the fuck's gonna happen, so you be scared of it. But it's probably pretty dope, being that it happens to everybody. But what's gonna incentivize you to live if you know that death is fun? You know it may get scary, so with the unknown people are afraid to approach it, but once you get there it's not that bad.

I'm not scared of it because that's all I know, and I'm just not impressed with any of the people. Like, I really didn't like the way Lyor used to be fronting. It would make me mad 'cause he's, like, a little dude. He's like a big fish in a little pond. But, like, in a big business, he's not respected because he can't make money outside the culture. "So why come fronting on us?" I used to hate that shit because I used to know what he was doing. It's like if a dude hustles, and you know if somebody's getting money or not, and they on the block acting like they getting it, they copping ounces, but they acting like they copping keys. Lyor is copping ounces. He never used his own money, he was never anybody's boss. He ain't never, ever one time put up his own money for anything. So how come he was given that much power? Why was he given money? So, that would be my issue with the whole corporate thing.

Number one: they make you thank somebody from another culture like you need them, like you gotta have them involved. Like, 'I need you to tell me how to sell music to my people. I need you to take me to another level.' We never needed those dudes, ever. They made money off of us; they made money off tricking us into believing we needed them, and I always knew we didn't need them. That's why I never respected them and I always carried them the same way. Just like the Backstage tour and the Hard Knock Life tour, we put that together ourselves. That's why I was so aggravated that they tried to take the credit for it. I did that myself. I'm not saying that I didn't have a team, but they had nothing to do with it. They just showed up. I was like, 'Yo, we can put a tour together ourselves. We don't need them to do a tour.'

And it just so happened that we were all underneath the same umbrella through distribution, but that was a total coincidence. And it just so happened I fucked with them; and it just so happened that I fucked with the Ruff Ryders. Like, Dee and Waah, we were all cool. So we just put it together, and I was like, 'Don't try to come over here trying to act like you know what's up.' That's why I was so tight about the jackets in the movie. I was like, 'Don't act like y'all did this like you always do.' The reason why that was bothering me was because they made it seem like we needed them to do that tour, I wanted people to

know we could do a tour as big as anybody else. And it sold out, and at that time, rap wasn't on the road like that. People were shocked because before the Hard Knock Life Tour there was a lot of violence happening at a lot of the Hip Hop concerts before we went on the road. But violence was taking place because of the way they were doing it. People didn't have respect for each other. But I think when we were on tour because we didn't have any guns on the road and the security was Muslims with bowties, it became a respect thing. We all respected each other. We knew that it was us doing it, and we also knew that we had a responsibility because if that would've fucked up, it would have definitely fucked it up for everybody else. It was like that was the tester to see if people could do it and make people feel safe.

I then asked Dame if it's easier to go on the road as an independent.

All you need is a booking agent, that's it. You don't need anybody else. A booking agent, that's all you need. The "Label" doesn't even book your shows. You can promote your own shows.

Gems:

Every artist makes most of their money from their shows and merchandise.

Any independent artist looking to increase visibility should concentrate on developing the core demographic of their brand by answering these three questions: Who is my target audience? Why is that my target audience? Where is my target audience?

In today's market, it's easier for an independent artist to blow up now than it was back in the day. All you need to do is put more effort into your show by opening as well as starring in your own events, and developing merchandise and releasing all the digital content you can.

No one can operate or build an empire by themselves. You'll need a team to increase the visibility of your brand.

WEED, DMX, HOLLYWOOD, THE DEVIL

After Red and I ran through Dame's crackers and cheese, we started to talk with him about a lot of random things, from marijuana legalization to the Devil. Red set it off when he asked Dame, "Do you think legalizing marijuana is a bad idea?"

It's not bad. The only thing that made it bad is that lawmakers are saying it's illegal. It really was never meant to be illegal. It is safe for the economy, just like liquor saved the economy in the last recession. Alcohol at one time was illegal. Then they made it legal, they taxed it, and as a result, the economy grew. Back then a lot of people that were labeled as criminals got made into upstanding citizens, and for that decade, it was run by criminals. So, they're not going to let that happen again. Obama's very strategic. He's not dumb. He can't just say, "Weed is legal," like that because everyone that's a so-called criminal will become legal upstanding citizens. With something as serious as marijuana legalization, they have to feel it out

and do their own census. Trust me, they're going state to state slowly to feel things out, pause. If you pay attention, you'll see it's very strategic. I think it's smart. I mean that's how I perceive it; that's how I'm looking at it. If I were the President, I wouldn't make weed legal in a day because I know it would cause pandemonium. It would cause murder because a lot of criminals would be out of a job. Then you would also have to deal with outside opinion like the Republican Party, the one that's called "the unrealistic side." They'd be making up shit like it's the doorway to chaos, continuing to say weed was crazy in the first place. So, you can't just throw that on them all at once because it gives them a platform to talk shit. It has to be done gradually.

Red then brought to our attention that the American Government still has marijuana listed as a schedule one drug, next to cocaine. Dame being hip to what Red was talking about replied.

Yeah. This is just like investing in a new business model- you cannot do it overnight. If you're completely invested in an old business model, you can't even invest in a new business model until you make your money back from the old business model, which isn't clicking anymore, and this is a new business model. A while ago, I was trying to make a hybrid car with Malcolm Brickland. The Tesla and Karma was our competition. We called ours the 'Brickland.' I was trying to learn the business, and the problem with that was that if they changed the hybrid they would have to change all the parts; including the factory where the people would have to learn how to work with the new equipment. So you can't just do that overnight, especially when you just invested ten billion in an old thing. You would have to sell off all the old stuff before you can transition into hybrids or into electric cars because you have to change every part. So now whoever invested in the original hybrid or electric cars at one time had an industry to supply them with those parts, right? People were making screws, nuts, and parts for the old model. Now, people aren't going to buy the old parts anymore. What happens when it breaks down? Where would you get it fixed? Nobody could

Independent Cheese With Corporate Crackers

fix it! Unless you have the people that can facilitate whatever happens to those car models. If not then you're fucked up. So you can't just build an electric car; you have to build the support system for the electric car. You have to build the factories, you have to make the parts, and you have to educate people on how to fix it. Everyone's used to working out of Detroit. So, it's the same thing with the weed: they have to figure it out and really regulate that shit. By the time it's completely legal, they'll have a handle on how to monetize it, have people pay taxes, and get the so-called criminals outta there. They're just figuring it out. That's how I see it. I mean it's logical. That's the math.

Red said he was doing a documentary on marijuana and Hip Hop, and that's some good info that he could use. He then asked him what he thought about the cannabis movement?

I love it! I'm a smoke to it right now. Well, the thing about weed, with me, is I didn't smoke at first.

While we watched him spark and steam his herb, Red asked him how long has he been smoking?

I've been smoking heavy since the Big Pimpin video. That's when I started smoking. I used to smoke and get paranoid because I was very insecure.

About Taking Advice

I asked Dame if he still feels like he has something to prove?

I've already proven things in business, so when I walk in a room, I don't have to prove myself anymore. My history speaks for itself. The only thing now is that I don't have to listen to anyone because until you've made Jay Z and Kanye, and helped with Cam, Kevin Hart, and Rachel, then it's not really too much you can tell me. You can't tell me I'm doing anything wrong because you haven't done what I've done. That's another thing about advice: "Never listen to someone

giving you advice on shit they haven't done, ever in life." Like, if someone would try and tell me what to do, my response would be, "Have you done it? Then why are you talking to me about this?" It kills me to hear the opinions I get. So, you want me to apply your blind vision to my professional business and lose money?

About the Devil

Red asked Dame if he thought the CEOs of today were doing better business now than people from the nineties like Lyor Cohen.

Dame said, **"It can't work. I'm not gonna let them. They're lame."**

Red then asked, "Do you think the new generation is doing better business than before?"

Nah, they're not built like Lyor. That's one thing I have to give Lyor: he bangs out.

In response to what Dame was saying about Lyor Cohen, Red said that Lyor was always cool with him and Meth. But Dame wasn't trying to hear none of that.

Yeah, but that's the way they get you. The nicest niggas to you are the ones that's [Gesturing being stabbed in the back]. You can't stab a nigga in the back in front of him. You can't tell a nigga you about to stab him in his back. That's the thing about the Bible to me, right. They say the Devil came as a snake in the garden. Like, how the fuck? I would've ran from that. He had to come as a funny bunny rabbit or something; he had to trick her. You don't come as the Devil when you're the Devil. You come as something that's nice. The Devil never comes as the Devil, my nigga. When a nigga come and kill you, he's smiling. Evil is fucking intelligent; it plays on the things that you love. It's the only way it can survive. It has to cheat; it has to be strategic, just like a nerd. That's why I call the Devil a nerd because nerds don't fight. They get you back sneaky and don't want the credit for when they get

you back. But they'll get you back in their way without taking credit because they're too scared. They don't care. They have no ego or no pride.

About Integrity

After knowing Dame for way over ten years, I asked him about integrity because I've always wondered how he keep his integrity after being involved in the corporate world of Pimps and Hoes that will do anything for a dollar.

I don't know, man. I think God blessed me with nuts for a reason. He gives you nuts to fight. He wouldn't give you nuts to not stand up for yourself and fight. "You don't wanna fight? Give your nuts up." Pause. I got nuts man. I have compassion for women because they don't have nuts. I excuse them for everything, but I don't excuse men, pause. I know what I would do as a man. When you start acting like a woman, I ain't got no burn for you, and you'll notice that women don't have no burn for a man that acts like a woman.

When he said that, not speaking for Red, but I totally agreed with him because I believe with women, any man that acts like a woman will always get charged to the game with the quickness.

You think they loving you, but you an herb to them so you don't care. [A herb] "I don't care." Herbs know they're getting herbed, but they don't give a fuck, and a nerd doesn't give a fuck either. They have no pride. They'll do anything for the money because they can buy everything.

About DMX

I sat out on this conversation because Red and Dame are both friends with the legendary DMX, and both of them have their own stories of him—both agreed that DMX is a Rock Star. The conversation shifted to DMX when Red told Dame he should do a movie with DMX.

See, the thing about working with DMX is that there's an art

with that as well that you have to enjoy. You have to enjoy the process. So, if I'm in the mood for that, I would. Like, if you notice, I generally do stuff with people just because I enjoy whatever I'm doing with that people. So, like, even with the 'Hard Knock Life Tour,' there were certain challenging situations. But I enjoyed it; I bought into it. So, when I'm ready to buy into all that, I would work with him. I remember seeing him when I was shooting Paid in Full. He was shooting something in Canada and he was tearing that town down. He was on the front page of that town every day. They were damn near getting ready to kick him out of there. They were like, 'Yo, he gotta go!' On the first days, the articles were nice, but by the end they were like, 'He gotta go. He's bugging!' He was definitely bugging. But he's a Rock Star, so you can't be mad. I loved watching him be himself. There's no compromise with him. You have to love that about DMX. He's completely authentic and he wears it all on his sleeve. He's completely honest and that's what people love. That's why they'll always love him because he never hides anything. And he's insightful–very insightful," Dame said. "Like when you catch him when he gets into a rhythm, he says some very intelligent, deep shit. His perspective, at times, is really surprisingly on point, but it's the delivery that scares people. But whatever, man, that's how he communicates."

About Hollywood

Red said, "I noticed that doing business in Hollywood is kind of skeptical. It's actually harder than the music business. I mean maybe it's easy to you, but do you bring the same tactics from the music business into the movie business?"

I use the exact same tactics every time. Hollywood sucks because they move slower, and they're arrogant, and it's someone else's business. It's another culture's industry at the moment. They've created their own industry, and what you're trying to do is fit into what they want you to be, and all they want is to make money off of you because they could care less about you.

About Rebellion

I don't wanna be on a crowded block. In my first experience, I tried doing business the corporate way. It's just too demeaning. It's too fucking humbling for me. I've just done too much to have to be talking to people who don't put up their own money. In Hollywood, no one's putting up their own money. They're all making money off of people, but they're employing who they want, and it's whoever is going to listen. But a real 'Rock Star' doesn't listen. So, once you get signed and you start acting corporate, all of that being a 'Rock Star' leaves you. What makes you a 'Rock Star' is that you're rebellious. Once you get put in that corporate formula, a formalistic environment, you're not a 'Rock Star' anymore. You don't have an opinion, you have no point of view, and you get told what to do. I hate to see a 'Rock Star' get tamed. I hate that. That shit breaks my heart to watch someone who didn't give a fuck all of a sudden care about everything, and I've seen that happen often. I hate when it takes the 'Rock Star' right out of the Rock Star. Once you start listening, and getting patted on the back for money, the 'Rock Star' will leave you. [Gesturing to Redman]. Right or wrong? I know I wouldn't wanna see a 'Rock Star' that's known for being rebellious all of a sudden be subservient and told what to do by somebody that's not from the culture just because the check is big.

Damon, Kenyatta, & Redman
PCH- Malibu, CA
11:02pm

Gems:

Be cautious taking business advice from people who haven't experienced what they are telling you to do, unless you want to lose money. Never apply blind vision to your professional business.

Success will always follow the man or woman who has integrity.

A person with integrity will never go against the standard of doing right by others.

The person who will do anything for money, even if that means robbing people to come up, lacks integrity.

Hardship will always follow the person who lacks integrity.

You possess what I call an inner "Rock Star" that can create and achieve the impossible.

Kanye, Damon, & Q-Tip
Calabasas, CA
8:14pm

I TAUGHT JAY Z AND KANYE SELF SUFFICIENCY

I once had a barber named Jay who wanted to work as an apprentice under my license while he was finishing Barber College. I had just touched thirty, and he was about nineteen and ready to start his career as a barber, so it was an honor for me to help him come up in the hair game. The first week, I had Jay cutting kids' hair to see if he was cool enough to graduate to cutting adult hair. Once he graduated from the kiddy fades, it was off to the races. His haircuts were cool, but he kept pushing people's lines back with no chill. For two weeks straight, it was a lot of work fixing all of his mistakes, from "McDonald Arched" line-ups to giving out Hitler mustaches. To make matters worse, he couldn't handle criticism. He would always get bent out of shape when his customer would tell him something wasn't right. I always intervened when I would see him getting sensitive because I could see he paid more attention to getting paid than making sure his cuts were on point. Whenever I would see that his customer wasn't pleased, I'd lean over to him and tell him he didn't have to pay. Then one day, this gangsta dude came in and asked him for a shave and a line-up. Everything seemed like it was cool until Jay handed him the mirror and dude said, "Awww, Cuz! You fucked my mustache up! On Crip, look at my line!" Jay kind of laughed at how dude said that, but homeboy wasn't amused. It got crazy on some Boyz in the Barbershop movie type shit in an instant. Gangsta dude put the money on the counter, threw the mirror down, snatched off the cape, hairline and mustache hair flying everywhere. He said, "Cuz, I'll be back!" Since I didn't wanna die over a thin mustache and a bad line-up, I reacted fast.

On his way back, I could see he had a gun, so I calmly stopped him at the door, first giving him his money back, and then "politely" asking him if there was any way I could help fix the situation. He looked around at all of the people looking at him in fear, and said, "Naw, it's all good, but you need to tell that nigga don't be laughing in people's faces when he mess up, or he can get a real problem, on Crip!" After Jay's "Big Pushback," I immediately pulled him out of the deep end of the haircut pool and placed him in the shallow end to teach him the basics on how to not only cut a fly fade with a crispy line-up, but also how to conduct himself as an independent businessman.

The first lesson I taught him was how to conduct himself with customers. I taught Jay the difference between a customer and a client. I told him, "A client is a person who chooses to patronize your services on a consistent basis, and a customer is someone who has the potential to become a client once they admire your work, and both deserve respect. When both client and customer ask for a specific style, it's your job, as a barber to make that happen, and if they're not satisfied with your work, it's your job to rectify the situation with sincere concern. Humor is a definite "No', 'No' when a person isn't satisfied. A smile to an unsatisfied customer looks like you messed them up on purpose and you're trying to be funny, as you saw when Gangsta dude came back." Jay said he got it.

Then one day, I noticed he was getting at damn near every female customer that came through. I told him to chill on dating clients because if the relationship fails you're taking bread and butter off of your co-workers' tables. But, like all young men in the player stage, there was no chill. He started dating one of the beautician's main clients. For months it was "all good" until they fell out, which made the stylist lose money because the client stopped coming in. I was about to U-Haul his apprenticeship, but I could see he sincerely felt bad for messing up his co-worker's money. Jay said he got it and that it wouldn't happen again.

The week he passed his State Board test, he was excited to get back in the deep end of the haircut pool by renting a booth, but before I could let that happen, I had to put him back on kids for a minute to make sure he was paying more attention to his work than the money at the end of the service. He passed the test. I let him get down without his apprenticeship since he was licensed, and the rest is history. After eight years in the game, Jay now has his own shop and is one of the most sought after barbers in LA. I must admit I feel proud that I helped him on his journey to becoming a successful barber in the hair game. The truth is, back then, helping him helped me locate my shortcomings, fix them, and not only become a better barber, but a better businessman. Word up!

Continuing to look on in third person, Red asked Dame what his key was to bouncing back from being down; he explained why he could never be down after helping so many people become self-sufficient. In this chapter, Dame reflects on how teaching people to become self-sufficient is important in advancing the culture.

In my mind, I was never down. I just left a business. Let me ask you a question: do you know how big Rachel Roy is? It's a fifty million dollar business. The whole time they were bombing on me, I was never without that business, so how could I be down when I have a fifty million dollar business, if every single second I was down I've always had at least five people working for me? I employ people. How could I be down? Just because I'm not doing music or I'm not doing what y'all telling me to do, doesn't make me down. That makes y'all down.

The mentality of someone that's a corporate slave or someone that has a job usually tries to make the person that's independent look bad because of the freedom that comes along with having your own company. But still, what they don't realize is that the independent is always flipping, buying inventory, so there might be a time when a bill is paid late due to timing issues. So, to the corporate slave, their perception is that the independent is broke. When things don't hit in the marketplace, I call it "timing issues." I was never down, not one second.

The only curveball I didn't see coming my way was the taxes,

'cause I was paying people money to watch my taxes. So I didn't see that coming. In the process, the tax problems cut off the credit I needed to move forward. So, I had to get back on my regular hustle. As any entrepreneur knows, in a tax situation, you have to pay your taxes because credit is important. I had to become complete cash and carry during that period, but in the long run that was better because it helped me sustain the patience it takes to build any business. At that time, I was focused on building my companies, which is why when you heard people so-called bombing on me, I wasn't correcting their perceptions of me because I just didn't give a fuck. That's the reason why you never heard me defend myself about my finances for the past five years.

I never got into the "I'm not broke or I am broke" conversations because I didn't have an agenda to do so. That wasn't my focus; I was doing fashion. It's just that every second of my life became publicized by corporate media outlets to downplay the power of my independent businesses. So, they never talk about me in a positive light, like you've never seen an article back then about my art galleries all over, or the BlakRoc project with the Black Keys. Even when I did music, it was better than what anyone else was doing at the time, but I just wasn't trying to monetize it. I never stopped doing anything business-wise. I never disappeared. I just came back in front of everyone else just because I had to come back to save the culture and to expose the people that are content with robbing the culture.

What happened was I left the industry because I felt I couldn't help it anymore. All the people that I was employing, I was going it independent, so I was like, 'Yo, I can't pay y'all outta my pocket. Go let them pay you. It's not their money anyway.' So, whoever took the job could now be responsible for giving everybody else who I had love for a job in the industry because I couldn't give them a job. I refused to use other people's money. So, I went to do my own thing and let everybody live, but what I did start to notice was that people weren't in a better place, the culture wasn't better. Hip Hop is suffering on a whole because the people aren't making money like they're supposed to because they're getting robbed. So, when I was doing stuff for fun, like making music with Curren$y, and I saw how Joie played him and Tood Maskovitz played him, I'm like, 'Damn, they still doing this shit.'

And the reason why they're still doing it is because I didn't regulate them the first time. I'm looking at it like, 'They still trying this shit with me. I can just imagine what they doing to everybody else.' And yes, people are still dying; they're still making money off beef, and I don't see them squashing nothing. Did Lyor ever sit anybody down and squash beef? Did you ever hear of him doing that? Putting two black men in a room and say, 'Stop fighting?' Have you ever heard of that? Well I've done that many times. Did you ever hear Lyor say, 'Don't act stupid, man. It's embarrassing for your culture'? Did he educate you? Did he ever tell you whatever you were doing was impacting children? Or did he ever ask you if you were giving back? Did he ever even ask you those questions?

Red said "no." Then Dame asked Red if he ever asked him about his culture? Without hesitation, Red said, "He didn't have to." Still pressing the issue to see if Lyor cared about the culture beyond making money off the culture, Dame also asked Red did he ever see him giving back to the culture? Red responded, "I wasn't in his business like that."

No, it's our business," Dame said. "He's making money off us! Naw, you make money off me, give back! The same kids you make money off of, make sure they have a positive influence. Make sure that the rappers you make money off of, when they get older, that they're protected! Did he ever tell you how to save your money? Did he ever sit you down and tell you that?"

Without hesitation Red said, "No."

"That's crazy!" Dame said. "He wanted you to run out of money, 'cause then he could control you."

After patiently listening to Dame's thoughts on Lyor, Red said, "I didn't think it was his job."

It is his job! If I'm making money with you, that's my job.

Anytime I'm making money off you, my responsibility is to make sure that you're protected. Like, in a company, my job is to make money for my partners. As a businessman, it's your job to worry about other people before you worry about yourself. I know I sat down with all my artists and made sure that their bank accounts and that their bookkeepers were doing right. I wouldn't even sign an artist if I knew he was getting robbed. Like, if somebody came to me that was signed to a production deal and the management was robbing them I would say, "No, I'm not doing that. I'm not helping you fucking rob this kid just so I can make money off him." I would never do that. If I see somebody spending too much money, I'm telling them. I used to bark on Jacob like, "Why you keep fucking letting my artist go down there and spend all their advance money?" That shit isn't right. That shit's not right, to make money off of people and not educate them. You think that's right? Come on, man, especially if you're a stranger in another person's culture. You don't think you should have to fucking help that culture you're making money off of, and you're not making off your own culture?" He's fucking definitely donating shit to his culture with our money. Who is he helping with the money he makes off us?

Dame's breakdown about the moral reasons why someone should help the person who they're making money off of to become self-sufficient caused Red to ask, "So, is it that he's the smart one and we're not smart to recognize that?"

For certain people, out of fear. What it is—is that he's smart enough to give you this illusion and make you think he's helping you when he's hurting you. It's the devil's trick. He acts like a nice guy, but he doesn't help you. Has Lyor ever helped you?

Without even having to think about it, Red said, "Hell naw!"

Alright then. What's so nice about that? Because he's robbing you 'cause he's making money off you, but when you need him he's not there. He's not going to educate you how to protect your future, even though he's protecting his own. That's what I'm saying. I need that conversation with him. Why won't he? I want

to talk to him publically and ask him why not? Why? How does he justify robbing this culture like that without any explanation? And what did he do to deserve that, besides rob Russell? Why? You shouldn't be looking at him as a boss in something that's our culture. You gotta ask him to put out records to your people, and it's your music. Does that add up?

That just puts that mentality out there that we need them. That's what he's doing. He's not working in front of you and telling you this; he's putting that in the back of your brain. He's doing it sneaky. 'You need me; you're my slave; and you work for me. Be happy, be happy you're getting money. Spend all of it so you can need more and be more in debt so I can have more control over you.' I mean is that not the math? That's not an emotional thing. He can't do it to me, so I'm not mad at him for doing it to me, I'm mad at him for doing that to y'all! For making you worry when you don't have to, for not telling you how to do the business. Right? Why wouldn't he tell you how to do the business and don't be a slave? Like, 'Yo, Dog, let me tell you how to do this.'

See, what you notice about everyone I work with is I teach them how to do it without me. So, Jay can survive without me; Kanye can survive. I taught them. They could never tell you I didn't teach them. I teach you how to go ahead and win without me. Go live. 'I don't want to run your company all your life; I'm not you.' To me that's wack. I don't like that, managing other men. I don't like doing things for dudes. I just don't. I don't think men are here to work with men; I think men are here to help women. Men are supposed to help themselves. That's how I had to make a conscious effort to put money into me, and my point of view, and my brands, and my movies, and me directing, and put my name on it. I need to make money off me right now. I don't like making money off niggas too much. I'll make money with a nigga. We partners, but I'm not making money off a nigga. I don't like that, that's not me, I'm not a fee guy. We can fucking eat the food we kill together. I'm just as equal as you. When that thing happened with Jay, he was like, 'I need more.' I was like, 'Naw, I know what I do.' And that was the end of Roc-A-Fella because I wasn't negotiating. I know my worth.

After Dame said all of that, Redman fell back in his seat and said, "Shit..." as if he was amazed by the clarity of Dame's speech. Dame finished going into how he helps people become self-sufficient.

I mean it is what it is. I know my worth. I know what I do; I make people rich so I can't be down. As long as Jay's rolling, how can I be down? As long as Kanye's rolling, how can I be down? Nobody beat them yet. I have no reason to come back out of retirement. Just 'cause they doing it without me, that's still me right there. Every time I see that nigga I'm like, 'Shhh... I'm not mad. I'm happy.' The bigger they get, the bigger I am. Unless my ego would get involved, but that's fucking corny. I don't have a vagina.

I don't want that nigga to go away; I want him to win. The more they win, the more I look good. That's my motto: "The more your crew got, the better you look. Am I right or wrong? So I look like a good boss. Do I look like a bad boss or a good boss? Everybody around me was rolling, and they're still rolling without me. 'Go ahead, go get independent.' I never locked none of them niggas up like slaves. Right or wrong? They could all walk away, which they all did, and I'm alright with it. I wanted them to. I make you self-sufficient, then I let you do your thing. Go ahead. I'm not even letting you. Please, go ahead and do your thing. I got my own life to live. I made money off you, so my present to you is to teach you how to make money off yourself. So, you don't need a middleman anymore, and they all went independent.

Dipset, Cam, Jim, Jay, Kanye, they're all living, right? They're all eating because I taught them all how to do it, and every time I see them getting robbed, even if I don't have shit to do with it, I'm like, 'Naw, that's not how you do it.' Period. None of my friends are getting robbed on my watch, and as a result you know this, at least on the Harlem side. It's like me and Cam are all good. It's like we get money every day. It feels like we're cheating life because we're having too much fun.

Gems:

By any means necessary, a corporate slave will always downplay independence because they envy the freedom that comes along with having your own company.

An independent entrepreneur is a person who continuously buys and flips inventory.

A boss must develop the characteristic of patience while moving with passion.

Being self-sufficient is the foundation of independence.

Every accomplishment is self-bestowed.

The measure of your success is the measure of your belief in yourself. Confidence is key.

Your belief in yourself is your belief in God, and your belief in God is your belief in yourself.

Raquel & Damon
Vernon, CA
1:06pm

POLITICS AS USUAL

Before we started filming the "Politics As Usual" chapter, while the battery was being replaced in the camera, we were building on why envy is hard to avoid when you are having so much fun as an independent business owner. We also explored: How can one find someone to go into business with you without that person feeling the need to outshine the voice of the company?

It's hard to find someone to work for you when you're having so much fun, especially someone who is not going to eventually want to be you. Like look how managers end up being fucking rappers or end up on reality shows. It's really hard not to get absorbed by all that attention and all the money that comes from it. So you have to find someone that has no desire in being you, and that's hard. That's why I generally like to work with women because they don't want to be you. They want to help you, but dudes, they always want to be you.

Culture Vultures

Gems:

The best managers are the people who don't have a desire to be an artist.

I've found that the best managers for men happen to be women because women have a desire to help a man be the best he can be.

CORPORATE OPTIONS

This was Redman's first time being an independent artist after being signed to Def Jam for over twenty years. He asked Dame if an artist has a distribution deal, does that interfere with them owning their music?

That is 'owning' your own music. That's just paying somebody to put your music out. That's like somebody cleaning your house; that doesn't mean that's their house. I'm not saying that you can't work with corporate; you just can't work for corporate. There is an option, and I'm not saying I won't work with corporate. Like, I hear some people saying, 'Well you wasn't saying that when they was giving you money.' Man, they didn't give me shit. We were partners. We put money in that shit. You acquire something that we fucking brought value to. We brought that; we ain't giving you nothing. Y'all wasn't fucking with us when we wasn't rolling.

Red then asked him if being a partner be the only way he would do business with corporate?

A distribution deal, in essence, is hiring them. They won't want you to say it like that, but that's what it is. You own your own masters, and when you don't feel like working with them anymore, you take your masters with you. They might give you an advance against what you're going to sell, but that's so they can make money off you. Like, the distribution deals I've done, I don't even want them to give me any money until I hand them the product. I don't want them acting like I owe them anything. I don't want to owe anybody money. I want you to make your money back day one. As soon as I give it to you, it's on you now. Basically you're giving me the money to make sure that you do your job 'cause I'm trusting you with something valuable.

Gems:

A distribution deal means that the distribution company works for you because you own your masters. They might give you an advance against what you're going to sell, but that's so they can make money off of you.

I've learned to never take an advance from the distribution company until I have my product ready to hand them. That way they can't front like I owe them anything.

Basically the distribution company gives you money to be involved in distributing something valuable, which is your product.

Filming The Secret To Ballin Journey Kenyatta, Redman, Michelle Gentle, & John Whittaker, Crenshaw, CA
6:12pm

PCH - Malibu, CA
6:58pm

BEACH CHAIR LIFE

Dame stood up, dusted the ashes from his clothes, and walked to open the balcony door that was facing the ocean. As soon as it slid open, the fresh air moved in and the sound of the ocean immediately filled the room. When Red heard the screech of the ocean, he said, "Them waves sound like a car crashing."

You get used to it; there's no better sleep than sleeping next to the waves because the ocean has a rhythm, it's a beat. It's a pulse. That ocean breathes, man. The ocean is dangerous. That ocean is full of nothing but energy, there's nothing but pure energy in the ocean. Period. It's a lot of shit going on in the ocean, B. That shit is dangerous; that shit broke my collarbone messing with that ocean. In the ocean, you have to go with the flow. You can't ever go against the flow of the ocean. That's why when you look at the sea, you just feel relaxed; it makes you relax. If you get nervous in the ocean and go against it, you gonna get broke. You gotta turn into that shit and just move with

Culture Vultures

it, like life. Life is like surfing: when the waves come, I just roll with them. If you go against it, you're gonna get hurt.

Red then said, "Sometimes going against the grain is not bad."

It depends on which grain it is, though," Dame said. "Like, if somebody creates a grain, fuck that grain. That's why I'm not listening to any fucking shit contrived by some human man. What man can tell me what to do? As long as I'm not hurting anybody else, I don't believe in rules by people that fucking enslaved me, and tricked my culture, and robbed me. Those rules don't work for me. Those rules don't mean I win. So, I don't play by none of those rules, but that doesn't mean that those are rules. The real rules are God's rules. Period. Like, at the end of the day, let's say that there was a law, whatever that law was, and if you broke that law you went to jail but at the end, you went to Heaven, or wherever it is. Like, that was supposed to be what you were supposed to do. Now you're going to hell because somebody told you what to do when your test was not to listen. Sometimes, the test in life is not to be told what to do.

Gems:

The real rules are God's rules. Period.

Raquel M. Horn
Rincon, PR
1:13pm

Biggs, Claudie B, Damon, Alex
Lower East Side, NYC
3:57pm

CAN'T KNOCK THE BLUEPRINT

The way I do business is I start companies. I build them then I let somebody else run them. Or I might even start a company for someone by getting it started. When I start a company, I have to run the cash register first. Like, if I have a block, I have to click on that shit first; I have to pitch myself first; I have to know what's going on. I have to interact with the customers; I have to make sure I'm not getting robbed and I have to know everything. You have to do that first, but I enjoy it. I love the concrete. I also love the ocean, that's why I come here and just chill. But when I hit the city, I'm on the pavement. I'm hitting that concrete because I enjoy it. I sell one company; I invest right in another one, but that's me. Everyone is not built for that. But I also like to be creative as well; the way I do business is also creative. Like, I can get high every day. I smoke weed every day, and that's not for the kids, but I have ten businesses that are all independently owned and I'm doing it like this. [Gesturing to how he's dressed]. I don't have to wear a suit and tie. I get up whenever I want and I employ whoever I want.

I could see that Red was one hundred percent with everything Dame was saying when he said, "That's the best kind of business to fucking have."

"It's the only business I know," Dame said. "I remember they were trying to conform at Def Jam and I was like, "Y'all bugging! You ain't ever gone tell me what to do, never!"

Red then asked Dame if he still has anything to learn from the music business?

Yeah, from business in general. Not from the music business. I mean I think what's happening right now is revolutionary. So yeah, definitely, this direct-to-consumer thing and not needing a label—I'm loving the evolution of that and the freedom it's giving people. So yeah, I have a lot to learn always. Like, every day, I have a lot to learn. I don't have what I want; I'm still fighting for it. I'm still in the fight. I haven't won yet. My fight, to somebody else, might look like I'm winning, but my fight, I haven't won that fight yet, and it's a long fight. I don't want to win yet because I know I'll get bored. That's why I keep making my fight more complicated. Like, if my fight was to be a Hip Hop mogul, I would've did that shit ten years ago. So why the fuck would I do that now? It's boring to be a Hip Hop mogul after the first five years. That's what I tell people because I know how it is. It sucks because you get grown; Hip Hop people get older, and also the demographic for Hip Hop is really fifteen to twenty-five. That's the age of your fans. I'm not trying to be talking to kids that aren't my age. I want to evolve with my peers. Like, I wouldn't want to be on Hot 97; I'm ready to go to WBLS. That's just me. I'm fucking forty-three years old. I don't want to be the old dude in the club. I never did. I want to be the youngest dude in the club. If I'm the richest person in the room, I'm in the wrong room. I'm getting robbed. I have nothing to gain there. If I'm in that type of environment, all I can do is give them something, or they're going to take something from me. I'd rather be the poorest nigga in the room. That's always been my motto, and I don't want to be the youngest; I don't

Independent Cheese With Corporate Crackers

want to be the oldest dude in the room either. Not that I won't hang out with old people, I want to be around my element; that's around my age. The thing that happened with me was I got successful so young that I looked older to people my age, and to older people, I was far beyond my years. But to some executive, I was always looking crazy because at the time, I was a twenty-three year old millionaire flipping on everybody. But I was twenty-three, so that was a part of the immaturity I expressed in that environment, which was totally opposite in the streets because in the streets, I'm calm, but in business, I'm the wildest nigga. I'm known for being calm in the streets, not wild. I'm known for being wild in corporate. The so-called wild shit that I used to do in corporate America is normal in the streets, like being honest, being direct, wanting to get paid for what you do, and not wanting to get played. All of that is normal behavior in the streets.

Plus I'm from the snobbiest part of Harlem. I was down with a crew called 'The Best Out.' When we were outside, we were getting money, and we was laughing at niggas that wasn't getting it. When crack first came out, we were outside hustling, and we were super arrogant. We were Harlem arrogant because our crew consisted of a lot of dudes from different blocks, and what we knew was that we always looked better as a team. So, we always knew that when we hustled together, if there were more of us that had shit, it made us look "ILL." We always looked better than everybody, and we always voted for each other. We always wanted each other to look big by trying to make each other rich. It's a different motto. Like, my motto is 'Make Your Friends Rich' because if you had something to do with making that happen, how could you go broke? How could I ever go broke if I helped my friends come up? And I know that if I need something, I could probably even call you just because you're a cool dude, and if you have it, you would give it to me. I've done a lot for my friends; there's far too many people that I've helped for me to ever go broke. That's why I make people rich because it secures that I could never go broke. Like, every time I have a timing issue, I just call Cam. He sends it right over with no problems because timing issues do happen."

Culture Vultures

He smiled as Dame talked about Cam'ron saying, "Killer Cam, that's my nigga right there."

"Yeah he's fucking burnt out in business; you don't even know. He loves to hustle. All he wants to do is flip money."

Gems:

When you start any business, it's important that you remain hands-on until you fully understand how you make your money and how things work.

When I start any company, I have to run the cash register first. Like, if I have a block I have to click on that block first; I have to pitch myself first. I have to know what's going on; I have to interact with the customers; I have to make sure I'm not getting robbed and I have to know everything.

My motto is "Make Your Friends Rich" because if you have something to do with their success, how could you ever go broke when you help them come up?

Cam'Ron & Damon
Poppington Gallery, LES
9:23pm

L

SHAME IN THE GAME

While Dame was reminiscing about the Hard Knock Life Tour, he asked Red:

"Back in the day when we were on tour, what did we used to do? They didn't drink, so they used to drink with me, and I didn't smoke, so I used to smoke with them." Thinking back, Red said, "That's right. That was wild."

"So, every day we would be looking for each other. Like, "Where you at? What's up?" We'd have a battle every time." Thinking back over the good memories, Red added, "But it was a straight up black-owned tour, man. That's what I dug about it the most. Everybody on the tour was straight up homeboys from different camps, and we were getting it in."

I told him that Red told me about the time he had to put hands on somebody that was talking flagrant on the Hard Knock Life Tour. Red said, "Oh yeah, Dame got hands. He don't play those games."

Yeah, I had to dress him up. I told him, "Yo, don't do it, B.

I'm a fuck you up. I'm not playing with you." But that's also a part of being a freedom fighter, every freedom fighter should know how to fight. Defense is necessary because everyone is trying to rob you. Trust me, anybody that's a good dude has to know how to fight; you have to be dark. There's no being good because people will take advantage of you. So what do you do when people take things from you? How do you defend yourself? You can't talk your way out of certain scenarios. That's another thing—back in the earlier days of Hip Hop, it was a lot of fighting. It was serious because people were coming from an extreme environment. That's what was selling at the time. It wasn't a peaceful time. Motherfuckers were selling their experiences from selling drugs and killing, so it was a lot of egos in the room, a lot of overcompensation. But we were young. What the fuck, we were kids with a whole lot of money…

Red then asked Dame if he thinks people stick together like they used to back in the day.

"Nah, I think they stick together way more now. That's why I was fucking with the young niggas because they were hanging with each other. Like Curren$y, Wiz, and Smoke were all hanging out and they were from different places. That's what I've always liked about them. I think with this independent thing, there's a very even balance that's going on right now. I think before, it was ridiculous to be independent. Now there's half-independent and then there's half-pop. To be honest, I feel like the people that aren't independent feel ashamed that they're not independent. It seems like whenever I see somebody that's plugged into the corporate system, they be looking guilty. They don't even want to look me in the eyes."

I thought about the heat I heard listening to Red's new Muddy Waters 2 album in the car prior to these interviews. I asked Dame how Redman, who is from the "Golden Era" of Hip Hop, could market his new album to the people.

"Strictly online, selling your music through the Internet,

and then the only way you're really supposed to market your music is at your show."

Red agreed, saying, "Yeah because there ain't anymore 'Mom and Pop' stores like it used to be when we came up."

"Again, the way you market your music is through your show," Dame said. "That's the marketing event: your show. That's the way you market yourself. You go into a marketplace and you set up shop. You physically go there. That's what a 'Promo Tour' is. You're going in there to sell what you're doing. You have to get with the people; there is no other way for music. Most people think the only way to market is to make sure your product is good enough that word gets around, which is true to an extent, but for me, I don't care if your music is good. I want to know about your show because anyone could sound good in the studio. It's about the show."

I think anyone that has seen Red perform can agree that whether he's solo or with Method Man, his stage show is always on point. That's why at this time, I stated that his shows were official. Dame went back saying, **"I ain't gon' lie, the first time I seen you perform was in Long Island, and this was a long time ago. He had a hockey stick or some shit like that. It was like the first time anyone heard about Redman. It was like when you first got signed. It was like a Jones Beach kind of thing. It was some promo shit. That's shit was crazy, and you tore that shit down. We was like, 'That nigga can rap.' But you had to back then—you had to know how to rap. Like, now you don't really have to know how to rap because people buy into people. But in his day [referring to Redman], you had to be very lyrically inclined, and a lot of what you were saying had to be truthful. You couldn't be lying. Telling the truth was what Roc-A-Fella was all about. Like, our thing with everything was that everybody was lying because we were really getting money, so we was talking about money, but we was really getting it. So, we saw all the rappers talking like they were connected, and we were like, 'Y'all niggas ain't getting money. We're the connect.' But it was a different time back then. Like, you had to have skills.**

Like, it was Nas; it was Jay; it was Redman. I mean it was crazy. You still can't fuck with these niggas."

Still digging for more information on independence for the homie, Red, I asked Dame: Does Red now have to build his brand from an independent foundation?

"You just have to work hard, that's it. But he's good. He's a brand; Redman is already a brand. He's made movies. He's toured the world. Everybody knows Redman. Him and Meth were the first Buddha heads that weren't passive. They were the first funny, aggressive Buddha head thugs. That was a group back when it was like a backpack thing. They were the Cheech and Chong of rap for that time, for that moment, and a lot of people have patterned their careers after them. So he can go into any Smoke Fest, any Cypress Hill Tour, or any Smoke Dza show, or anywhere the Buddha heads are happening, and he's God. It's culture now. It's a culture. That shit is legal; it's like alcohol now."

Gems:

The best way for anyone in music to market themselves is through their shows.

It doesn't matter how good your music is if your show sucks. Anyone can sound good in the studio; your stage show is all that matters.

Taylor, RedMan, Bianca, Raquel, Damon & Kenyatta
Bel-Air, CA
10:19pm

Deon, John, Josh, & Damon
Poppington Gallery
Lower East Side, NYC
12:06pm

Independent Cheese With Corporate Crackers

FRIEND OR FOE

There's nothing better than getting money with people you've known for over twenty and thirty years because they know you and you know them. But it's not your responsibility to be the best artist and the best businessman, you'll have to create a team that knows business and eventually, you'll have to check them. You have to check them because you can't trust anybody with your dough. Human nature will always kick in on some level, at some point, and you never know your money's short when you're rolling. You only know when shit starts slowing down. You'll be like, 'Got damn, that bill ain't paid. Why? I thought I had this much.'

When I got a late bill, that's how it happened to me. I was like, 'Where's my money? I thought I had five million dollars in the bank. This accountant nigga told me I had five million dollars.' I found out I didn't have it. It was a promissory note that needed to be liquidated for five million dollars, and I told them, 'I'm not going to do the deal with Roc-A-Wear unless you can liquidate the five million dollar note because I need all that liquid to buy goods for Rachel Roy, so don't do the deal.' It's crazy because even on my ledgers that he would send to me, he would send it to me counting that five million, so I always thought I had it. I was like, 'Yo, where's the money?' And he was like, 'Well... I didn't...' I said, 'I told you not to do the deal unless it was liquidated.' He told me it was liquidated. Come to find out, it was unsecured which means if I needed the money, I had to liquidate it. I had to sell it for fifty-cents on the dollar. So, my five million, man, turned into two-point-five. This is what an accountant did. I lost two-point-five behind that. The only way you can rectify shit like that is to go to court, and it takes a long time, and a lot of people ain't built for that, but I am. I never do that fee shit with lawyers. I got everybody on payroll. That paying by the hour shit isn't good for lawyers. I don't play that fee shit, fuck that. When you pay somebody for time, they going to waste it all day, especially a lawyer. You pay for everything. They wait out every moment saying, 'and, and, and, or, or, or' just keeping you on their clock. The more they talk, the more you have to pay them. Period.

Gems:

It's always a wise move to create a team of individuals who know more than you do in business.

Never trust anyone with your money. Human nature will always kick in on some level, at some point, and you never know your money's short when you're rolling. You only know when things start slowing down.

Never pay a lawyer by the hour because they will usually waste time to collect more fees. I have everyone on payroll because when you pay someone for their time, they'll waste it, especially a lawyer.

Lawyers that are paid by the hour wait out every moment saying, 'and, and, and, or, or, or.' Their mission is to keep the clock running because the more they talk, the more you have to pay them.

Damon & Kenyatta
Los Angeles, CA
12:06pm

ON TO THE NEXT ONE (THE OCTOPUS)

I ain't gonna lie, watching Dame over the years put an equal amount of time into all of his businesses, without getting overwhelmed, is a trip, especially because he keeps a clear vision of where he wants each one of his companies to go. He told me how he runs so many companies without getting confused.

Well, my business model is called 'The Octopus'. "The octopus, pause, has a head and eight legs, but if you cut one of those legs off, it grows back. Nothing happens to the head; it grows back. So that's how I look at business. I have a lot of different companies. If one fucks up, I cut that bitch off. Nobody even notices because all the other ones are there. It doesn't affect the head. See, I was always invested in movies, invested in fashion, invested in different things because I never wanted music to define me.

I learned that from Russell because there was a time that

Def Jam wasn't making too much music and they weren't hot at all. But the Def Comedy Jam show was keeping Def Jam hot. And he told me, 'Yo, as you see I'm not doing anything in music right now, but everyone's still saying my name because I'm doing Def Comedy.' And I was like, 'You right.' I'm never going to fall off and not be hot because I'm always going to be doing something that's hot. So I haven't made any music at a level to monetize in a while. I still own brands like Rachel Roy. I'm always doing something to increase the value of the culture, so I will never be dependent on one thing. That comes from being insecure. I don't trust one thing. I don't trust anything in one business because I feel like, at all times, it could go down.

I don't ever want to be dependent on anything. I've always planted a lot of seeds as something else is rolling. Like, while the music's making money, that's the time I could be reckless in something else and lose money because I have so much money over here in this other business. So, the reason I went into Roc-A-Wear was because it was so much money coming in from what was happening at Roc-A-Fella. Then once Roc-A-Wear started making money, I started investing in Rachel Roy because Roc-A-Wear was making a lot of money. Basically, I'm always planting a seed and letting it struggle while I'm comfortable someplace else. But what happened with Rachel Roy, where I got fucked up, was that I invested a lot of money in Rachel Roy, but when I sold half the company to Jones I didn't get the money that I put into the company back. So, I didn't have any money to put into something else, and then I had tax problems, which also meant I didn't have the credit I needed to move forward. Then on top of that, everyone was being sneaky and using other people's money to bomb on me because they had jobs. So, I couldn't fight that, and I really didn't even care because it wasn't affecting me. I had to just flip and buy things with no credit while I was waiting to get my money back from Rachel Roy. Now when the money came back from Rachel Roy, all of a sudden, I had ten new companies that had no debt on, and I'm one-hundred-percent independent. I was like, damn, I can do this with nobody, with people bombing on me, with tax problems, and still build ten businesses and have no debt on any of them, and now I'm in a better position

than I've ever been. My foundation is solid. That's why I really have no respect. I don't need them to make me wealthy I can do everything. As long as my work is good, they're buying. As long as I continue to do quality things and I'm consistent, it doesn't matter what anyone says. Of course people are always going to talk, but that means nothing to me.

Gems:

Stop relying on people outside of your culture to make you wealthy.

Invest more time into developing your brand. As long as the product you're selling is good, people will buy and continue to buy.

Damon & Kenyatta
Bel-Air, CA
8:49pm

THE 360 DEAL

Redman said to Dame and I that in the beginning of his career, he didn't care about the ins and outs of his contract. He just wanted to be signed to a deal.

"We were young, and it was the first time we was doing it. You didn't know that shit. You not supposed to know it at that age. You were just enjoying what was going on. You were just happy to be in the game. That's a dream come true at that moment. You're enjoying it."

Looking at Dame, Red said, "You gotta admit it was way better back then when we came in. Deals were better than they are now. Nobody was really thinking of independence. I know I wasn't thinking about being independent back then."

"But listen, you know what happened," Dame said. **"Remember when crack first came out and they were selling**

twenty-dollar bottles. That was because everybody didn't have it. The block wasn't crowded yet, but then it got a little crowded, so people started selling dimes, then it went to nicks, then there were trays, then it went to two for fives. It's over, and basically it just got oversaturated. It was a lot of competition, so it's just like that in the music industry. The artist today gets less while corporate profits the most. So everyone was starting to compete for the same slot. It just got oversaturated for that business model, but also the Internet came into play. And also people weren't as bright. There weren't that many independent people in the business back then. Roc-A-Fella had a co-venture. We were never signed to anybody. We kept our independence."

I never knew what type of business arrangement Dame had when he owned Roc-A-Fella, so I asked him if his deal with Def Jam was strictly for distribution.

"No, it was strictly a co-venture. We were partners. That's why I'd be like, 'Yo, stop treating me like y'all paying for shit when you haven't funded anything. We've already generated that money! We've already put money into this. Y'all just acquired some equity under a certain condition. That doesn't mean we should be appreciative, and on top of that, it's not your money!' At the end of the day, it was never any of their money. It used to trip me out because I didn't get how somebody could make decisions about your life, and they're not even putting up the dough, they're just making a hired decision. That's too much power to give to someone, especially when they're not putting up the dough. They don't know what to do. They're taking hired chances with your career. That's your life they're playing with.

I mean think about it, there've been Civil Wars over that shit," Dame said. "People get tricked into being slaves, but it's just a different kind of slavery at this time in history. It's more psychological now. But again, I think it's getting better because people are creating from a totally even playing field because of the Internet, and they're winning. Like, you don't necessarily have to have a 'Hit Record.' You can just create a following, pack a venue, sell merchandise, and win. For real, an artist can make crazy money on the road like Rock Stars do. That's really the business model for music and a lot of other things in entertainment—it's the road. That's what Rock and Roll has always been about, and Hip Hop today is Rock and Roll."

I told Dame that Red says he constantly stays on the road, and Dame said, **"That's what you do. That's how you make your money. That's how you pay your bills as an artist: your shows and your merch."** So does that mean now that Red is independent, he has to stay on the road to sell his records?

"Yeah. But that's why I don't like the 360 for a creative because then corporate takes some of your show and merchandise revenue. They take your merch, your show, and they also take your endorsements," Dame said. **"That shit is crazy. Lyor invented that bullshit. That's why it was better before the 360 deals hit the game."**

I asked Red if he was ever signed to a 360 deal, and emphatically he said, "Hell no! That's unheard of. I wouldn't have made any money if I was signed to a 360. I'd be trying to rob y'all motherfuckers if I was a 360 nigga. I'd be out there doing dumb shit if I had a 360 deal. Yeah, that ain't the move. I heard that shit is going on though. Yo, that shit ain't cool, man." Amused by Red's response, Dame said, **"The 360 deal is like diabetes: it doesn't kill you overnight, it breaks you down over time. When you get older, you gonna be like, 'Yo, I need all that.' It'll be like, 'Oh shit, where's my publishing? Why do I still have to ask niggas what to do? I'm a grown-ass man.' The 360 is the ether B…"**

Gems:

Because of the "360 Deal," most artists today have less money while corporate profits the most. The "360 Deal" eats your show money, your merchandise money, and it also eats your endorsements. The "360 Deal" is like diabetes: it doesn't kill you overnight; it breaks you down over time.

Independence starts with investing in yourself.

I think it's better to do business with corporate than to work for corporate expecting them to provide you with the platform to create a legacy.

The Internet has created an even playing field that's allowing more teams to win. You don't necessarily have to have a "Hit Record." You can just create a following, pack a venue, sell merchandise, and win.

Independent Cheese With Corporate Crackers

I'M A BUSINESSMAN

After Dame finished rolling up, Red asked him what's his real motivation in business?

"I like to run around the world because I want to know culturally what other people are doing. I really think I'm the coolest guy in the world. So, I want to travel around the world to see if there is anybody cooler than me that I can learn from them, and I haven't found that guy yet. But I have found some people that are as cool as me. But another thing is that I have A.D.D. (Attention Deficit Disorder). I can't stay in the same state for more than a couple of weeks. After I'm there for a minute, I'm out. I can't stay still for too long. Even when I'm in America too long I be like, 'Yo, I gotta get outta here' because I've been here too long. I get bored. I don't want to see the same things. It's like going to the same club over and over again with the same girls and the same people, with the same outfits, with the same agenda. There's no growth, no evolution. In business, you're supposed to grow ten-percent every year regardless. If you don't do that, then you're not doing good business. But that's me. I'm a killer for business. That's all I do—I flip. I started out hustling, and I still hustle as an independent which is buying something and selling it for more than I bought it for. Whoever sells it for me I know what I need to pay them; I know I have to put the money back into the goods, and re-up, and buy and buy more goods."

Red told him that it seems like he has the right connections and Dame said, **"Well, you have to make those connections and turn them into good connections. Like, in business, people really don't fuck with you unless they can make money off of you. So, when you're rolling, people are going to try and make money off of you. That's just what it is. It's just like that in the streets. When you buy a car, all of a sudden, your stock goes up. That's why I used to always buy a car before anything because that used to make so many more people want to get money with me. Soon as I bought a car, everybody I knew either hit me with some work or wanted to get hit with some work. All 'The Connects' started coming because they knew I was getting money. Buying a car is like branding yourself.**

I also realized that the key to my success has been to make money off of the things I love like my lifestyle. I monetize my lifestyle because I don't just do anything for money. Even right now, as we speak, we're monetizing this moment for this book as well as the film. I look at every second of my life as a way I can make money. Why not? We build brands to do so, and when the cameras are on us, it's our responsibility, socially, to say something positive, something that teaches because we've learned from trial and error. So, why not allow people to learn from our experiences? Monetize the moment; that's all I've ever done throughout my life in business. The code I live by in business is to care more about other people than myself because I have an Executive mindset. Selfishness is for the artist. As a rule, they only worry about themselves. See, as an artist, you have to worry about yourself, and as a businessman, you're always worrying about someone else. At all times, I've always put other people before myself. I pay other people's bills before I pay my own because I need my employees to work; I need them to continue making moves for me. I look for long-term benefits when it comes to business. The businessman that's looking at immediate satisfaction is only looking for their own pay day while overlooking everyone else that's important to the big picture.

Executive responsibility was something I got used to before

Roc-A-Fella because I've had custody of my son since I was nineteen. He's lived with me since he was eight years old. Even to this day, I'm conscious of every move I make. I'm always worried about how it affects the people I love. So, that's another thing about being a businessman, you have to learn not to really give too much of a fuck about yourself. But I'm sick of that shit. That's why now I'm being my own artist with my own point of view because people don't like when you make money off you. Like, an artist really doesn't like when someone keeps making money off their creativity regardless. I know they be thinking like, 'Goddamn! Every time I make you money, I have to give him something!' In business, anytime you tell someone what to do you're only telling that person to do something for your own agenda. Don't get it twisted; the creative will eventually begin to resent that. I know what that feels like. I've seen it firsthand. At this point in my life, I want to be respected as an artist, but I had to create the team that can help that become a reality just so I could play for it. But still, the only way I'm playing the game is for my own team. I'm in the tournament. I'm never going to play the game the way they want me play it. No one is going to 'let me play.' I don't like being 'let' to do anything. I create my own arena; I create the team, and I give out the plays. I don't need to compete with everybody. I'm only competing with myself. I'm not looking to be as big as anyone in business. I just want to continue to have enough to be completely independent and do what I want to do."

Dame continued, **"That's another thing about business: as arrogant as you have to be, you have to humble yourself enough to be broke because you have to go broke in business. There's no other way. Any entrepreneur that puts up his own money gets cracked, even hustlers. Sometimes I see a nigga's jewelry in the pawnshop, and he's proud of it because he's like, 'Nah, I'm a pawn that shit, but I'm a get that shit back.' And when he gets it back, he feels better because everyone gets fucked up in business at times. It'll always happen when you're an independent. There is no being an independent and not getting fucked up at some point and time. You have to embrace it and shake it off. In the beginning of any venture, you have to lose money. So, my point is, you have to be humble enough to take a loss even when you're used to winning. Every time I start a new business, I have to take a loss. I have a television network and I know I'm not going to make money day one. The support base and following has to be built. So, in the beginning, I'm already aware that I'll take a loss, but so what, it's** expected. When I started clothing lines like Roc-A-Wear, I didn't make money day one, it took time. For Rachel Roy, I had a business plan. I knew that I had to lose two million dollars a year for four to five years before I could make my money back. That's part of the game when it comes to building a brand. Building a brand means you have to be consistent. But when it comes to fashion, it's entirely a different story. To build a fashion brand, it's smart to do a designer line just so you can get editorial coverage, which is for perception. Anna Winter told me herself, 'You're going to lose money for ten years. You'll have to have deep pockets if you're going to play in this fashion game.' That's why you see niggas open up and shut down fast in fashion. Fashion's not a game. That's a whole 'nother game, believe me. But that's business."

Days before we did this interview, Dr. Dre wrapped a mega deal with Apple that was said to make him the first billionaire in Hip Hop. Red then asked Dame if it made sense for Dr. Dre to sell his Beats by Dre brand or should he have held on to it.

"I mean if it's profitable, it all depends on what you're doing business for," Dame said. "It depends on what he wants to do. If he wanted money then he was good to sell it. If he enjoyed being in the headphones business, then he wouldn't sell it. So, if you have a multiple, let's say you're making two million dollars a year profit in the multiple of seven times, your company is now worth fourteen million dollars, but it's not your company anymore. You just got fourteen million dollars, but it's not your company. For some people, fourteen million dollars is great. I'll take that, run with it, live my life, and you don't have that business anymore. But for other people, they might say, 'Fuck fourteen million dollars, I love my business.' Period"

Gems:

One of the best ways to grow and evolve in business is to travel around the world and see what people are doing in different societies.

In business, you're supposed to grow ten-percent every year, and if you don't do that, then you're not doing good business.

Hustling as an independent means you buy something and then sell it for more than you bought it for.

I've learned that when you buy a car, your stock goes up. That's why I used to buy a car before anything to create the image of success which would make a lot of people want to get money with me. Buying a car is another form of branding yourself.

The key to my success has been to make money off of the things I love like my lifestyle. I don't just do anything for money. Even right now, this moment is being monetized for this book.

An executive's mindset cares more about other people than they care about themselves.

Always look for long-term benefits when it comes to business. The businessman who looks for immediate satisfaction is only in tune with his own selfish desires instead of looking out for the people involved in the big picture.

Keep in mind that everyone has ups and downs in business. There has never been an independent that hasn't had a problem in business.

In the beginning of any venture, you will have to lose money in order to build its infrastructure.

A good business plan will help you prepare for the unpredictable forecast of any business.

Damon Dash
Forbidden City
Beijing China
2:26pm

SECTION 5:
ONLINE BUSINESS HEALTH

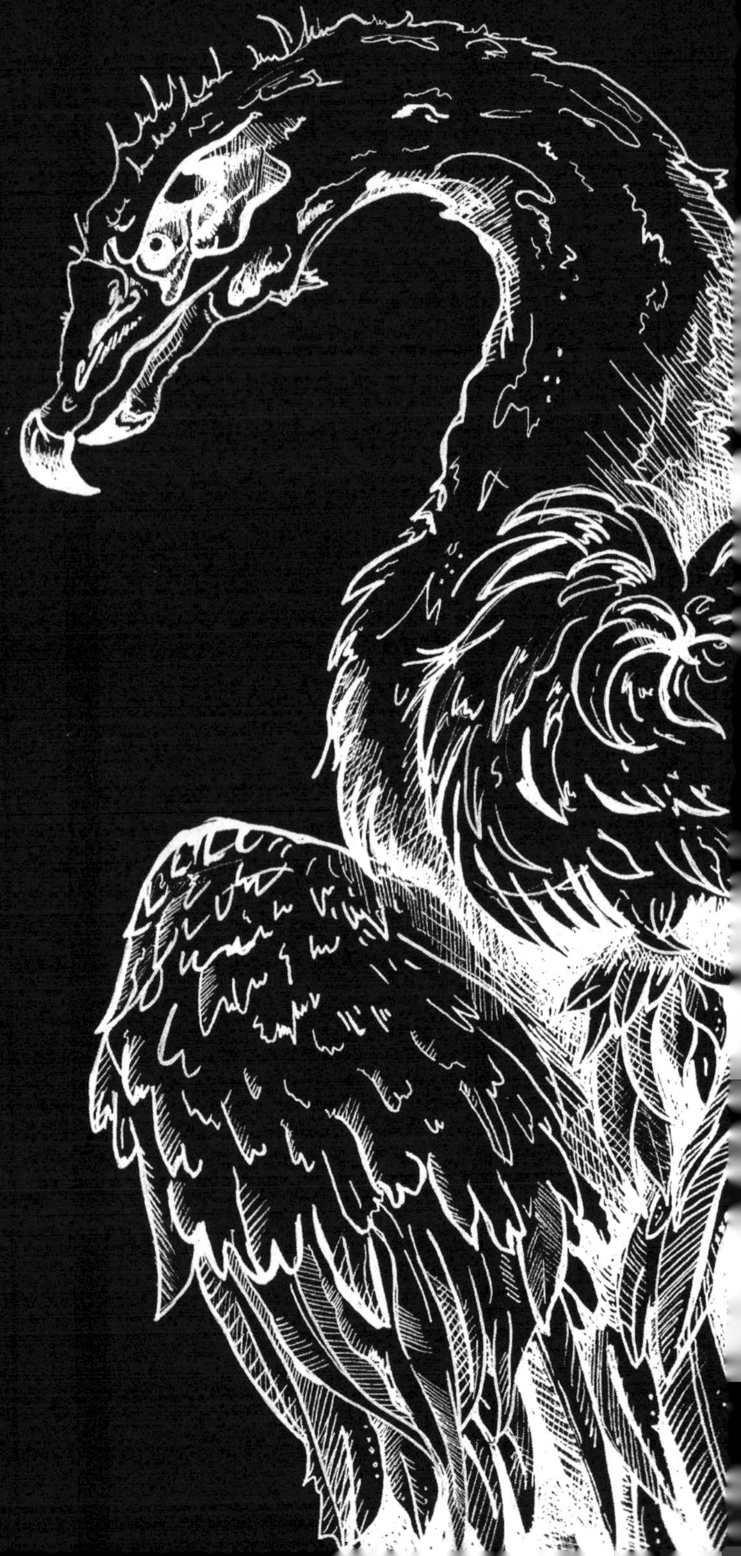

TORTIOUS INTERFERENCE & O.D.B. LAWSUIT

We started this section of chapters on Dame's deck in Malibu with his lawyer, Josh. He hit me earlier that day and told me he needed a shave and that I should bring the Hip Hop Motivation crew to capture a conversation between him and DJ Vlad, CEO of VladTV, who was coming through later on that night. Back at the barbershop, one of my clients named Q showed me an article that said Ol' Dirty Bastard's estate had a lawsuit going against Dame to retain masters of unreleased music from O.D.B. Even Dirty's son chimed in during an interview, saying he was looking for Dame so he could talk to him about getting his father's masters back, but said it's been hard getting in contact with him, even though his gallery is located in the SOHO district of New York.

Like I told you earlier, Vlad TV is coming through. He's independent, and the thing is if someone's going to interview me, I'd like to be able to talk to them about their perspective on things, especially when they've talked to me about my perspective. I want them to be fearless about their opinions, just like they expect

me to be fearless about mine. I think it'll be dope because Vlad is an independent entrepreneur as well. See, my thing is getting independent people to stick together as a culture. Even though he might not be black or white, I believe we're still a part of the same culture which is Hip Hop.

When you hear me calling out 'Culture Vultures' it doesn't have anything to do with race, and it's crazy because nobody's hollered at me still. I still don't hear any explanations from Lyor. He's still not saying anything. I'm going to keep on until you talk to me, Lyor. You have to explain yourself. It is what it is, man. I have questions, and I don't want it to be emotional. I want it to be honest. I want people to witness it and understand the things he's done from his perspective. I just don't agree with his movement. It's almost like if somebody molested some children, I'm not going to just stand by and let it happen on my watch. And the way I look at it, Lyor has molested our culture. And the way that Joey said on The Combat Jack Show, 'I don't care,' to me that was disrespectful to the culture because my question isn't a question. That's just my question. It's a question that culturally we all want the answer to. That's why there's so much support behind it.

We all want to know how you can justify being called the 'Head of Urban,' and how you can justify giving a man that's aggressive my number, knowing that you're going to make money off of whatever happens that could be negative. Like, that question was never asked or answered on The Combat Show, and that was why I was disappointed in Combat Jack because he didn't ask him any questions that challenged him. It was almost like he had a script. It was almost like Joe IE told him the questions to ask. It was just too contrived, and I thought we were all being honest. So, I was disappointed in Combat Jack because it wasn't about his radio station, it was about an agenda. It wasn't about business. This is not an emotional rant; I'm speaking up like this for business answers. So, it was just disappointing, but it's another example of why and how we never stick together. Culturally, we don't stick together. Combat Jack let his personal agenda get in the way. He wanted his show to get more recognition. It was very disappointing, but that was the position he chose to take. I was like, 'Damn!' That

Online Business Health

shit was apparent, and it wasn't even sneaky. But then again, now that I think about it, it was sneaky, but not that sneaky. But it makes sense when I think back to why I stopped using him as my lawyer in the first place: it was because he made contracts where I was robbing Ski and everybody for their publishing.

When I read it, I was like, 'Yo, I'm not taking their publishing. Give them back their publishing.' So I gave it back and made him revise the contracts. That was Combat Jack. On the real, that was my issue with Reggie Osse. I told him, 'Yo, you got me robbing kids!' He was also the one that did the contract with Priority Records. I remember telling him off the top, 'Yo, it's two-percent fee off the net, not off of the gross.' It's a big difference between net and gross. Net is profit. An example of the net would be if you grossed a hundred million dollars, but you didn't profit a dollar, then you did not net anything, but you grossed a hundred million. If you made a hundred million and you netted three million dollars, then you made three million dollars, but you grossed a hundred million. So, my contract was supposed to be off the net where they would get a two-percent fee of the net, but instead it was twenty-four-percent off the gross, not twenty. And actually, Jay caught that mistake reading the contract. I'm not gonna lie, Jay was like, 'Yo, this does not say net, it says gross.' Jay and I gestured at each other that we were finished. That was Will Sacholaf and the people at Priority. That's why we went to Def Jam because they were trying to rob us, and I was like, 'I'm not having it.'" So, of course they tried to make it look like I was crazy and all that other shit. But I was like, "Yo, dog, you just flat out tried to rob me, and you ain't put a gun to my head."

Like, if you're doing something wrong and somebody brings attention to it, the person getting accused brings attention to something else. That's always it. When somebody puts attention on something else, they're taking attention off the point. And that's what they always do. I never had a beef with Jay; I always had a beef with Lyor. They made it look like I had a beef with Jay. My beef was with Lyor. He did that bullshit. He knew what he wasn't supposed to do; he wasn't supposed to give that man options like that. Jay was never supposed to have the option to

Culture Vultures

say whether or not he could have Roc-A-Fella with us or without us. They gave him the option, which is why when everything went down Jay was like, 'Yo, it's just business.' I was just like, 'Alright,' and that's what happened. That's why I don't blame Jay; I blame Lyor. I don't expect everybody to be cut from the same cloth as me because I'm made of a completely different fabric.

What Lyor did with Jay is called tortious interference, and it's illegal. That's the reason people don't understand why I'm getting at these 'Culture Vultures.' I always have a lawyer on deck. Really, if it were legal to have a company full of lawyers, I'd have it. See, when we bang out were fighting over a dozen cases. We're definitely defending more battles than we were attacking. See, it's never in the newspaper that I have a lawsuit against somebody. Even when I sued everybody at Warner, the newspapers didn't say a word. The world doesn't know about my lawsuits against Barry Klarberg for three years. And they don't know about how we're fighting Ol' Dirty Bastard's lawyer because he doesn't know what he's doing, and he got his son thinking that I got his masters. Really, it's retarded what Ol' Dirty Bastard's lawyer is doing. That lawyer is robbing Ol' Dirty Bastard's estate. They're making them do dumb stuff and charging the family for it. So, every dollar that Ol' Dirty Bastard's estate does make it's going right into legal fees for nothing.

Smiling at the details of Dame's dialogue, Josh said, "If their lawyer really wanted to do right by his family they would've had a trial by now."

"I'm so frustrated with these lawyers! What happened the last time I was in the same room with Ol' Dirty Bastard's lawyer?"

Amused by his question, Josh said, "You got deposed."

"They wouldn't let me back in because I was flipping out, we were on that lawyer telling him, "Yo, why are you robbing that family? You know you're robbing that family!" Their lawyer is Scott Kessler. Hear me clear, Scott Kessler is robbing Ol' Dirty Bastard's family, I suggest y'all look at his books. Please believe he's robbing you. I don't have any masters. He never

completed the album; he died. It's ridiculous because the lawyer has convinced them to chase things that don't exist, and every time they do that the lawyer gets paid for every acquisition that's made. The lawyer is telling the family some bullshit and gets the family to think I have masters. The Black Keys were on to produce the Ol' Dirty Bastard album because I got the vocals. I don't have any masters. Plus, before you master something you have to pay producers. Those producers never got paid. I tried to put it out through Koch, then they sued Koch, so then Koch wouldn't put it out. This was years ago. So, every time I was going to do something with the Black Keys to produce the album, Koch kept saying no. It was crazy, but it worked out because the Black Keys signed up to create BlakRoc."

Gems:

> *There's a big difference between net and gross. Net is profit. An example of the net would be if you grossed a hundred million dollars, but you didn't profit a dollar, then you did not net anything, but you grossed a hundred million. If you made a hundred million and you netted three million dollars, then you made three million dollars, but you grossed a hundred million.*
>
> *Don't expect everybody to be cut from the same cloth as you.*

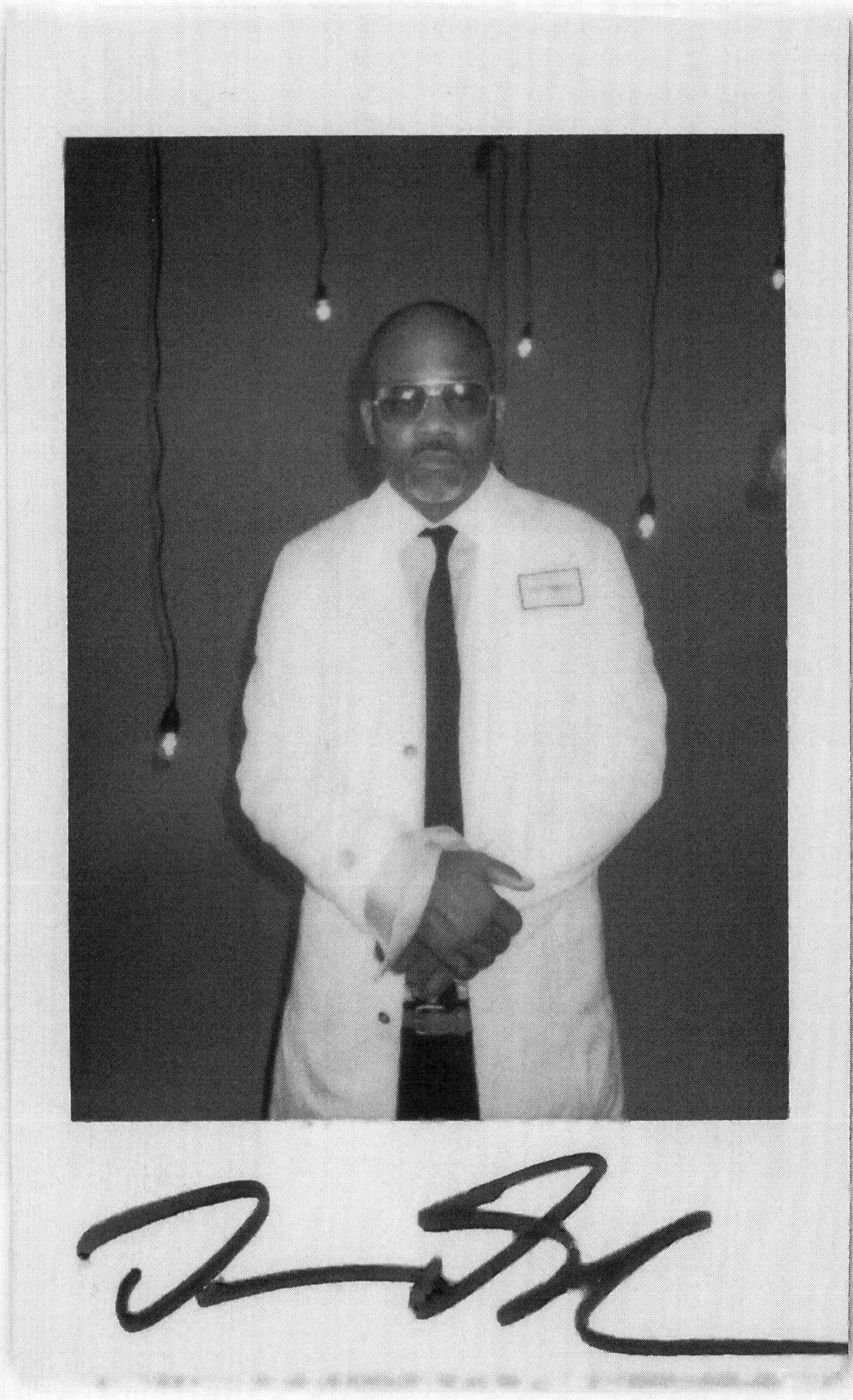

BEING A DIABETIC

The first time I heard about someone having diabetes was in high school. I was bumping A Tribe Called Quest's album The Low End Theory on a song called "Buggin Out" where Phife said the infamous line, "When's the last time you heard a funky diabetic?" At that time, I was ignorant to what and how someone becomes diabetic and it wasn't until I saw my grandmother shooting herself up with insulin a year after hearing that song that I actually saw the reality of diabetes live in the flesh. In 2003, my mom was diagnosed as a Type 2 diabetic which can be treated with oral medicine, proper diet, and exercise. My grandmother and Dame are both Type 1 diabetics which means their pancreases produce little, to no, insulin. They have to take insulin either through injection or through an insulin pump. Type 1 diabetics also have to test their blood sugar levels four or more times a day to avoid an extreme increase in blood sugar. But, with a combination of insulin, proper diet and exercise, a Type 1 diabetic can maintain healthier blood sugar levels.

About a year ago, I told Dame about my mother who is no longer a diabetic because she lost over 155 pounds from a change in diet and adding exercise into her daily ritual. I asked Dame if he could do the same to get rid of his diabetes, and he said, "Naw, I'm a Type 1 diabetic." We stayed on that conversation for a minute. In the process of this dialogue, I learned that there were different categories of diabetes, and that one of Dame's major goals was to create products and awareness for diabetics all over the world. This interview came to mind watching him shoot insulin into his leg, on his deck, while overlooking the ocean in Malibu. I asked him if he was still going to develop products for diabetics.

"I keep forgetting to talk about that because I'm openly diabetic. I take my shots anywhere. I don't care. It's a 24/7 thing for me. It's no bullshit. Diabetes isn't a disease that kills you overnight. It kills you over time because what happens is when your blood sugar is high it becomes like sandpaper to your organs. In a healthy person, the pancreas produces insulin, and in a diabetic, the pancreas doesn't distribute enough insulin to balance the blood sugar levels in your body. You're actually producing little, to no, insulin when you have the one I have, which is Type 1. Your shit breaks all the way down. My pancreas has been broken. It doesn't work and it's nothing I can do. I don't care what anybody says, I've never seen anyone go from having an unhealthy pancreas to having a healthy pancreas. If you have seen someone do that, I need to talk to them. I keep hearing about it, but I haven't seen it. It doesn't happen. You just can't cure it. You have to put insulin physically into your body, plus you have to know how many carbs you're putting into your body. So, you can cover the carbs with insulin, but then you have to know how certain carbs react differently in each situation. It took me to become 43 years old before I was able to speak this intelligently about diabetes. Like, when I first got it, I didn't know what the fuck was going on. I still think about it, like, back then it was like a dope fiend needle with the syringe and all. It was crazy.

At some point, I'm going to get around to developing products for diabetics. And I definitely think it's my responsibility on a social level to let people know and lead by example about the dangers of diabetes, I've lost friends to diabetes. They just simply didn't take care of themselves. If you don't take care of diabetes it's gonna get you quick and kill you. I'm not saying overnight, but

Online Business Health

if you take care of it, it won't become an issue. See with type 2 diabetes, I don't have to eat any special diet. I just have to know what I'm eating, then I have to cover it with insulin. [Gesturing as if giving himself a shot]. And then I have to always make sure I work out on some level. You have to have some type of workout regimen because while you're working out, you're not diabetics, for some strange reason. It's weird.

As far as making products for diabetics I would do test strips; I would do testers and I would do all the insulin, and I might create a pump, but I don't use the pump. So I would just make everything that I use, then I would also educate people on diabetes. My plan is to do a lot for diabetics. It's gonna happen, but at this time, I've just had so many other things to do. It's such a part of my life that I have to do something for others with diabetes."

Dame's hustle is non-stop, but I wondered if his diabetes interfered with his businesses.

"Why would it? If I let it interfere with business, it would, but nah, hell nah. I mean don't get me wrong, I've caught reactions, which means my blood sugar goes too low. Like while I was on stage or on television. But nah, I keep up with what I need to do to not fall off. When my blood sugar goes low, I feel super duper hungry, light headed, and then sometimes you feel cold sweats. The problem is I smoke weed, so when you're high, you don't know when your sugar is low. But honestly, my approach on diabetes is that they make you so scared of your sugar. But I think it's worse when your sugar goes too low, which is why I don't think people understand why candy is a big part of diabetes because your blood sugar goes so low that you always have to have candy around you. So, you basically end up eating more candy than the average person because you have to get your sugar level back up. So, when you go low, it's like a game. It's like drugs; the prices change every day. Your blood sugar changes like the wind. Yeah, it's a crazy thing, but like I always say, 'You're dealt your hand, so you have to play it cool.' Everybody, at one point in their life, gets dealt a fucked up hand, but my hand really isn't fucked up to me. I'm just so

used to the hand I was dealt that I don't fold under pressure."

Still ignorant to the diabetic lifestyle, I asked Dame if a Type 1 diabetic has to shoot insulin or can they just take pills.

"Yeah, a Type 1 diabetic has to give themselves shots. That's what I'm saying. Sometimes I get confused at the types, but yeah, that's Type 1. I mean you could take pills, but it's not gonna help. You have to put insulin physically into your body and then you have to be able to measure how much you need. There's no pill that could measure the amount of insulin you need to get into your system like that. They've been trying for years to do that, but nah. I heard there's like some new pumps that are supposed to be able to test your blood and distribute the insulin you need, but I don't know how that's gonna to be. Plus, I don't like being all wired up like that. I move around too much, especially when I box. I sweat a lot, so I don't think that'll work for me."

Gems:

A Type 1 diabetic's pancreas produces little, to no, insulin, so they have to take insulin either through injection or through an insulin pump.

Type 1 diabetics also have to test their blood sugar levels four or more times a day to avoid an extreme increase in blood sugar. But, with a combination of insulin, proper diet, and exercise, a Type 1 diabetic can maintain healthier blood sugar levels.

A Type 2 diabetic can be treated with oral medicine, proper diet, and exercise.

Filming of Dash Diabetic Network
Los Angeles, CA
3:32 pm

Filming of Dash Diabetic Network
Los Angeles, CA
12:06 pm

Damon & Aaliyah
Long Island, NY
3:36pm

AALIYAH

When we conducted this interview, the Lifetime Network was developing an Aaliyah movie. There were a few people talking about it in the shop, but it was mainly women who had more to say about her life and legacy being televised than the guys in the shop at the time. Everybody agreed that Aaliyah's legacy was bigger than a television movie and should be released as a feature film worldwide. Aaliyah definitely meant a lot to many people who came in contact with her, whether it was through her music or from family to friends who loved her on a personal level. Dame, of course, was one of those people who had a personal relationship with Aaliyah that remains in his heart still to this day. So, I thought if anyone had an opinion on this Lifetime production of Aaliyah, he would be the right person to share his honest feelings on its development. That's exactly what he did. To me, Aaliyah was talented beyond her years and was lost way too soon. The peaceful sound of the waves in the night air created the best energy for Dame to openly reflect on his feelings about Aaliyah.

If someone needs an Aaliyah movie on a screen and not

television then somebody should put it on a screen. Like, if that's what they wanna see. But of course, I wanna see it on a screen. I mean at some point, I will make my own perspective of my experience with her. No one can tell me what to do with that. But it's such a painful thing for me because of the memories. Not to say painful, but it's just very, you know, it's very…To relive it is painful for me. Even when I see a movie where someone loses someone they love like their girl, their wife, or their husband, I know how that feels. I just went to this movie with my daughter, Ava, called The Fault in our Stars and that movie had me lightweight emotional for a couple of days. Not because the girl had cancer, but because she had lost someone that she cared about, and I know what that feels like.

Even now, as I'm talking about it, it's like I don't like to feel that way anymore. But that's what happens when you lose someone you love. It happens to everyone. Death is a part of life; that's a definite thing. Everyone's going to experience it at some point in life, or they're going to die before it happens. You have to be able to deal with loss in a certain way. Like, I think you never get over it, but you live with it and it defines you. It makes you stronger; it elevates you to another level. Like, to experience that kind of pain, made me completely focused because you have to think a lot when you're in pain. When in pain, you do a lot of reflecting and a lot of reading. It's a very psychological thing. Like, for me, I accept pain. Pain is supposed to happen, so I don't resent it. I just let it happen and try to just entertain myself as much as possible while it's happening, but I never try to escape it. I just don't want to feel that way because my life is so much fun that I just can't let anything stop me from having fun. I'll just have to have fun with pain.

I would have to say it was 'the' worst pain I had ever felt. Like, when I lost my Mom it was like, 'I lost my Mom…' I loved my Mom, but I wasn't talking to my Mom every day. Aaliyah was my best friend, so it was crazy on that level. It was like not only did I lose someone that I really cared a lot about, it was someone that I was used to having in my life every day and I was used to hanging out with. I was used to a lot of phone calls. We used to talk every day. But I'm not trying to relive that shit right now. We got the waves going and all, and you don't wanna start crying.

But like I said, when I get to it, I'll get to it, and when I get to it, it will definitely be from my perspective. But I have to be ready for that. It will be a very psychological and emotional thing for me. I don't really have too much expectation of anyone doing right by that on a television level because there's a formula. The people that are making it on T.V. aren't making it to make the best piece of work. They're trying to make it so that they can sell it and make money from it. That's their agenda. Plus, like, if they don't talk to me and I don't know what the perspective is, but I'm not…whatever. But again, if that's what someone wants to do then that's what they'll do, and if someone doesn't like it then someone needs to make a real movie. Period. I'm not going to sit there and judge it. I hope they make a great movie, and if I'm in it, or if they mention me, they might not even mention me, but if they do, I hope they got someone with super swag, or else it's not going to be believable. But it's probably going to be one of these fucking nerds that I disrespected, or they're going to have some square play me, if that happens.

But I'm not making sure of nothing they can do what they wanna do, but then I'm going to make a movie about whoever wants to make a movie about me, that's all. That's the power of having a television network: I can just get you back the same way you get me. If you make me look crazy, I'll make you look crazy, and see how you like it because I'm not going to be worried about it. Actually, I'll probably enjoy it. I'll probably laugh. But again, it's sad, so I don't know. I don't know what they're going to do, but they'll never get anyone to play Aaliyah on point. Nobody can do that.

Her family is pretty protective of her legacy. Aaliyah affected a lot of people. It's hard to say that no one can speak about their experience with her, but they should do it in a way where it's respectful to the family. But there's so many people that she touched, that if they have a perspective on the way that she touched them they should be able to express that freely. And as long as that's in respect, I think that's fine. Like, nobody can tell me about my experience with her, ever. **No one can tell me how to talk about it because that's my experience. But I'm always going to have respect for her family, which is probably why I haven't done anything with my perspective of Aaliyah. I know how they feel about that, and like I said, I respect that."**

Gems:

Make sure you cherish every moment with your loved ones. Reach out and show love as much as you can.

Everyone will experience loss at some point, or they're going to die before it happens.

The degree to which a person continues to grieve will affect the very cells of their body, which will eventually cause a variety of ailments and disease.

One In A Million.

Wiz Khalifa, Curren$y, Stalley, Mckenzie, & Damon
DD172
Tribeca, NYC
12:11am

Online Business Health

INTERNET HUSTLE

I asked Dame what he thought about the Internet hustle.

"There're certain dudes that are in the music business that I'd tell, 'If you wanna do something, let's do something' because I genuinely liked hanging out with them and I liked their perspective. Guys like Chuck Inglish are really cool, but I wished they worked a little harder because I want pop culture to experience them. I think they have a lot of potential. It's just a new vibe. My son put me on to them. The crazy shit is that my son and my nephew, Da$h, used to put me on to Curren$y, Drake, and Wiz Khalifa. I always knew exactly what was going on because they were on the Internet every day. I learned about Wiz after my son checked him out on YouTube. He was one of the first to really exploit the viral direct-to-consumer model, the same with Drake. Everything that affects pop culture right now basically started on the Internet. Remember, Drake had that mix-tape that was crazy. Lil Wayne was even putting records out every single day on the Internet."

I've totally reemerged from being online, everything's online, but I've been doing everything silently. I wasn't announcing it to pop culture because I wasn't ready and because the 'Culture Vultures' would've tried to steal it like they're trying to do now. See, this is why I'm getting at them right now, for real because now they're trying to exploit the Indie Hustle. What they're trying to do is exploit the Independent Hustle by taking it and making it corporate. Basically what is happening is corporate is trying to monetize the Indie Hustle with the 360. So from there, it destroys the independence of the business which means someone owns your ass again. I'm not going to let that happen. I feel like if people become aware of what's going on in business, they can free themselves from the slavery of the 360. I can't front; I was really tight to see Wiz sign a record deal because he already had his career laid out. He didn't have to sign with anyone; he did every single thing right. And it's the same with Curren$y. They were brilliant in their approach. From there, I saw corporate trick them into thinking that they needed them by making them change into creating a formula record so that they could monetize it. But they choose that path, and I guess that's fine for them because it's not like I didn't choose that path before I gathered awareness. They're young, but for me, it's just a tough pill to swallow.

See, back in the day, there wasn't that much real-estate on MTV, and you really had to spend between two to three hundred, sometimes a million dollars to make a video, and you really did have to spend a million dollars to work a record at radio in order to be heard. But today because of the Internet, the middleman's cut out, which makes it easier to be heard. That sets up the ability to tour your records. You don't need radio anymore; you don't need to make videos anymore. Everyone that's not digital is trying to transition into a digital platform, just like cable T.V. When you look at everything, all that counts is what's going on on the Internet. All that counts are your numbers on the Internet, and then eventually it will hit pop culture. But radio and television usually get it last. Because that form of communication is slow;

it takes so long to get here and there. The Internet is worldwide-fast and it hits bang, bang, bang, bang. People are on the Internet every day getting their information."

I agreed with his analogy of the brain's appetite for more, relating it to my own belief that the brain is a muscle that, when trained, expands the size of our vision. Acknowledging his lawyer, Josh, Dame said:

"He's my head of legal with banging it out. And of course because he is a lawyer, his approach to business is like a lawyer, and because I'm not a lawyer, I don't approach business that way. I'm always like, 'Nah, I'm not approaching it like that.' Sometimes we bump heads, but so what? That's business. It's crazy when I'm in business meetings with lawyers and they're like, 'Ah, this is too crazy, you're crazy.' My response is, 'Come on, man. What are you, a baby? This is business. Do you understand what business is?' That's like getting in a ring, getting punched, saying, 'You're not supposed to hit me.' Business is 'Dog Eat Dog.' Period. Nothing that's great in life is given to you. Everything that's great has to be earned. Period. I've never been given anything that was great. Roc-A-Fella wasn't given to me; Roc-A-Wear wasn't given to me; Rachel Roy wasn't given to me; DD172 wasn't given to me; Dash Motors wasn't given to me. Down to Vampire Life. Like, we would be in situations where people would threaten my life and his. Right or wrong, Josh?"

Josh responded, "Yeah, that was after we had those issues with the Russian Mafia."

Dame continued, **"Russian Mafia. Yeah, whatever you wanna call it because that's how they be trying to act. That wasn't the mafia. I wouldn't be walking if that were the mafia. Just like we have fake businessmen, there's fake gangstas, and they be selling that shit. So what happened, Josh?"**

"I sent them a cease and desist," Josh said. "One of them to the factory, one to all the customers, one to all the sales people, and told them we were taking over the business. And that's what we did. They tried to act tough. I wasn't there, but I was told they came by and you had them on tape while

Culture Vultures

they were screaming…"

"They tried to come by dressed in black, looking like they had guns on their ankles. I was like, 'Get the fuck out of my spot!' I kicked them out on tape. 'Get the fuck outta here with all that tough shit. I'll give you a fair one.' And that's what they was about to get. I'm into fair ones, fuck all that. I was like, 'I'm a give you a fair one. You're gonna come to my spot and disrespect me bluffing!'"

Josh went on to say that they called him and said that if Dame's dogs weren't there, he wouldn't have lived.

"Yeah, saying if my dog wasn't there they would have thrown me through a window. And my daughter was there. Man, I was hot, so I taped him getting humiliated just in case he wanted to talk shit. 'You know who you are.' I was like, 'Run the cameras.' It's funny because when I see someone getting ready to play themselves or act a certain way, I be like, 'Run the cameras!' so you can watch this because it's going to be funny. There's no reason for bluffing, and there's no reason for violence. There's no reason to be acting tough because you'll go to jail. It's business; you can't be putting your hands on people. They just be bluffing; they know they can't do anything. It's business. It's just like when people beef on records. It's like, 'Ok, now that you're on a record, there's nothing you could do.' Period. Since it's on record, you must not have a real beef, and if it is a real beef, somebody needs to give you some better advice. You shouldn't be documenting what you're about to do to somebody, especially if it's illegal."

Gems:

When corporate gets involved in the independent hustle, some form of a 360 deal will appear.

Corporate tricks people into thinking they need them to survive by placing the spotlight on the lows of the independent hustle.

Today because of the Internet, the middleman is cut out, which makes it easier to be heard. You don't need radio anymore; you don't need to make videos anymore. Everyone that's not digital is trying to transition into a digital platform, just like cable T.V.

All that counts are your numbers on the Internet.

The brain is a muscle that can expand from the fast pace information of the Internet.

Nothing that's great in life is given to you. Everything that's great has to be earned.

Business is like getting in a boxing ring: you're gonna get hit, so always prepare and train to have a great counter attack.

Vlad, Damon, & Kenyatta
Malibu, CA
12:49pm

WEB CURRENCY

Vlad had arrived. As he walked into the house, he introduced himself to everyone; he raised his hand and said, "What's up" to all present. I extended my hand saying, "Kenyatta." He returned the pound and said, "Vlad". Him and Dame went outside on the patio and talked for a minute off camera as we chilled in the living room before we started the interview. For those of you that don't know, DJ Vlad is the same DJ who made the dope Biggie mixtape Rap Phenomenon that became a hood classic back in the day. When the interview finally began, Dame said to Vlad, **"So, explain how you make your money. I need to pick your brain because I have a television network now."**

Vlad explained, "Well, with VladTV, I own three web properties: vladtv.com, sneakerwatch.com, and the VladTV YouTube channel, so the three of those work together. I'm partnered with Complex Media Network. We're 50/50 partners. They provide all the ad money; my job is to build traffic."

"So are the ads based on the traffic you have? And how do they gauge that? How many views do you get?" Dame asked.

Vlad said, "We do seventy million page views a month on vladtv.com, and sneakerwatch.com does twenty-three million page views." When Dame asked him if he could explain what a page view is Vlaid said, "When you go to a page and there's a video, ads, or blogs all around it, that's one page view. Vlad has an audience of one-point-two million unique visitors."

"So, if someone looks at the front page, that's a view?" Dame inquired.

"Right," Vlad said. "And then if they click on the article, that's two page views, and if they start going through the pictures, each of those pictures is a different page view." Shaking his head, as if he understood, Dame asked Vlad how does he monetize his page views? Vlad answered, "Well, every time a new page comes up, new ads come up, and that's based on the deal that Complex makes with each company. We have one-point-two million unique visitors, and out of that one-point-two million unique visitors, we get seventy million page views. And then there's also a breakdown between display views which are like banner ads, and video pre-role, and that has a higher rate."

"So are these all running on your YouTube channels?" Dame asked Vlad.

He responded, "It runs on my website. My YouTube was through another company called Full Screen, but that relationship is ending in the next couple of weeks and Complex is taking that over as well."

As I was sitting there listening to the dialogue between Vlad and Dame, I could hear the respect both of them have for each other as independents. Dame's interest was on high as he continued to ask Vlad questions. Dame asked, **"So, Complex is a heavy weight? What are they, are they like the Viacom of the Internet?"** Vlad responded, "Well, they're focused on males eighteen to thirty-five, which is my demographic. Because they have such a vertical, they're able to get higher ad revenue. So, for example, on the YouTube side we do, like, twelve million video views a month, and we have over six hundred thousand subscribers."

When Dame asked Vlad what he meant when he said 'Subscribers," Vlad seemed shocked that he asked that question, but then realized that Dame was asking all these questions for the people who don't understand what certain terms mean. Vlad patiently explained, "On YouTube, a person can subscribe to a particular channel." Dame asked Vlad how much does he charge people who subscribe to his channel, and he said, "It's free. They don't pay to subscribe, but there are paid subscriptions with certain companies like Sesame Street who has a paid subscription model where a person can pay five dollars and their kid can watch episodes anytime." Dame replied, **"I think that's how I'll do my site. That's all Netflix is doing."** Vlad added, "Yeah, Netflix is the same type of thing, but with us, we have subscribers and we give away stuff for free, but you have to watch the ads in order to watch the content."

The valuable back and forth dialogue kept going when Dame asked Vlad what his five-year plan was, and he said, "My five-year plan is to keep growing the company. For the last few years, I've been having fifty-percent growth, fifty-percent revenue growth, year after year." Dame concurred: **"That's because you've learned how to monetize it more."** He said, "Yeah, I learned how to monetize, but I'm also growing my traffic." Dame asked him if his growing traffic was due to being in business with Complex. Straight to the point, Vlad said, "Pretty much." Dame said, **"Is that because they have a network of ads?"** Vlad replied, "Well, they have a network of clients who buy ads."

Impressed, Dame said, **"Obviously they have good sales people."** "tYeah, it's different for different sites," Vlad said. **"So, for example, you got VladTV and you have Sneaker Watch. VladTV has more traffic than Sneaker Watch, and ultimately it does make more money, but on a page view, for page view basis, Sneaker Watch makes more money because it's more of a vertical market. What's crazy is how many people have websites and have no idea how to monetize them."** Vlad agreed as Dame continued, **"That's the same thing that happens in rap. But because you've been in the game for as long as you have, with VladTV you were there the first five years of the Internet, from its inception on the ground level."** Correcting Dame's calculation, Vlad said, "Actually, the first year of the Internet. The Internet has been around longer, but the World Wide Web came around in the nineties."

Dame then told Vlad, **"I had a site called Block Savvy five years ago, but we were trying to chase MySpace. But we always knew what content to put up and what it was about. MySpace just got corny,**

Culture Vultures

I think." Agreeing, Vlad said, "Yeah, MySpace just got ridiculous. It was an uncontrolled environment where you go to someone's page and everything just went crazy." Dame further described MySpace as being the Internet of an eight year old. Vald added, "To me there was no reason why Facebook really should've taken over. MySpace should still be on top."

"Well, Facebook probably learned from MySpace's mistakes, and MySpace was probably heavily invested in corny shit and taking too long to develop it," Dame said. "And that's the thing— the Internet is so fast. So, it's hard to invest in any development because somebody can develop something 'ILLER' the next day." Vlad said, "I think a lot of the reason why I became successful, and I really kind of leap-frogged past a lot of other blogs, other Hip Hop sites that have been around longer than me, is because I actually have an engineering background. So, like, really VladTV's a technology company as much as it is a Hip Hop company." Dame asked him, **"When you say technology do you mean platforms and stuff like that?"** He answered, "Meaning that we built our entire platform from scratch." Dame asked Vlad if he built it himself, to which Vlad replied, "Well, me and my programmer. Like, I used to program, but I architected everything with him." Dame asked him if he did coding, and Vlad said that he used to do coding. Dame said, **"So basically you're lightweight super smart; you're a computer genius?"** Vlad immediately said, "Not anymore. Yeah, but really, my first few years out of college, I was coding until I realized it wasn't really for me. Still being modest, Vlad said, "I'm O.K." Dame expressed that he definitely respected that. Vlad continued hipping us to his game saying, "Yeah, so really, like, with a lot of these other Hip Hop sites, you have Hip Hop fans who start a site, and they just start. They don't want to have a real job, and they just wanna do Hip Hop shit for a living, and the sites really kind of stay around four/five million page views, and kind of just stay there for a long time. You look at like a lot of these sites, like Rap Radar or 2dopeboys, like these are all quality Hip Hop sites, but they're not run by technical people. So they don't know. A lot of people think, like, you build it they will come. If I just put up content every day, it will keep growing, but it won't. You gotta really fight for every page view, and you gotta constantly reinvent the back end. Like, I've spent probably over a million dollars building my websites."

Dame asked Vlad what was it that he had to do, and Vlad replied saying he and his team we're constantly changing things. He added, "Well, for example, when we launched VladTV there was no Twitter, there was no Instagram. Facebook was still in its infancy. So, it's like as new technologies came, we had to figure out how to incorporate those new technologies into the site. The technology is constantly changing." Dame said, **"But it doesn't cost a million dollars to put Twitter in it."** Vlad responded, "But you're talking about everyday—there's constant development into the sites. I mean this is six years in. I'm not talking a million dollars in six months; I'm talking about a million dollars over six years."

"See, that's good that you make money that way, but the way I would approach it would be through the brand, since you have six years of wire T.V.," Dame said. "So, I would focus on all the ancillary things as well. Like, VladTV merchandise and VladTV notebooks, or anything you could sell because that would put the brands in the streets every day. I would not only have VladTV, I would create VladMovies as well. The way I've always approached making records was to make it a commercial for everything else I'm selling. The way I've approached making movies was as a commercial for everything else I'm selling. So if I don't sell a record, but a lot of people see what I'm selling, I don't care because we would make money on the road selling t-shirts and other merchandise. That's why the model really wasn't record sales; it was in lifestyle sales. But because corporate was involved, they made every artist worry about the record sales when all that matters is how much money you make performing and how much you make selling merchandise. Then if you're getting paid for your celebrity, what would matter is how much you get paid for endorsements. And that's basically why I don't like the 360 deal because now the label gets a piece of all those things. See, before, if your record didn't sell, it didn't matter or even if they spent a lot of money and tricked a lot of it off, it still didn't matter because you would make so much from your show. But now they've figured out a way to take that through the 360. That's why I'm not with all that 360 bull.

Really it's the same model for everything, which is to build your brand and sell ancillary things. For example, with Rachel Roy's high-end, we don't make money off the high-end. That's called a loss leader. But what you do is you put it on Michelle Obama,

Oprah, and other big people, and then you get editorial and product placement, which creates a certain kind of traffic. But really, you make money from the stuff that people can afford. Like I said, Rachel Roy's designer line is the loss leader because we sell two thousand dollar pants, but really we make money from selling sixty-dollar pants that you can buy at Macy's. That's called diffusion. Like, Mercedes doesn't make money off 600s and Maybachs, they make their money off of 230s. Ralph Lauren doesn't make his money off of the purple label; he makes his money off of off price Polo.

So, if I had a VladTV and I have six years in, where I have seventy million people, I would sell them a lot of stuff besides television. But that's the way I would approach it. Then if you never make money over here at VladTV, you're still good because you have other ancillary things to get off. But if you can create a way for your loss leader to make money, of course, that's also good. When I had Roc-A-Fella, to me, the record was the loss leader because if I put out a record, I didn't care if it sold any copies. Even if I lost money making the album, I knew we would make so much money from touring, endorsements, and selling merchandise that it didn't matter if the record sold anything. The loss leader is the commercial for all the other stuff you have to sell. That's how I would approach it, but that's me. Like, with PGTV it's gonna be a lifestyle channel. It's not going to be just about the content; it's gonna be about all the ancillary things that come from the content. It's just like how YouTube is now throwing these festivals for people on YouTube. Like, there's a whole other way to make money that's just opened up because of the Internet. There's like YouTube festivals, and if you have a hundred million views, somebody's going to pay a bunch of money just to see you do what you do on YouTube. It's a whole new way of touring. It's crazy."

After listening to Dame's input, Vlad said, "That's how VladTV started: it started as just a YouTube channel. I was doing mixed-tapes, and I loved it, but I was actually selling mixed-tapes at the time. And number one, it wasn't totally legal, and number two, the money was going away. So I got into doing DVDs, and that was cool. I did some documentaries and shit like

Online Business Health

that, and then DVDs kept going away as well, and I was trying to figure out what I was gonna do next. And then, in 2008, YouTube introduced a partner program where you could now get paid. YouTube was already around, but you couldn't get any money off of it, so I never bothered with it. Then in 2008, they introduced a way where you could get paid per view on YouTube, and it wasn't that much money, but I saw the big picture of it all. So that's why I dropped everything that I was doing. I stopped DJing, I stopped doing DVDs, I stopped doing documentaries; and I just focused completely on that and the whole model was 365 days a year, new content every day. And now, basically, the last six years I've done that with e-mails going out every day."

"I can definitely dig it," Dame said. "Yeah, everybody gets an E-mail, I respect that. I'm a copy you. I'm definitely gonna look under the hood, pause, and check out everything, and figure out if there's any other way I can incorporate the stuff I have to sell. So, how can we work together, as independents? How can we come together and do something that no one else is doing? I feel like if independents would stick together, we could become the new corporate, but it'll be an indie corporate, and we would share with each other. The issue I have is when people go corporate, they don't share. I feel like if you're gonna sacrifice being corporate, you have to lookout for everybody. Just like if you work for the jail and your friends are prisoners, you have to look out for them. They need to get something out the kitchen. But that's not what I see. So, it's time that the people that don't share get outta here. Like, whoever was in corporate power that wasn't sharing with the people should get out or rob corporate like they're robbing us. Let me get some of that money. I don't mind spending some of that money, but I'm just not working for corporate."

Gems:

A website is called a "web property."

Even if I lost money making an album, I knew we would make so much money from touring, endorsements, and selling merchandise that it didn't matter if the record sold anything. Remember, the loss leader is the commercial for all the other stuff you have to sell.

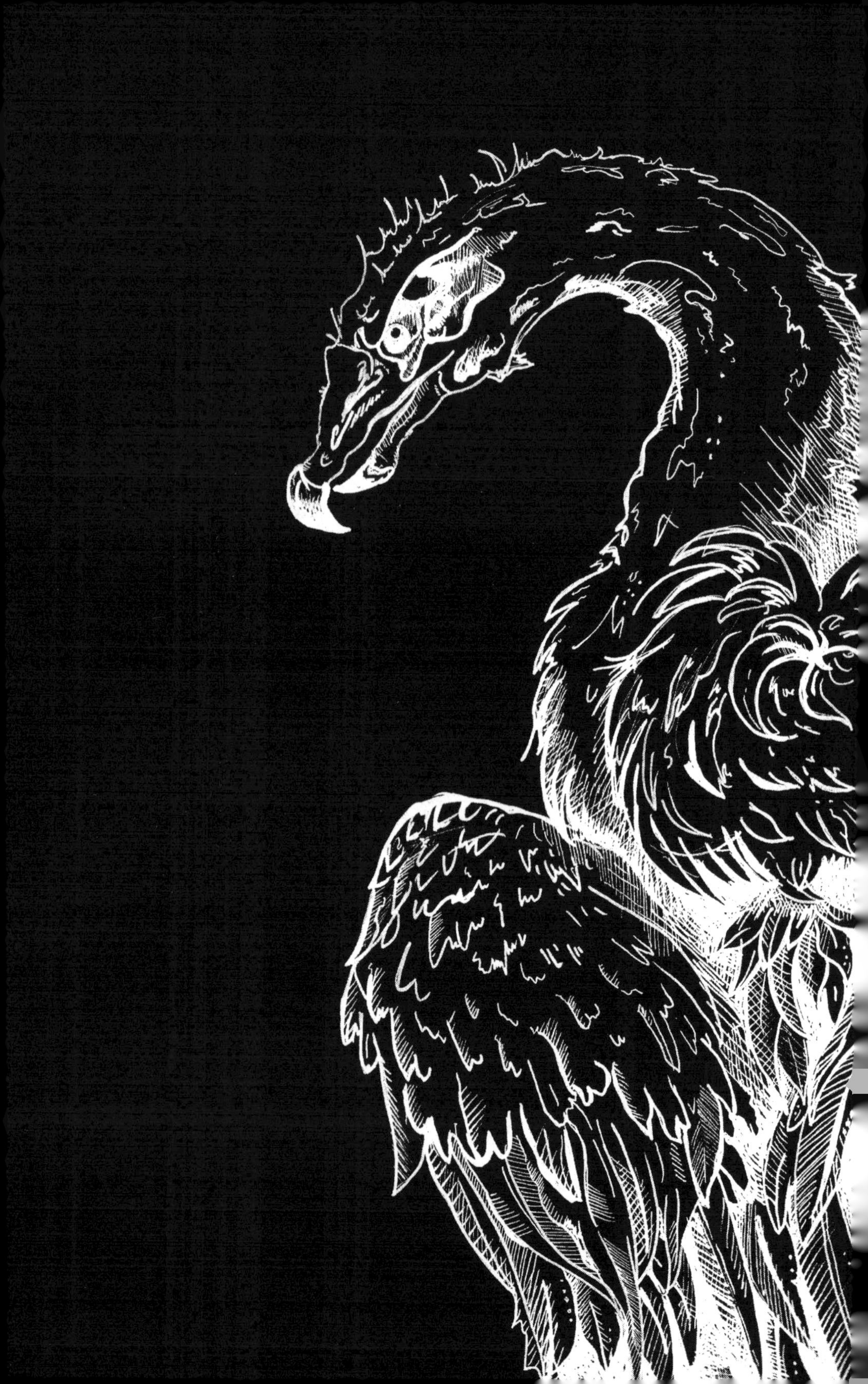

CULTURE DISRESPECT

This chapter should've been called "Clipper Disrespect," because as I was giving Dame his shave, I realized how little respect he has for the clippers and his own mustache. Like I said, I've been cutting Dame for way over ten years, so I already know how he gets down when he's in the chair. As a result, I've given this dude French, Hitler, and Tom Selleck mustaches. I've left Shags on the back of his neck, Duck Tails with no triangle, eyebrow edges chopped off square face style, and on mad occasions, I've almost had the clippers knocked out of my hands from him jumping out of the chair to do whatever comes into his mind. When Dame's in debate mode and the cape is on, barbers beware. You can't tell him to sit still when he's trying to give his opinion. As his barber, anytime I see him animated, I fall back and chill, or chance destroying his mustache game, "Ground Zero." Once you read this chapter, you'll understand why Dame was so hyped up when talking about the things and the people he perceives as "Culture Disrespect." Word up!

Looking directly at Vlad, Dame said, **"Let me ask you a question: Why does Joe IE of Interscope have the title 'President of Urban'? I need someone to explain what that title means because to me that title means 'President Of Black People.' The title 'Urban**

Music' is usually what corporate uses when they refer to black music, right?"** Vlad agreed, saying, "Right, Hip Hop and R&B." Dame said, "So the title **'President of Urban' means he runs the 'Black Music Department' at Interscope, right?"** Vlad responded saying Jimmy Iovine gave him that title. Dame pressed the issue saying, **"Well, yeah, Jimmy Iovine gave him that title, but why do you think Jimmy Iovine gave him the title 'President Of Urban'?"**

Vlad said he felt he was given that position because of his previous history at Asylum Records. Dame, still confused, said, **"So, why did he even get that title at Asylum?"** "I don't know how he got his title." Vlad said. "Really, I have no idea. I met him when he was at Asylum." **"See, my problem with it is that it would be like me being the 'President of Rock and Roll,'"** Dame said. **"It doesn't make sense. It just doesn't."** Vlad then asked Dame, "But what if you live a Rock and Roll lifestyle your whole life?" Repeating his question, Dame said, **"If I lived Rock and Roll my whole life? But I haven't."** Vlad asked again, "But what if you did?" And Dame said, **"If I did, yeah, maybe. But I haven't. I'm not from that culture."** At this point, it felt as if we were recording an episode for VladTV when Vlad asked Dame, "So you don't think that Joey has any history in Hip Hop?"

He responded, **"I think he has a history as far as making money off of Hip Hop, but I don't think he has history in Hip Hop,"** Dame said. **"I don't think he made any sacrifices for the culture; I don't think he's lived it. I think he's monetized it his whole life. He's a party promoter. That's what I think he's done, and I think because he couldn't survive in his own culture, that's the reason he came to our culture. If that's the case and that's valid, then what has he done for Hip Hop that he hasn't had to do? Like, what has he done besides work from Hip Hop? Everything that he mentioned seems to be something that he was monetizing."** Still in VladTV mode, Vlad asked Dame,

"So, you're saying he was never a DJ and a rapper?"

Dame said, **"I'm saying that I don't think he's one-hundred. I think he said he couldn't even tag; he couldn't even draw right there. I think he might have known graffiti artists, but if that** was the case, show me pieces. He didn't bring any pieces to the show, and they said tag something, he said he couldn't. So no, I don't think he's telling the truth. Also, I personally heard him lie. But anyway, my point is what has he done for Hip Hop? Like, what has he done for the culture? If he's making so much money off of it, and he's living it, how is he living it? What front line has he been on for Hip Hop?"** Those questions changed the channel back to The Poppington Network when Vlad replied, "I haven't heard of him doing anything."

"Well, that's my point," Dame said. **"Which is why I said it wouldn't make sense if I was running Rock and Roll every day, and I don't live Rock and Roll every day. That doesn't make sense."** Vlad immediately said, "But these are corporations." Dame seemed annoyed at Vlad's explanation. **"He's not a corporation. A corporation hired him. Why did they hire him?"** Vlad further explained his answer in relation to Dame, saying that a corporation hired him. Vlad said, "That's what I'm saying. So if you work for a corporation, and he had a history of monetizing music, then why not?" In debate mode for the Culture, Dame's comeback was, **"No, he didn't have a history. He only had a history of being hired to monetize black people's music."**

I saw a light bulb come on in Vlad's facial expression as he agreed and Dame continued: **"That's what he has a history of doing with Todd Moscowitz, who is a lawyer that I personally know who doesn't know shit about music,"** Dame said. "Todd Moscowitz knows nothing about music. I told Todd Moscowitz, 'You know you have a group called The Black Keys on Warner?' He told me, 'I don't know who the Black Keys are.' I said, 'Come to the show.' I forgot where it was exactly, but it was during fashion week. I had them perform at the Gramercy, and I was like, 'Come to the Gramercy and look at them.' And I also told him that he had a kid named Wiz Khalifa, and he was like, 'But y'all dropped him,' and he was like, 'I don't know Wiz.' They don't know shit about music. I've also witnessed Lyor do the same thing when Michael Jackson was gonna hit the stage for Summer Jam. I was like, 'Yo, you coming, pause. What time are you going?' And he was like, 'Oh, I'm not going. I don't need to see that.' Michael Jackson is gonna be at fucking Summer Jam stage with Jay Z and you're not gonna go? I thought that there was gonna be a bomb or something. I thought he was about to kill everybody. I'm like, 'What you about to do?' He just had no interest in the culture whatsoever. So, my point is why do these people that have no interest or proven history in the culture get jobs over people that live it every day, that have made sacrifices for the culture, that if given a position, can help will give back to the culture? Why is that? That's my question."

After thinking about it, Vlad answered, "Well, I mean there's always been, I mean historically, I mean music, and media, a bunch of other shit, and there's only been a couple of people that could do it." Still appearing irritated by the lack of a response that made sense, Dame said, **"No, no, no. There's only been a couple of people that could do what? Make money off black people? Or make black people make money?"** Vlad explained his opinion further. "Like, on major labels there's only been a couple of big media companies, and there's always been a better entry for people to do it up until someone leaves them. VladTV wouldn't have been possible without the Internet. When I moved to New York in 2002, it was like I had to fuck with XXL, I had to fuck with The Source, I had to fuck with MTV, I had to fuck with Vibe. And if I did not fuck with any of these outlets as a DJ, which was what I was doing full time back then, there was no way for me to actually advance my career unless I went through like these four media outlets."

"There was another approach you could have had then," **Dame said. "That approach would be to incubate yourself at a club, do a residency, and get a thousand to a million people just to come see you perform. Not to say a million, but like if you're moving around festival wide. You can control your own platform; it just takes a lot more work. You didn't need XXL to get that. You just wanted that. At the time, that was your business model. You didn't have to do that."** Speaking from his own experience, Vlad said, "My business model back then was to promote myself. I became one of the biggest mixed-tapes DJ's of the time. I won mixed-tape of the year from The Justo awards and all this other type of shit, and it worked for what I was doing. But at the time, like, I had no way of creating my own media platform. I had to go through the other established means."

Dame agreed, saying, **"That's true. But keep in mind the Internet is what gave you that freedom. The Internet's amazing!"** Vlad then expressed that as of today his network VladTV is way bigger than Vibe, way bigger than XXL, and way bigger than The Source. Dame replied, **"Yeah because you've been invested in that business model for ten years before everyone else. You got there before everyone, so you were consistent. I'm saying before everyone else because people are just getting hip to the Internet now as we speak. Like, you understand the power of the Internet. Still, to this day, conceptually it's hard for some people to understand."** Vlad said he attributes much of his success to his Computer Science background after going to UC Berkley.

Dame called him a rarity in his lane, further telling him, **"Also what you have to remember about the Internet is a lot of people were heavily invested in the old business model, and that wasn't the Internet. So a lot of people that had money in other ways of doing business have to get their money back from investing in that old way of doing business to invest back into the Internet. Everyone that was only doing physical business are trying to go digital. All that counts right now is digital, and, with you, you've built a brand. You've been consistent, and that's all it is. Think about it: if you do something over, over, over, over and over again all day for six years, and you don't get nothing, then you need to do something different. I've never seen that happen. You were consistent and you built your brand. You didn't need that corporate infrastructure, and that's why I'm fucking with you now because you chose an independent path. Regardless, culturally, we are the same, from the Hip Hop, we also share an independent perspective about surviving."** Vlad said, "I'm just not a good employee. I've never been good at working for other people, so I had no choice."

"I don't think anyone should be a good employee," Dame said. "Hell, Kunta Kinte wasn't a good employee. If you work for something that you don't own, to me that's slavery, and if you work for someone and help them get something, and they don't give you the opportunity to have your own, that's

also slavery." Vlad added: "I remember when I was in college, I had an internship at Intel, and it was a cool job, but then I remembered sitting around watching my manager, who was real cool dude, and he had been with the company for like ten or fifteen years, and he was probably making fifty, sixty thousand a year. And as I was looking at that goal, I was like, 'This just ain't enough for after ten or fifteen years.' I just couldn't sacrifice working to build someone else's company."

"It's like Flex working at Hot 97 for the same time slot for twenty-five years straight and not owning any piece of the company," Dame said. **"To me that's crazy! What did you think about Angie Martinez jumping? Remember, I talked to you about that when you interviewed me."** "I didn't even know about that until you mentioned it," Vlad said. "I didn't fully comprehend what you were saying until I looked it up after the interview. Um, I mean no matter how you slice it, Power 105 is killing Hot 97." **"Why do you think?"** Dame asked. **"They got people that have been working at the same job for twenty-five years. Like, how could you evolve? Like, anyone that would want to do the same thing for twenty-five years would not be someone you'd want a hundred million people to be listening to every day and be influenced by. Complacent. That's just too complacent."** Vlad said, "I think with a lot of companies, I think that they set all their morals with what they've done before."

"If it's not broke, don't fix it, and they don't care about the evolution of the culture," Dame said. **"They care about what they're going to get from Ad Reps, period. They don't care about how stupid they're keeping people. Actually, the stupidest stuff sells the most, and that's the shit that they're putting out. That's the stuff they report the most, the dumbest shit. It's just dumb. If we put smart stuff in the air, people will become smarter. When we put stupid shits in the air, people get stupid. All that shit is contagious, all of it. When people laugh, you laugh, and when people are grumpy, you get grumpy. When people are broke, you get broke. When you're corny, that's shit's contagious too. That's why I stay far clear from corny niggas. I don't want that shit to get on me at all. That shit is a disease you can catch, it really is. Everything is contagious. Energy is contagious.**

Period." Vlad said, "I think with Angie, she wanted to go to a place that was more up-rise."

"Yeah I'm sure she couldn't take listening to Ebro anymore," Dame said.

Vlad replied, "Well, Ebro 'was' the Program Manager." Dame was shocked. **"Wait, What? He quit?"**

"He might be an Interim Program Manager," Vlad said. "He's no longer the Program Manager at Hot 97." Dame said, **"So, what does he do now? Is he just an artist?"** Vlad told us, "He's a personality for the morning show."

Sarcastically Dame said, **"Oh, I thought he was a 'Big Boss'?"** "Well he was until a couple months ago," Vlad said. "Like, he might be the Interim boss."

"I wonder who's going to be the boss now?" Dame said. **"That never made sense to me. Let me ask you a question: why do you think they would have someone that's not from New York programming New York music?"** "I talked to him about this at one point," Vlad said. "Um, I mean, he told me that when they interviewed him there weren't a lot of people that were willing to really just move their lives to New York because they were interviewing nationwide."

"But why would you not, on a smart level?" Dame asked. **"Like, put it like this: when I first started funding Rachel Roy, and I knew at some point that I wanted to sell it to a bigger corporation, at least half of it. I went and hired a President who was the ex-President of Givenchy and at one time Nike France, and it was the biggest mistake because she wasn't from America. She really had no idea what was going on in America. It was different. Shit is different in different demographics. So, if you have New York music, don't you think that person should be relatable to New York people, like they should have a New York experience? Because that's basically who you're trying to service. So why would it make any sense to hire someone that's not from New York? I just don't understand that math."**

"I've never been a fan of radio," Vlad said. "At the end of the day, these radio stations are big corporations. Emmis Communications owns Hot 97 and they also own Power 106 in LA and a couple of other stations. But they aren't as big as Clear Channel and Radio One."

In conclusion, Dame said, **"My point is just because you're big you don't have to be poorly dumb. Why would you hire someone that's not from that town, not even from that coast, to run New York radio? It's like setting him up to fail. It just doesn't make sense to me, but you wanna know why? Because corporate tends to hire people that will listen. They don't hire the smartest person; they hire the person that's the most subservient, the one that will fight for something they don't own. That's why. Period. That's why I've never been offered a corporate position because they know they're not gonna make me subservient. The first thing Lyor did when I signed that deal at Def Jam was try to make me fight someone he had a beef with."**

Gems:

If you're doing something over, over, over, over and over again all day for six years, and you haven't grown in business, then it's time for you to do something different.

When you work day in and day out for something you don't own, to me that's slavery, and if you work for someone and you help them become wealthy, and they never give you the opportunity to build your own wealth, that's also slavery.

Associations, mentalities, and energy are contagious, so be cautious of who you hang with.

Corporate usually doesn't hire the smartest people; they hire the people that are the most subservient, the people that will fight for something they don't own.

The Dame Dash Show Filming
Kenyatta and Damon
Los Angeles , CA
8:21 pm

Damon, Kenyatta, Vlad
PCH
Malibu, CA
10:39pm

WARREN BUFFETT

While giving Dame a shave, he initiated a conversation about real estate investments saying, **"Every time I buy property, and then sell it, I always make money".** To which Vlad responded, "Really? I always break even." **"You know why?"** Dame said. **"Because when I saw the economy about to crash, I was dealing with my man, Giseppi Chippiani, who was always building something. So, he was always with the banks. He was like [in an Italian accent] 'Yo'"** because he speaks Italian, **'It's about to be a disaster.' It was good because I needed the liquid to fund some of my companies. So, I had this crib in Beverly Hills that I sold right before the economy crashed. But at a certain price point, when the economy crashes, it doesn't affect everyone because the rich stay rich. They're just not making as much money, but they still have a stash."** Vlad said, "Yeah, I've been putting all of my money into the stock market the last couple of years." **"Really? I don't fuck with that,"** Dame said. **"But have you been able to pull out the money you make?"** Vlad said, "Yeah, it's all liquid. You can pull it out whenever you

Culture Vultures

want. When I first started making money, at first, I had a financial advisor, and then I realized he was full of shit. And then I started reading Warren Buffett's books. I read his autobiography and then I figured out the book that he learned from, was by this guy named Benjamin Graham, which was the guy he studied under. He made more money in the stock market than anyone ever in the history of the world, and I just started kind of basically doing what he did."

Dame asked if Warren Buffet makes his money off of stocks, and Vlad answered, "Most of it. Well, he puts a lot of money into stocks and then he buys certain companies as well. He owns Geico, Dairy Queen…" Inquiring about the strategy of a Billionaire Elder, Dame asked, **"But when he buys it, does he buy them based on a multiple, or does he buy it in distress, liquidate and license it? Like, how does he have money from the companies he buys?"** He responded, "His thing is to buy really high quality companies and keeps them forever". Dame asked, **"So just get a company that makes profit?"** He said, "Yeah, like something that's usually simple. He really doesn't put money into text stocks." **"Do you know what he pays for it? What his multiple is or what his formula is?"** asked Dame. **"I mean, usually when a company gets sold it's based on even dial, like the profit times whatever the multiple is."** Unsure of the exact number, Vlad said, "Like a seven multiple or something like that."

"Yeah, so like say if you're making five million a year, it would be like five times seven, that'll be thirty-five million," Dame said. "Like, how does he gauge?" He said, "His thing is he keeps shit forever. He doesn't flip shit."

Correcting his own question, Dame said, **"No, I'm saying how does he buy it? When he acquires it, how does he rate what he sells it for?"** "I don't know. He never really releases that information," Vlad said. "He kind of works out a lot of things in his head."

"Like, for example, let's say Geico was fucked up. So now he can buy it cheap, liquidate it, pay all the debt, and then just license it out and make money forever," Dame said. "That's what corporate does, really. They buy companies in distress, or at a multiple, and then license them out, and just get the revenue from them forever. That's what corporate does." "He's huge on insurance", said Vlad. "So what he would do with insurance companies, he would basically take all the money that comes in from insurance and he would put it in the stock market, and then he would pay out whatever he needs to. But basically, he's investing other people's money." **"Got you. Is that shit fun though?"** Dame asked. **"How can you have fun with that?"** Amused by all the questions, Vlad said, "I don't know if it's fun, but watching my money grow is fun."

"I don't really like watching my money grow, pause. I like to watch my companies grow," Dame said. **"For me, if it's not fun, I'm not doing it."**

Does Warren Buffett even have fun?" Speaking from the perspective of Warren Buffet's autobiography and not knowing him personally, Vlad answered, "Yeah, I think he does. I mean he's the best that's ever done it." **"I guess that's your perspective of fun,"** Dame said. **"Does he have music in his life? Does he like listening to music?"** Vlad told Dame he plays the ukulele, and he heard he sings a little but nothing more than that he's eighty-five. **"So."** Dame responded. **"When I'm eighty-five, I'll be boogying. I don't give a fuck. I would rather not be a billionaire than not have music in my life. Would you trade in music for money?** Vlad began looking around as if he was putting some thought into the underlined sacrifice being asked in the question. He said, "Ah, I don't know, man." Dame was shocked that Vlad would even think of giving up music for a billion dollars, saying: **"What! Nah, ain't no way. "See, that's not fun. I couldn't imagine life with no music."** "I mean I grew up in Hip Hop." Vlad said. "I was a Hip Hop kid since elementary school." **"So would you trade that experience in for a billion? With no Hip Hop in your life at all, you'll be lame with no swag or nothing,"** Dame said. **"With no Hip Hop in your life?"** With a look of indecision on his face, Vlad said, "No Hip Hop? What about Rock?" Dame said no music. Vlad looked up into the ceiling in a daydream still unable to make a decision. Then he said, "No music? I don't know."

"I need to get on his Instagram and see what his life is like. Like, what did that billion buy you? Like, if it buys you reading books all day, nah, I don't wanna do that shit." Vlad expressed that he's thirty billion deep, and Dame immediately said, **"But what's he**

doing with it? Does he have a rollercoaster in his backyard?" Smiling, Vlad said, "Nah, he's super cheap." **"So what's the purpose of having the money? You know that's crazy, right?"** Dame said. **"Don't you find it interesting that people with the most money don't spend it? So what's the purpose of having it?" Vlad told Dame,** "Well, you can't spend it." **"Yes you can. Oh, I can spend it; I can definitely spend thirty billion. I know what to buy. I'm just not gonna buy nothing that's less than a billion. That's a football team, a basketball team, a couple of jets, a yacht."**

Vlad then told Dame that Warren Buffet bought Heinz Ketchup. He said, **"Ketchup ain't fun! He better catch up. When was the last time he danced? When the last time he danced?"** Dame asked. Vlad said, "He was at the 40/40 Club at one point." Sarcastically, Dame said, **"Exactly!"** When Vlad asked Dame if he ever saw the picture of Warren Buffett throwing up the Roc symbol, Dame said, **"Well, they party a little different. That's why we stopped partying together. We have a different party here. The 40/40 is not where I used to hangout. No disrespect, but we just have a different perspective on fun. But that's what I think. If you gonna have a billion dollars, it ain't no reason to have it if you're not gonna have fun with it. If you just gonna save it and get more money, that's nasty. I mean for me, I don't like holding on to money. I like having fun with my money. I have to see my kids enjoying it; I wanna see my friends enjoy it; I have to enjoy it. I'm gonna create opportunities for my friends. Does he hang out with his friends? He's eighty-five?"**

Vlad said that Bill Gates was Warren Buffett's best friend. So, Dame asked him if he thought they were best friends because they like each other or because they're both rich, and Vlad answered by saying he thinks they like and respect each other. **"Of course they respect each other. Do you think that they talk and joke and laugh?** Dame asked. **Or do you think their bond was built because they both like each other because they're both rich? I don't hang out with people because they're rich. Like, I would pick Bill Gates' brain to death just because I wanna know this or that, but I don't know if we could go partying or nothing like that just because he's Bill Gates. He can't hang out with me. Bill Gates can't hang out with me, B."** Dame laughed. Vlad said, "Warren Buffett's the fifth or sixth richest person in the world." **"But who's having the most fun?"** Dame asked. **"Being rich is quality of living. That's rich."** "I would say that Chief Keef is probably having the most fun on the planet right now," Vlad said. "He's eighteen years old, and hot to death."

Dame asked Vlad what Warren Buffett was doing when he was eighteen and Vlad said, "He was investing in stocks at eighteen" **"So he never had any fun?"** Dame asked. **"He's never been irresponsible?"** Vlad said, "He owns a private jet company." **"But he ain't got any girls on his jet,"** Dame said. **"He didn't get a party going. Did he pop bottles on his jet? Did he hotbox it?"** While he was laughing at Dame, Vlad said, "No, I didn't ask him that, but probably not."

"What's the purpose of having all of that shit if you're not gonna have any fun?" Dame asked. **"It doesn't make any sense to have a bunch of money, and look at it and then pay taxes on it."** Vlad respectfully interjected saying, "Well, for example, the reason why Warren Buffett isn't the richest person in the world is because he's given billions to Bill Gates for Bill Gates to give away to charity." **"Oh, so now you wonder why they're best friends,"** Dame said. **"He gave him billions. So I guess their foundation's not built on money?"** "No, he gives to Bill Gates' charitable foundation," Vlad said. "They go on vacations together, and play bridge."

"So they're basically old ladies?" Dame said. **"For a billion dollars, I definitely would want that life. Nah, I'm just playing. I'd probably pay a billion not to have that life."** Dame laughed. **"Yeah because that wouldn't be fun. Now tell me about Hef [Hugh Hefner]. Now he's having a ball. I'm not saying I'm gonna do that, but if I'm at that age, I would love to run around and go out with a bang... ballin'. I'm not trying to be cool; I'm trying to help people, but I'm also trying to enjoy life at the same time. Like, that's what I'm saying, rich without fun is not rich. That's not wealthy. Money does not define a man. It's the quality of living and the amount of people that love him that define a man, and the way his children act define a man to me, Like, when it comes to my relationship with my kids, I wouldn't trade that for all the money in the world. At all. Like, it wouldn't even be a question. Saying, 'You could have Bill Gates' money, and his**

money combined, but you won't have kids you hang out with.' I'm not doing that." Vlad said, "He has a pretty good relationship with all his kids. As a matter of fact, one of his kids traded his stocks to purse a career as a music producer. He did all the original music for MTV, and I think he did a bunch of Broadway plays and stuff like that." He responded, **"That's dope. So, his kids are having fun. That makes sense, but I would still wanna have some fun though. So, in all of Warren Buffett's many companies, is anybody black running any of them?"**

"I don't know," Vlad answered. "He has so many companies. I don't know who's running his companies."

"I'm curious," Dame said. **"I'm not racist like that. I'm just curious to know if he does anything culturally? But, yeah I forgot, Warren Buffett actually does things for the whole world. I can't knock that…"** "Yeah, well think how much Bill Gates has helped the world," Vlad replied. "Like, Bill Gates probably gave more money away than anyone else." Unmoved, Dame said, **"Yeah, but he makes more money than anyone else."** Agreeing to disagree, Vlad said, "But he still doesn't have to give it away though." In conclusion, Dame said, **"Yeah, but he also doesn't have to make it. He does have to give it away. He has a social responsibility just being a good dude. If you make the most, you're supposed to give the most."**

Gems:

Large corporations buy companies in distress, or at a multiple, then license them out and receive revenue from them forever.

I don't really like watching my money grow. I like to watch my companies grow.

Make sure you create opportunities for your friends and family as you move up the financial ladder.

It doesn't make any sense to have a bunch of money just to look at it and then pay taxes on it.

Being rich without fun is not rich; that's being broke.

Money doesn't define anyone. It's the quality of living and the amount of people that love you that defines your status.

Those that make the most should give the most.

Damon Dash
PCH - Malibu, CA
10:41am

SECTION 6:
A FRIENDLY GAME OF LIFE

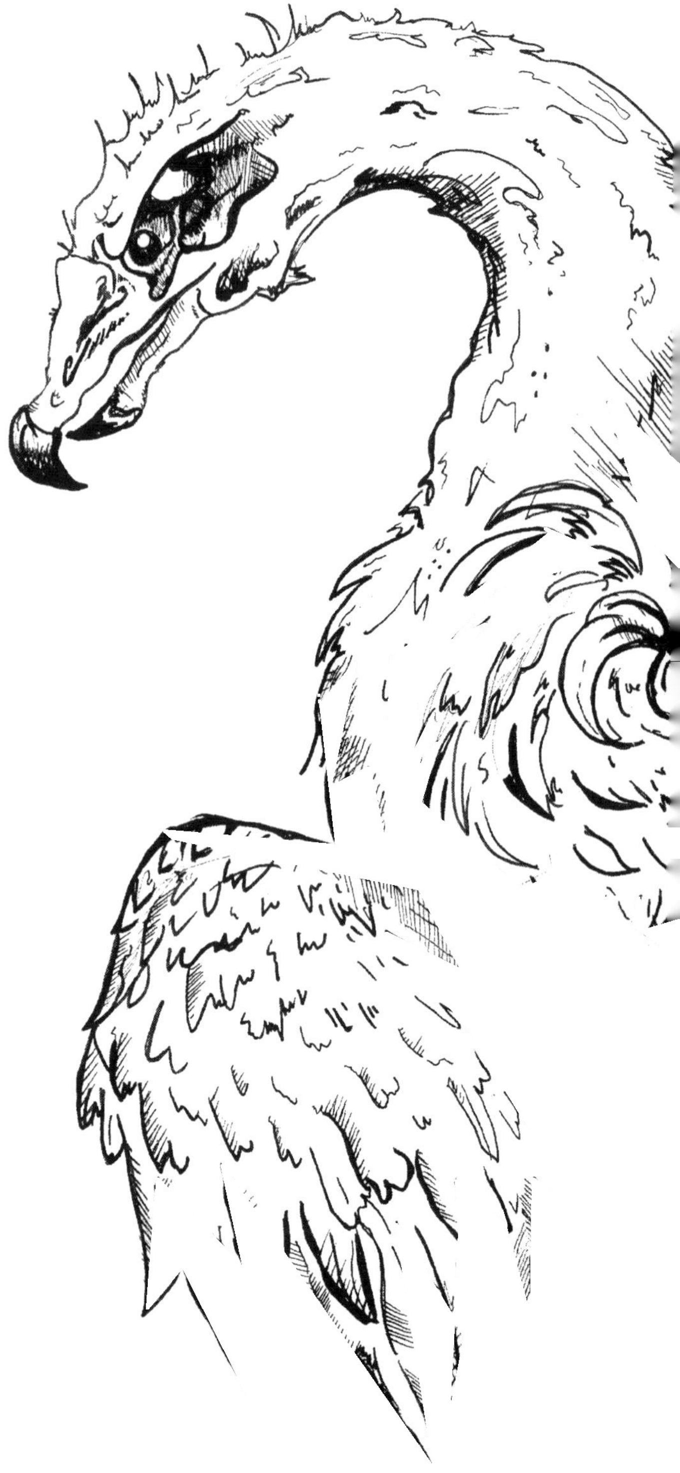

CULTURE EMBARRASSMENT

It's wack when you lose a friend or someone you had love for over a misunderstanding. The cold thing about over-projection is that once words leave the mouth, it's hard to retract what was said, as if it wasn't truly how you felt. Words used with the intent to harm turn into something similar to stray bullets that hit its target with total disregard for the spiritual or mental injuries that follow. Jim Jones posted a picture of Dame calling him a "Culture Vulture," also dropping the "F-bomb" that usually proceeds with violence in random situations, especially in the streets. Initially, when I saw this, I was shocked at what was going on because Jim and Dame have been friends for many years and both take pride in being from Harlem where the people live by the quote, "Harlem sticks together." After reading Jim's Instagram post, I went over to Dame's page to see what was going on. There was nothing but a picture of his wine brand that he launched called "Dusko Blu" with a comment underneath that said how excited he was to get back into the alcohol business. From there, the comment in response to Dame's post was from Jim calling him words that no man should ever call another man. Dame didn't respond, but instead posted another picture that showed him and Jim during better times with a comment that didn't feed the fire that was being thrown his way. Dame decided to take the higher road in response by saying, "I would never be ignorant enough to get on some tuff shit… That's what's killing our culture… I have nothing but love for you despite your disrespect…" After reading that, I called Dame to see what was going on and he said, "It's all good. I'll talk about it tonight after I get a haircut." And that's how it went down. In conclusion, my evaluation of this chapter taught me a life lesson on how important it is to always take the higher road by controlling emotions, whether it's business or a personal relationship even if, in the end, the people involved agree to disagree.

As soon as we started filming, I asked, "What's up with Jim Jones' Instagram post about you being a 'Culture Vulture'? How do you feel about that?"

"I mean whatever it is…I'm out here in Malibu, so I don't know," Dame said. "Whatever it is, that's family business. I know Jim; he's emotional. He's my brother and I don't know what or why, on any level, he would disrespect me. And in response to that topic, I don't want it to be about him, but what it's really about, which is business. I guess when it comes to black people, when they do business together, it doesn't matter how much good stuff you do if one thing is perceived as bad, it might even be misunderstood. Black people get very reactionary instead of talking it through, and a lot of times, it's usually a misunderstanding, and usually whoever's putting a battery in your back has their own agenda. But Jim's a creative, and again I know him. I've known him for his whole life, so I would never have any problems with Jim. I wouldn't ever have a problem with anyone on a physical level where I have to disrespect someone like that. I wish he would've approached it in a different way, but families have problems sometimes, man. They react. We don't hide our problems; we wear it all on our sleeves. So I guess when it comes to Harlem dudes, they're emotional, but that doesn't excuse it.

But anyway, on any other level, that tends to be something that happens. So, in terms of guys like Curren$y and Beans, I usually hear about their issues and it's never presented to me. I wish if they did have issues with me they would just come and talk to me about whatever's on their mind in a manly way because they should

know, based on my history from all the good things I've done, that if anything was ever done bad, it wouldn't be intentional because that's not how I'm built, and that's not what I do. And if I've done something wrong, I would hope they would forgive me for that one thing I did wrong based on all the good stuff that I've done. I would be alright having a conversation with anyone that says that I owe them money just as long as it's a civil conversation—as long as it's not overcompensation for robbing me someplace else. But my intent is never to do bad business in my book, and my books are always open. I make people rich; that's what I do. And then also when I'm fighting for something, I hate that it's always someone from the culture that will take that power from the person fighting for the culture. So I don't know why anyone would do that.

We have to stick together. The way to deal with things is to talk it out. It's never smart to talk violent, or be violent, or to be overly disrespectful. No one really deserves that. I'm not going to really call someone out of their name unless it's true. From my experience, I always say exactly what I'm mad about or what bothers me, and I'm always open for a conversation about it, whether it's private or public. But as long as we conduct ourselves like the men that we are. I just want the respect that I give, and if somebody's telling somebody something, I would hope that they don't believe that they should gauge whatever their thought is based on their experience with me on other things. I think I'm an honorable person, and I would challenge anybody to tell me I'm anything different, but usually when people say these things they always say it a couple of states away. It's never a direct conversation with me. I always hear about it; I never really know what's really going on. But again, it's usually a creative, and the people that have agendas put something in someone's ear or a battery in their back so they can make money off of them, which is what happens.

It's funny how heavily scrutinized the independent is, right, when corporate really does openly rob people all day and no one says anything. But it's always some sort of suspicion that I've done something that's vague, then it becomes some sort of an issue. And again, lawyers usually push issues because they get paid fees, and that's their agenda. They waste as much time as possible, and usually nobody wins but the lawyers. So, usually whoever pushes a legal action and usually, it is the lawyer that's pushing it, and then he wants all these unnecessary motions, and actions, and answers, and discoveries, and depositions. And at the end of the day, your legal fees are way more than whatever the damages are, and that lawyer gets paid because when you lose, that person has to pay the legal fees.

But also, being in business that happens. There's misunderstandings, and I never have an issue with going in front of a judge to objectively give a legal opinion. That's why I'm always in court because I always know that it's not about emotions in front of a judge. It doesn't matter how irate I am outside that courtroom. Justice usually prevails. It is what it is; the math is the math; and that's why I'm always willing to go to court. Even if I lose, honestly I really don't believe I'm wrong. I'm never gonna go to court if I think I'm wrong. That's dumb because I would have to pay my legal fees and their legal fees. But honestly from my experience, corporate will take advantage and they push you to go to court because they don't think that you have the stamina or the wherewithal financially to go through a three year process of five hundred thousand dollars worth of lawyers' wasting time.

In regards to the culture, I'm never going to have another beef with any man like that. If we do, we're gonna talk it out. It ain't never going to be violent. I'm not gonna be disrespectful because that makes the culture look retarded. And he's my friend; I love his son; I love his mom, like, I grew up with that dude. So that's where the forgiveness has to come in, but I would hope that if he has a problem he would talk to me like a man, and that's that, and that's really all I have to say about it. But that happens a lot when artists get mad and say things in the moment because they don't even understand what the business is. But they never apologize when they find out what the business is, or if they make incorrect accusations publically even after they find out you haven't done anything that they were saying you did."

When I asked Dame if he feels like there's a connection between being an artist and being emotional, he said, **"An artist is supposed to be** emotional, that's why he's an artist, that's why he's so good at his art. He's supposed to be. But a lot of people take advantage of artists, and if they see someone protecting an artist, they'll always make sure that they tell that person that they're making too much money off of them, or they can make them more money, or that they're robbing them. And also, when people create distance and don't talk, that's when you know they're about to do something bad because you can't stab a person in their back in front of them. You can't be with me every day and stab me in my back. So, once people start falling back creating distance, I'll be like, 'Damn, they ain't been around in a minute, they must be plotting or something.' But it is what it is. When it comes to all that shit, I don't really even care. Really I'm only focused on making movies right now. Whatever money it is, it must be short. There's not enough money in the world, I think, that could make you disrespect someone that's given you nothing but love their whole life, just because of a misunderstanding. There's a tolerance that I know about because it happens to me often. You can love a person from a distance; we just won't be doing business together because of that reaction. We can't do that, but as a culture, we can't deal with our issues like that. We have to talk it through; it makes us look so stupid in front of other cultures.

Could you imagine how happy Lyor was when he saw that? Other cultures always benefit from us having beef. There's not going to be anyone benefiting from us as brothers having a war or a disagreement, or whatever it is. That's not going to be the headline that everyone's going to make money off of: 'Our stupidity is based on emotion,' That's not happening."

Dame made a lot of sense in how to negate violence among not only friends but with all people—by taking the higher road of conversation instead of confrontation. I said, "That's the right way to approach it because he was once a good friend of yours." **"I mean just in general,"** Dame said. **"Not just him; anyone that has beef. First of all, we're all civilians. There ain't nothing we can do. That shit is dumb. We can't be tough in front of cameras, and on Instagram, and all that. There's no toughness when you're an artist. That takes it all away. That becomes dumbness because you're going to jail.**

And you're an example, everyone's looking at what you're doing. So it's twofold, karmically, it's tenfold. It's not good. If you're in front of the camera, you have a public responsibility to be a good example to the people that look up to you, especially from your culture. We all have to lead by example. We have to be intelligent. We have to do the right thing by each other, and that way no one else will do us wrong. Like, how can we expect other cultures to respect us and we disrespect ourselves? We can't be letting other people disrespect us; we're disrespecting each other all day. We have to stop disrespecting each other if we want other people not to disrespect us.

We can't keep checking other people for disrespecting us if we still disrespecting each other. We have to stop disrespecting each other. It has to be more love, man. Shit has to be about love; it can't be about beefing. Insecurity can't be about being tough. If you don't feel sure about something, get somebody to mediate it, or get an O.G. to talk it through with you. But all that over-projection makes the culture look crazy. We're smarter than that; we're all smarter than that. We all are; we know better. We all know love is better than war. We should all know this. That's way cooler, being cool and being peaceful. Having harmony is way cooler and more gangster than picking up a gun and busting it all day. That ain't it man, that shit is not it. That's not cool to me. All that shit is wack."

"Especially in the world we're living in today," I said. "When you listen to the news and you hear all the police brutality against black people that's going on it's sickening." Dame said, **"All the time, dog. We're at an all-time low probably, even though it's full on tilt and everyone's talking about it. Over the years, we been doing a lot more damage, and a lot more damage has been done to us. Right now, we're at a good time. Like, regardless to what's going on, we have a black President. I don't care what anyone says. I was looking at the last covers of Time magazine and it's a black man on the cover ninety percent of the time, and it's Obama. That sends a good message to the rest of the world, man. I don't care, let's say he's not here or there, so what?"**

I replied, "Hopefully the next generation gets it." **"We have to,"** Dame said. **"But we are evolving culturally because look how appalled we are at violence; look how happy we are about intelligence and peace. Intelligence is being celebrated, peace is being celebrated, and violence, unnecessary violence is appalling to people. So that's a good thing. I think we're evolving well, but we're definitely not going to be fighting each other. I'll never do that and it won't be me. I'm not going to be that guy that's going to make us look stupid. It will not be me, and it will not be anyone that I know that I can at least give advice to. Like, 'Come on, man, don't do that.' Pause. Hug it up, hug it up, B. Put down the guns. With all of that tough shit, disrespecting each other, that ain't it. Love is love, dog. Everybody, love is love. Everybody let's just pause and let's have 'Squash Differences Day.' I was going to say 'Squash Beef Day'. Like, everybody that has an issue on a tough level, squash it for one day, and just talk it out calmly, and I bet the world would be a better place."**

A few days after Dame's response, Jim did an interview with VladTV and expressed that his Instagram account was hacked and that he has nothing but love and respect for Dame. Shout out to Jim Jones for coming back for the verbal strays he let off. We've all been on the lower road in one way or another throughout life, but the jewel is that we all have the option to exit the lower road and take the higher road towards peace. Word up!

Gems:

The best way to deal with things is to talk it out when you have a problem in business. It's never smart to be violent or overly disrespectful. No one really deserves that.

Through the legal system, corporate will always try to take advantage and push you to go to court because they don't think an independent civilian has the stamina or the wherewithal financially to go through a three year.

An artist is emotional by nature; that's why they're good at their art.

When people create distance and don't talk, that's when you know they're about to do something bad because you can't stab a person in their back in front of them. You can't be with me every day and stab me in my back.

If you're in front of the camera, you have a public responsibility to be a good example to the people that look up to you, especially from your culture.

If you don't feel sure about something, get somebody to mediate it, or get an O.G. to talk it through with you.

Love is love. Everybody who has an issue on a tough level should squash it for one day and just talk it out calmly, and I bet the world would be a better place.

BIG PIMPIN' APOLOGY

Who doesn't remember the Big Pimpin' video where Dame and Jay were ballin' out on a huge yacht full of beautiful women? That video was immediately the breakthrough single that sent Roc-A-Fella records catapulting to the top of the charts, while etching their names in pop culture forever. Dame was turned up having a good time dancing with bottles of Cristal, taking sips, then pouring it on the ladies standing around. The video looked like they won a championship as Jay rapped and Dame poured champagne locker room style. I asked Dame how he feels about his actions in that video in particular.

"When you do something in your twenties and you're still paying for it when you're in your forties, it's an interesting thing to face because I'm a completely different person than I was when I was in my twenties. I'd be mad if I was in jail for something I did in my twenties. I wouldn't even know that person. It would feel like I was doing time for another person. And at twenty, you don't see that. You think forty is never coming. As we get older, we all become different people. So every time somebody comes through

Culture Vultures

charging you with your past, you'll be mad like, 'Damn, I wish somebody would've just told me when I was younger.' I've never really been in that position, but I can only imagine. Like, when I see things I've done in videos when I was younger I look at it like, damn, I was buggin. Champagne Dame. That dude was buggin' when he was younger. I don't even know that guy. Like, I would never advise anyone to do that. If my son ever did something like that I would be appalled. Appalled... But if I wasn't here to tell him it might happen, but I'm here to tell him I would be like, 'Naw, man disrespecting women ain't it. That's never alright."

Pouring champagne on girls? Hell yeah, it's disrespectful! I wouldn't want anybody doing that to my daughter or anyone I care about. I have to say I'm sorry to all the girls I poured champagne on... I'm not gonna say it wasn't part of what I was feeling at the time because it was Champagne Dame, but that doesn't excuse it, but I do apologize. I wouldn't advise that to anyone. I really do, I do feel a certain way about that. I wouldn't do that now."
As I was laughing, I said, "Yeah because that one girl you were splashing with champagne while she was on her back was drowning like, 'Oh, shit…'" Conscious of his past mistake he said, **"Come on, stop that, man,"** Dame said. "Don't be funny about it. I'm really apologizing. I did a lot of irresponsible shit when I was young that affected pop culture, and I think because of that I do have to pay for it karmically. At times, I feel like the message we put into the world when we were younger, besides being independent, really wasn't the most positive because it was about getting money by any means necessary. And my views have changed since then. I've evolved. It's not about the money; it's about your quality of living. It's not about money; it's about being a man taking care of your wife, kids, and family. That's the only gangsta thing I wanna hear about, and, of course, I wasn't saying that back then, but shit I was fucking twenty-five, what the hell was I supposed to say? And it doesn't make it better because we were a little more advanced because we were doing business at a really young age. You see, when you have a platform at a young age, it's dangerous because what you put into the world will be talked about in the future. It's crazy for me to see that this is still some people's business model.

Yeah, it wasn't the most positive thing to make a man feel bad because he doesn't make as much money as we did. And that was our business model: embarrassing dudes, making them feel bad because we had more money than they did, and our girls were better than theirs, and that we had better cars than them. And it made other people get it by any means. Even stabbing friends in the back to get it, and that ain't it. I've learned since then you have to do honorable things without cutting corners to get it. That's one of the reasons why I didn't have passion for the music business. That's why I stopped. People still ask me why I'm not back in the game. It just wasn't that positive to me; the message wasn't positive. That's why there was so much resentment and people hated me back then. I really didn't give a fuck to be honest, but I understand why now. I was fucking rubbing it in all their faces all day. It wasn't the right message. I get it. I wasn't supposed to be well received. It's good though.

But when you have kids, especially daughters, that changes you, man. When you have little girls, it's real. Little boys are a little different; you have to be a little tougher with them. But when you have girls you start to think about how you want your girls treated. With little girls, they're going to want to be treated the way their father treats them, so I'm like a slave for my little girls. I'll do anything for them because that's the kind of man I want them to have in their life. I don't want them to be use to abuse; I don't want that to be normal to them. I want them to experience butterflies, good smells, oceans, puppies, and fairies. That's all I want for my daughters. They don't have to be tough; I don't want them to be tough. I want them to be aware, smart, conscious, and balanced, but I'm never trying to make them tough just to survive. That's a terrible condition to have to live in, especially for a girl. I don't want a girl to have to worry about another young Champagne Dame. He was terrible."

I said, "Speaking of children, that brings me around to this question: I know having custody of Boogie when you were starting everything off helped you respect and appreciate women, or single mothers. [Because] wasn't it hard having custody of Boogie and doing business at times?"

"Well, the good thing about that situation was that I had the women and influence to support that," Dame said. "He was cool on that level. The hard part was being a mom. Like, I'm a good dad, but I'm not a good mom. At eighteen, I was barely a good dad. Like, he thought I was his age until he was, like, eight or nine years old. Like, I'm a playful dad. I wasn't like the dad type; I was a first time dad. He never had to go to bed. He doesn't even like dessert now because I used to give it to him first before dinner. I didn't give a fuck. I just didn't care, and that's why he's not indulgent. He's a very level dude. I don't think I did a bad job. I'm real proud of him and the way he handles things, including the way he conducts himself. So I must have done something correct. I don't think I'm an orthodox, traditional type of person. I'm definitely never going to be that. But I value my relationship with each one of my children. They're all equal relationships, and I have to make sure I have equal time with all of them and they all get treated the same, fairly. And that's all that matters is your children and how happy they are. That's how you rate your wealth, by how happy your children are. That's all that counts and if anything else counts in your world, that's not the cloth that I'm cut from, and I don't wanna be a part of any person that doesn't put their kids first. It's all about your kids, dog. It's all that matters to me. That's it. I don't care how much money you're getting; if your kids ain't happy, you're poor. Period."

Gems:

It's not about the money; it's about your quality of living.

What's gangsta is taking care of your wife, kids, and family.

I've learned that you have to be honorable in business, without cutting corners, to get peace in business. That's one of the reasons why I don't have passion for the music business anymore; everyone is cutting corners to make money.

Every little girl will one day accept and like being treated the way her father has treated her. I don't want my daughters use to abuse; I don't want that to be normal to them. I want them to experience butterflies, good smells, oceans, puppies, and fairies.

The rate of your wealth should be measured by how happy your children are.

Be cautious doing business with a person that doesn't put their kids first.

Damon Dash
Carmel, NY
2:01pm

TUPAC (B.I.G.)

From time to time, I wonder what would have surfaced from two of the most talented artists in Hip Hop. On the real, I think most of us agree that they were the best at the time of their passing. Pac was a poet that had love for his culture, and Biggie was a real M.C. that was visual. The day we conducted this interview was June 16, which was Pac's birthday. I never heard Dame talk about Pac's beef with Jay, so I asked him how he felt when Pac dissed Jay back in the day?

"I mean that was so many years ago. My mentality was so different back then, but my thoughts about it now is that I wish we could have all worked together. I wish Tupac could've lived. I wish that if he had any problems, we could have talked it out. I wish Biggie, Pac, and Jay could have done a project together, toured it, and made movies together. Like, my perspective on anything that would have involved any kind of beef is that I wish we could've squashed it. Like, if it's music and it's entertaining, keeping it at that level is cool. But people died, so anything that's associated with that situation has a dark feeling that comes over it because something that was

done genuinely as art and that made people happy really broke my heart. So whatever that shit was, it was wiped away, the fact that they passed away. But, I do think watching Tupac evolve as a person would've been really interesting. He was very intelligent."

Knowing that he was a friend of B.I.G., I respectfully asked Dame where he was at on March 9th of 1997. With a somber look on his face, he said: **"I was at my house in New York, on the phone with Jay. Jay told me, he said, 'Big got shot.' We were really apprehensive about going to LA at that time because of what was going on in the industry. Our advice to anyone was to stay home. I really didn't understand that whole situation because to me, you get into the music business to get away from the streets, not to bring it with you. Again, I like to laugh and have fun, and that wasn't fun. I really cried over that shit. So, I'm more about trying to figure out how to live than trying to figure out how to die. I'm here to enjoy life and take care of my children by preserving their happiness and making sure that they've got it. Good parenting is so important for a child, and it's important that parents make sure that the things that their children aren't sure about, that we make them sure about it because a child's brain isn't completely developed.**

I'd rather find the answers for my children than to have someone else teach it to them their way. I think it's very important to spend one on one time with your children by just letting them get to know you. What I know is that as a child, my mother and my father were my biggest influences until I became a man, until I made more money than them. But until that time, they were always my biggest influences. They were my superheroes. My father was my superhero, so if I'm anything like that to my kids, I'm a super, super, duper hero. And everything they see me do, or at least if I do something negative then I'm going to be able to explain my perspective on it because a lot of the negative things I've done on camera have been because of my insecurities and my desires to bring attention to myself from those insecurities. I have to explain that to my kids, and I have to tell my son why he can't be pouring champagne on girls' heads, but I did. I have to talk to him and explain why that guy's a clown, which is, of course, calling myself a clown to my children at that point in my life. Like, 'That person did what he thought he had to do at that age, but he's not doing that

anymore, so don't judge him by that. Judge him by this.' Don't judge a man by what he did when he was a teenager or in his twenties. That shit is crazy."

Gems:

I think it's very important to spend one-on-one time with your children.

What I know is that as a child, my mother and my father were my biggest influences until I became a man, until I made more money than them. But until that time, they were always my biggest influences. They were my superheroes.

I'm more about trying to figure out how to live than trying to figure out how to die. I'm here to enjoy life and take care of my children by preserving their happiness.

Studying the psychology of good parenting is not only important for parents, but for future parents if we plan on making the next generations better than we are today.

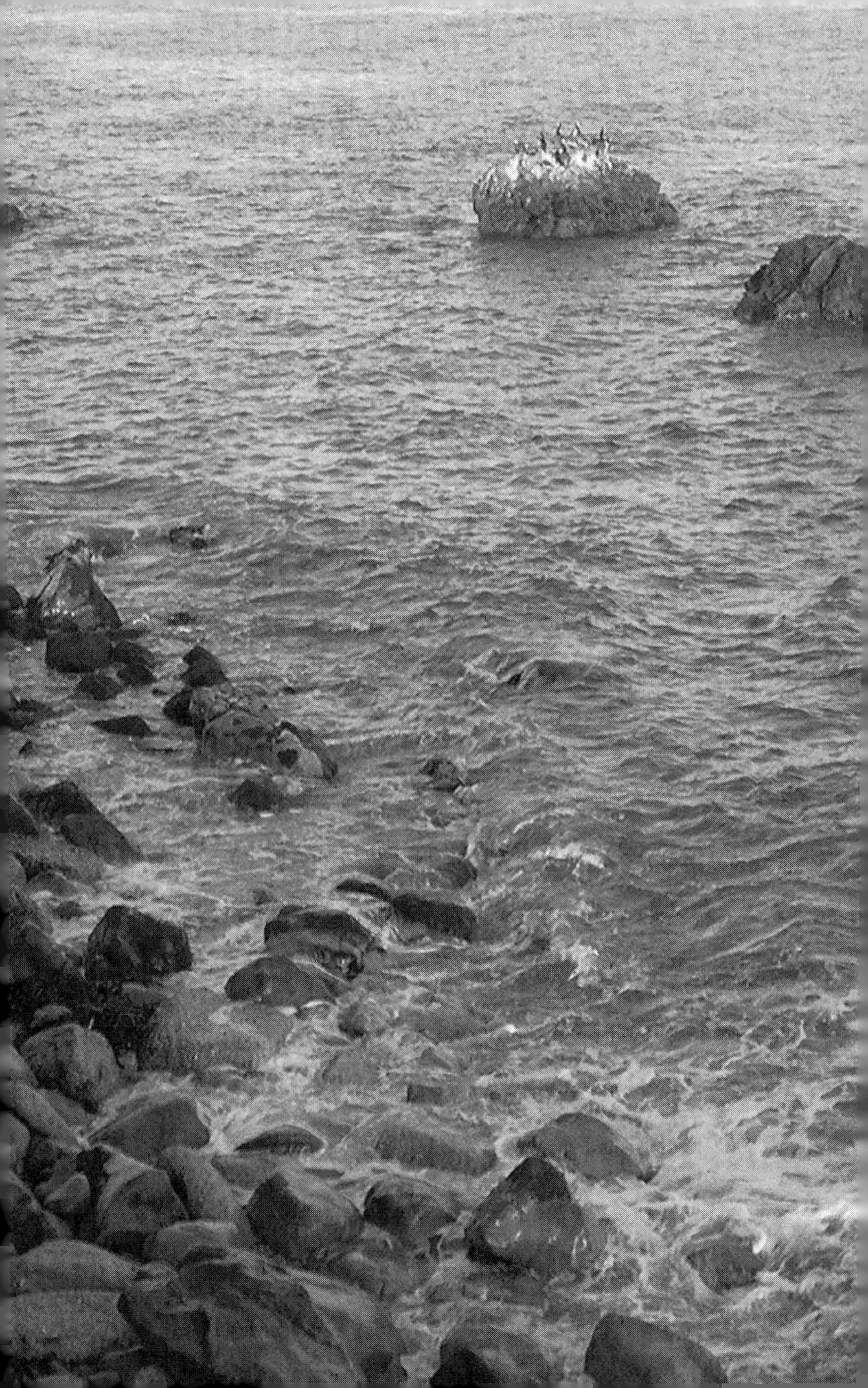

BLACK DISTRIBUTORS?

One of my partners in Hip Hop, Motivation John Robinson, asked: "Why do you feel there hasn't been a black owned distribution company in the music industry on a major scale?"

"That would take us sticking together," Dame said. "Meaning that a black distributor would start putting out a black artist, and usually when we start to do things like that, people start breaking us up in-between. With a brown paper bag some way, shape, or form; making us stab each other in the back. And I can't say making us; I would have to say influencing us, or testing us because no one makes another man do anything, really. But when that temptation is there for the short change, real quick, and it's not honorable, to some people, that's the easy route. For me, the non-honorable route, karmically in the end, I believe, will always get you. It's not about the paper; it's about how you feel about yourself. Again, if you're a wealthy person, meaning you have a lot of money, but you don't like yourself, then you're really broke. What's the sense of thinking you're rich if you don't like yourself? If you don't like yourself and your kids are unhappy? Think about it—they're probably unhappy because you don't like yourself. If you don't know how to like yourself, how would you comprehend liking your kids? We have to start dealing with our issues. It would make life a lot easier. A lot of people need a therapist, someone to talk to, that can give them an objective opinion without you getting mad at them. I've noticed that every time I try to give somebody guidance, they get offended. With us, as men, I guess it has to do with our masculinity. Like, usually if you tell a dude what he's doing wrong, he gets mad at the fact that you're making him aware."

Cracking up I asked: "Well, have you looked for a new way to adjust your approach?"

"Yeah, I stopped fooling with them," Dame said. "I don't need to be doing that shit. Like I said, all I have to worry about really is my children and my woman. That's all that counts. It takes too much time trying to help other people that don't want to be helped." Agreeing with Dame's philosophy, John said, "Yeah. The reality is if there's someone in my circle and they tell me something, I have to listen, especially if it's coming from someone I respect." **"Definitely If you respect them," Dame replied. "Sometimes resentment overrides respect, and that's ego. Ego's voice is loud, dog. You have to learn how to punch that ego voice in the mouth, like, 'Shut up!'**

The ego will justify disrespect, but there's nothing that justifies disrespect. When that voice says, 'Naw, fuck that! He did this, he did that.' You have to smack that voice like, 'That's not the right advice.' But usually your ego is telling you that what they've done justifies you getting out of pocket. It's your ego always. That voice is strong, man. That's the Devil. When I got a hold of him I was way better. Once you can recognize that voice and understand how to have a conversation with ego, it makes your life a lot easier. You have to put it in a chokehold. Just choke it out and put it to sleep."

Gems:

Throughout history, when certain cultures stick together, other people start breaking us up in-between with a brown paper bag in some way, shape, or form; thiw makes us stab each other in the back. And I can't say making us; I would have to say influencing us, or testing us because no one makes another man do anything, really

I believe when a person takes the non-honorable route, you will, karmically, get yours in the end.

If you're a wealthy person, meaning you have a lot of money, but you don't like yourself, then you're really broke. It's not about how much paper you have; it's about how much love you have for yourself.

When resentment overrides respect, that's your ego talking. That voice is loud, so you have to learn how to punch the voice of ego in the mouth and put it in a chokehold like, "Shut up!

Once you can recognize that voice and understand how to have a conversation with ego, it makes your life a lot easier.

Ava, Damon, Tallulah, Lucky, & Boogie
Carmel, NY
12:01pm

GOD & RELIGION

We are all similar to light bulbs connected to the same generator of power, and that generator of our power is God, the source of all things. This chapter is an interview segment on Dame's personal beliefs on God and religion. My belief in the Most High is that everything we see and everything we "Be" is God, and that we live in a mental universe which means consciousness is God, and that each individual's belief in themselves is their belief in God. What you are conscious of being becomes your reality, and whatever you add to "I Am" you become because "I Am" is God. That's why you have to be careful what you claim to be in love with especially if it's "CoCo". No disrespect to my family in spirit, O.T. Genesis, but peep game, "I'm" is an abbreviation of "I am" which means whatever you put behind it becomes your reality. Don't sleep, no one will be held guiltless to that law, so be careful. Check it out for yourself in Proverbs 18:21 where it says, "Death and life are in the power of the tongue and those that love it will eat its fruit." Believe that! When asked about God and religion Dame shared:

"I definitely believe in some form of a higher power that I don't

think our minds are completely ready to understand," Dame said. "But on a logical level, the thing about religions is most religions claim that if you don't believe in their religion you're going to hell, and there are so many religions. So, if there's a million religions out there, does that mean that everyone is wrong, and one religion is going to be right and everyone is going to hell? I generally believe in your intent and the evolution of your soul. What you put out there and the lessons you have to learn are concrete, and that's what you'll get back. I believe there are tests you have to pass in life, and the more things that you pass, and the more difficult test that you pass, the more things that you'll get. It's like gambling: the bigger the risk, the bigger the reward.

So, I do believe in your intent, your soul. I believe in a higher power. I'm not sure exactly what the formula is, but it's just hard for me to believe that one way is the only way. I think it's arrogant for someone to say that if you don't believe in me then you're going to hell, and that if every other religion is right that means that every other religion is wrong. I just don't know the odds of that. And I think that in religion, it's the tool that people use to be evil. I've seen people use religion as a form of control over the masses through money. Like, if I was the Devil, I'm going to come as a snake or something scary. If I'm the Devil, I'm coming as a bunny rabbit. I'm a come and try to trick you; I'm not gonna be that obvious. If I'm the Devil, I'm going to come as God. I think there's a lot of Devils pretending to be God, and it's like, 'Who is that?' There are some good ones, but I think there's more bad than good in the business of religion. Religion is too profitable to know if it's right or wrong. Too many people make money off of it, so it's a hard thing for me to gauge. I don't judge it, but it's just hard for me to have a definitive idea. I'll take the best ideas of every religion and put it together. Like, I like Buddhism, etcetera."

I thought it was interesting that he put together his own theory about God and religion from different ideas he collected over time. Then he went off subject while holding his puppy saying, **"You know it's good to have a puppy around. It's good to have something to love other than yourself. I have to make sure he eats, goes to the bathroom. Raquel, Ava, and Tallulah help out a lot. Everyone in the family** takes on the responsibility to look out. Like, Boogie is at home watching Dusko right now, but we needed a puppy to travel with, something I can pet all day."

I replied, "That definitely has something to do with success: "Taking care of other people besides yourself." **"Knowing how to give love,"** Dame said. **"That's my thing right there—is that it's more about giving love, that's it. The more love you give, the more love you're going to get back. The business model that I try to project is love, and love is tough. It takes love to give somebody an opinion they don't want to hear. I have to love someone to take the time to tell them something that might make them angry. That's why I tend not to do that too much with men because I don't want to be loving another dude like that. I don't love a dude enough to take him getting mad at me for telling him what's wrong, or giving him advice on how he can do something better. But with women, it's better; they don't have nuts.**

I'm just sick of trying to advise dudes that don't understand that it's all about being a man. They don't know what their nuts are for. Most men don't even know what they have them for. They think it's a new job to find a girl with money. No real man's supposed to want that. I'm not trying to be in the house where I'm not the breadwinner. That's wack. Like, 'My only hustle is to get taken care of.' God didn't give you nuts for that; he gave you nuts to go hunt and to lead by example. Would you want your kids doing that? Or would I want my son to say, 'Oh, my business model is to find a rich girl,' and be told what to do? Anytime a girl is paying a man's bills she's not fucking a real man.

Trust me, a women knows what a real man is and she knows what a 'Boy Toy' is, and some dudes don't care about being a 'Boy Toy.' I got nuts; I wanna be a man. I want my son to be a man. I want every man around me to be a man. I don't want people around me that think being taken care of is the motto, or that's a respectable way of living. That's The Vagina Monologues, and I'm not apart of that business model. Like, even a dog, if it walks in the room and he sees another dog, he wants to make sure that the other dog knows that he's dominant. That's just what nuts do, pause. That's what testosterone is; it's chemicals and it's a natural thing for men. A male dog can't hide it. He just has to go 'Ham.' I'm getting big with the dogs. They're very important, they really are."

Seeing Dame giving his dog attention, I asked Dame if he liked cats and he said: **"They're alright, but they don't listen. Cats are like women with an attitude. They don't acknowledge their name. You can't walk a cat. I don't mind having a house cat or a country cat where they can live outside and come in, but I need something that's going to give me some love back. That should be the natural perspective, especially when you're getting paid because you're good at something, to become completely self-absorbed. It happens to every one of my artists. It's unconscious; it's a human thing. That's why I tell my kids and everyone I care about that when the opportunities present themselves and you become successful the test is to care about other people more than you care about yourself. Pay attention to that. Start caring about other people by looking at things from their perspective. Like, the main thing that I do in business is I think about how other people would perceive things. So, if I'm talking to you, I'm already thinking about the answers you might give me and what you could be thinking. I'm looking at it from your perspective, if I'm not being fair or if your thinking is retarded, no offense."**

Understanding the natural law of polarity will take a person to new heights when they see that things like hot and cold, for instance, are different degrees of the same thing. The many degrees of heat are nothing more than the absence of cold, and the many degrees of cold are nothing less than the absence of heat. When you look at a thermometer, you can't tell where hot begins and cold ends because they are both different degrees of the same thing. Just like ignorance is a lack of knowledge, and knowledge is a lack of ignorance making them both different degrees of the same thing. As I listened to Dame, I could hear the balance of his ideas, which is why I asked him if he felt that it's wise to have a balanced outlook in everything you do?

"I just know every perspective, from the dumb perspective to the smart perspective," Dame said. **"The math—that's how I understand the person I'm dealing with. I always ask the**

questions to myself that I'm asking the person as if I was the person that I'm asking the question to. Then I think about what I would say if I looked at things from a variety of perspectives. I feel that if a person is not giving me the right answer, based on my perspective, then I know not to move forward. You can't be mad at someone for not agreeing with your perspective. You should be mad at moving forward with something knowing that you have a different perspective than that person just because your agenda is to make money off of them. That's annoying. But if I get into a room with someone and his perspective is to do it one way and my perspective is to do it another, we can just agree to disagree and not do business together. But because you want to make money off of me, you pretend that your perspective is like mine when it really isn't, eventually you're going to resent my perspective as you're making the money. You're not going to work well, and it's not fair. That's a very selfish thing to do, to be around somebody just because you can make money off of them, even though you're not doing right by them. That's wack."

As a believer of cause and effect, I know that what's done in the dark will always come to light. So my response was, "They can't get away with anything. It'll reveal itself regardless of how clever a person thinks they are anyway." Dame continued by saying, **"That's what managers usually do. My worst issue with artists is usually their managers. Their managers are usually the most 'High Maintenance.' Like, managers feel like if it wasn't for them the artist wouldn't be there, but the problem is if it wasn't for you that the artist wouldn't be there, then you need a new artist, and that's that. Period. These managers think it's okay to rob their artists because they politic the deal. It's not alright to rob your artists because you brokered the deal. It's alright to get your commission and keep it moving, but that doesn't entitle you to rob them because you feel entitled. The artists are artists. They have no idea. They're not paid to be good at business; they're paid for being good at being creative. And a lot of people make money off that and they take advantage of that by taking advantage of an artist's anxieties. Like, when an artist doesn't want to deal with something, they'll do anything not to deal with it. As long as you tell them it's taken care of, they'll feel good. So, it's going to be someone that's telling the** artist things are taken care of when not who will be the one that's taking money from them, making them spend money on stuff they don't have to. Period."

Gems:

We are all similar to light bulbs receiving power from the same generator of power, which is God, the source of all things.

Whatever you add to "I Am" you become because "I Am" is God.

"Death and life are in the power of the tongue and those that love it will eat its fruit." Proverbs 18:21

I believe there are tests you have to pass in life, and the more difficult the test that you pass, the more things you'll receive.

Life is like gambling: the bigger the risk the bigger the reward.

I think it's arrogant for someone to say that if you don't believe in me then you're going to hell, and that if every other religion is right that means that every other religion is wrong.

It's always good to have something to love other than yourself.

I've found that the pendulum swing of happiness reveals that the amount of love you give is the amount of love you're going to get back.

When the opportunities present themselves and you become successful, the real test is to care about other people more than you care about yourself.

THE FASHION GAME

In business, Dame is a guy that's worn many hats. Rocawear was a brand that he created back in 1999 that has reached way over 600 million dollars in annual sales. The topic of this chapter came to life when I asked him about the Ryan Kenny clothing brand he was helping former Roc-A-Fella employee Kenny Burns develop.

"Ryan Kenny was a line I invested in with Roc-A-Wear, and one of the issues Roc-A-Wear had was that I was investing in too many companies, and Ryan Kenny was one of them. They didn't understand that when you initially invest in any company, you have to take losses. I was trying to build Roc-A-Wear. I knew that Roc-A-Wear's existence was temporary because it was too logo-driven and it was based on a person, and that person can't stay cool forever. So, I was always trying to do other brands. That's why I had State Property, I had Rachel Roy, I had Charlotte Ronson, and Ryan Kenny was one of those brands. So, the other partners didn't understand my business model, but I'm sure they understand now.

It was hindsight, but we had to stop investing in that company. Again Rocawear didn't last because it was logo-driven. I further learned this looking at all the brands that went sideways due to being logo driven like Karl Kani and Cross Colors."

I wasn't all the way rolling with what he said because I've seen other brands that were logo-driven survive like Polo, Gucci, and Lacoste. I asked him if that's the case, how has the Polo brand been around forever with their logo?

"First of all, Polo never acknowledges black people. Period," Dame said. "If he does, it's someone black acting white because culturally we don't want something just "anyone" can get. We want something that's aspirational, and Polo puts a lot of money into their Purple Label brand lifestylewhich is a loss leader. Polo really makes their money from off-price Polo shirts because they make a margin because that logo means something. So there's a lot of money invested in lifestyle to sustain that, and usually whoever's behind these logo-driven urban brands, they don't have taste, and it's not built on lifestyle. It's built on the duration of the career of an artist.

Or, in a case like Karl Kani or Cross Colors, they were brands that were strictly logo-driven. And once everybody wears it, no one is gonna wanna wear it anymore because they weren't created as luxury lifestyle brands. And because they were people that were taking from the culture, they didn't care about the longevity of their brand, so they didn't invest in the lifestyle part and they didn't have a luxury loss leader. Everything with them was profit, profit, profit, profit, profit. But to sustain a real brand for a long period of time, you have to spend a lot of money in doing things just to showcase that you're cool and have talent. Like with Maybach, Mercedes doesn't make money from Maybach, they don't make money from 600s because not many people can afford them. Mercedes makes money from their 200s and 300s from people that are buying into a lifestyle that they can afford at a price point. So, there always has to be a loss leader. If you go to a store like Cartier Watches you'll see a five hundred thousand dollar watch, but if you ask them what keeps the lights on, they're going to say it's the stainless steel tank. People buy the three thousand dollar watch because they can't afford the five hundred thousand dollar watch, but if the five hundred thousand dollar watch doesn't exist, you don't want the three thousand dollar watch. But that's what keeps the lights on; it's the stuff that you could buy in volume.

There are luxury brands like Rolls Royce that don't compromise at all. They don't want the volume. You're buying that shit full price or Bottega Veneta. But with most clothing brands, their business model is selling off-price goods. So that's why they have to sell a lot of it just to make a little money off-price because it's guaranteed off-price. So if something cost ten dollars to make and you sell it wholesale for twenty dollars and they sell it retail for fifty dollars, if you could sell it for thirty dollars, you still make ten. But someone thinks that it's a deal, so they buy a lot of it. That's why it moves at that price point instead of making the full margin. So you also have to sell a lot of that. Like, I like margin. I like my work to look real good. I like to be destination and to be full priced-don't pay any sales. It's direct to consumer. We never go off-price because my work is good. That's my business model now; that wasn't my business model before."

If you want to sustain for a long period of time, your brand should have a luxury line. You have to have it. Like, there was no 'Rachel' by Rachel Roy, unless there was a Rachel Roy. We were in Bergdorf Goodman, and that's what got us into Macy's at a cheaper price point. But if we were never in Bergdorf Goodman, she would've never got into Macy's. We had to lose money first. So, for Rachel Roy, I had to lose two million dollars a year because I couldn't sell a lot of it. It takes a lot of money to develop it, and you only get into one retailer. We gave away for editorial so that I could be in magazines like Vogue and shit like that. So, you're really just paying for the developing, and the more people that buy it at that time—it's like a curse. You don't want everybody to have it; you just want a small group of people to have it. I just wanted to be in the most expensive department store in the world, which we were. I wanted to make that statement. So because of that, we currently can make a two thousand dollar pants. We could sell seventy-dollar pants and people will buy it. But then it gets into Macy's, that shit is cut in half anyway, it's forty-percent off.

Taylor, Damon, & Bianca
Los Angeles, CA
12pm

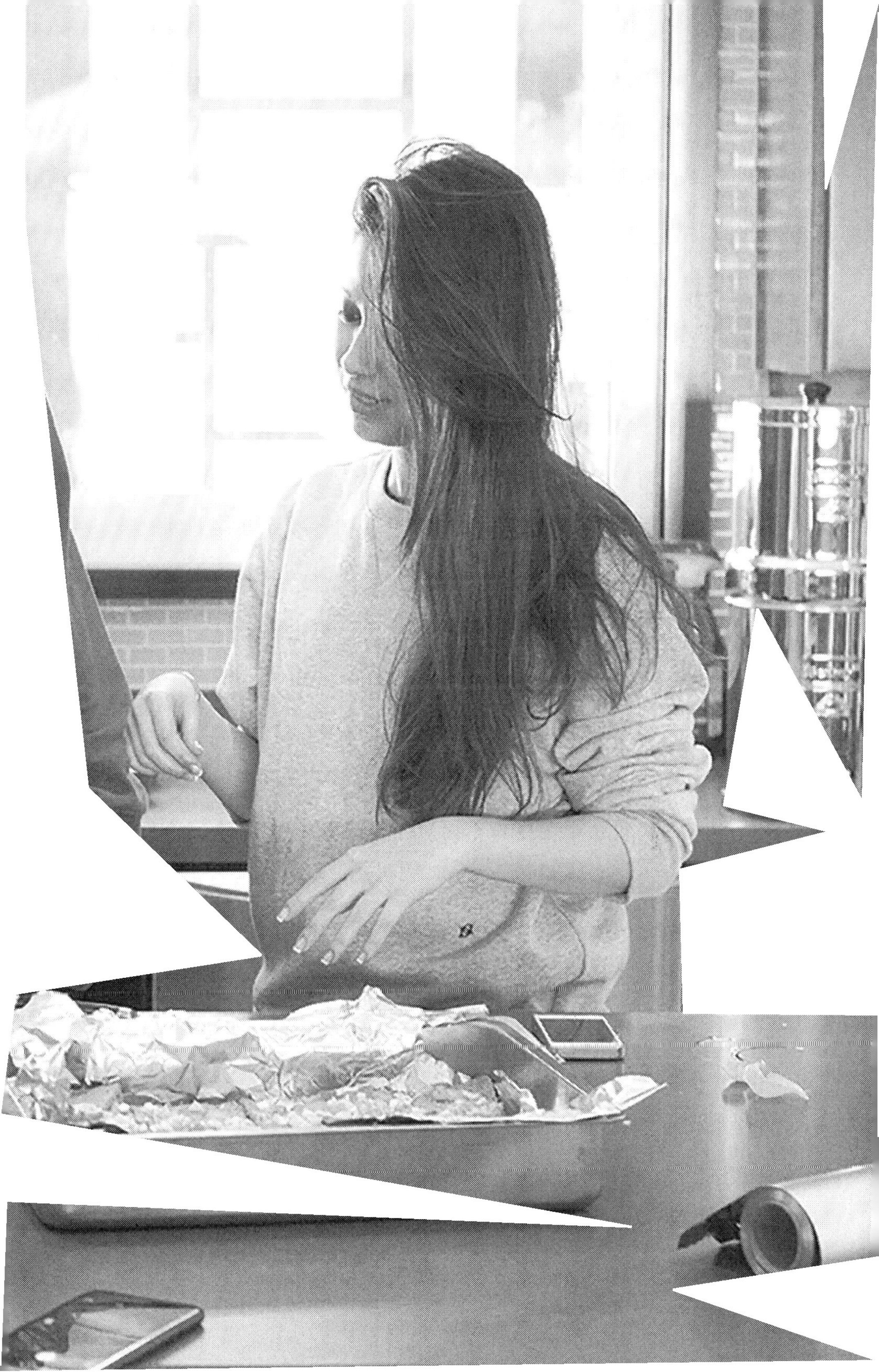

Macy's is nothing but a big-ass luxury off-price department store. You don't make any money being in Macy's. That's just for show. It's like advertising because people walk by it all day. You have to pay to be in Macy's. Not only does your brand go off-price, you have to give them twenty-five-percent for rent. You have to pay to renovate your shop in Macy's, and you have to pay the salespeople that work for them. That shit is a hustle. Macy's is nothing but a landlord. Ain't nobody making money in Macy's. You just seeing traffic go by. It's just a big ass moving advertisement store that a hundred million people go by everyday. Everybody is buying their shit off-price, that's why everybody goes to Macy's. Forty-percent, fifty-percent off. Where's your margin?

If you're lucky in fashion, you'll make a ten-percent margin. So, that means to make a one million dollar profit you have to do ten million dollars, and everything has to go right, and that barely happens. To make five hundred thousand, that means you have to do five million dollars just to make five hundred thousand. If you have a direct to consumer situation, you have a fifty-percent margin or more; from a million dollars, you make five hundred thousand. For two million dollars, you make a million. That's what I'd rather do. I don't care about perception; all I care about is taking care of my family. I want more margin. Why would I wanna hustle all day to make five hundred thousand, when I could just sit at home and sell it from my web store and make that same money, and not have to kiss anybody's ass, and never watch my stuff go forty-percent off, with my shit always full price? Why not? Destination is key. If your work is good, people will find you. You just have to make sure your work is good. Period."

Gems:

Always prepare to take a loss when you initially invest in any company.

Roc-A-Wear's existence was temporary because it was too logo-driven and it was based on a person that had to stay cool forever.

Most urban brands are not built on lifestyle; they're usually built on the career duration of an artist.

A clothing line will play itself out if it's not first presented as a luxury lifestyle brand.

In order to sustain any brand for a long period of time, a luxury line should be the main focus of that brand.

After the luxury line has been established, there should always be a loss leader that allows the consumer to buy into that lifestyle at a price point they can afford.

Macy's is nothing but a big luxury off-price department store. You don't make any money being in Macy's. That's just for show. It's like advertising because people walk by Macy's all day. You have to pay to be in Macy's. Macy's is nothing but a landlord.

Destination is key. If your work is good, people will find you. You just have to make sure your work is good at all times.

Damon, Kenyatta, & Carolyn
Evil Rock-N-Roll Cat
Hollywood, CA
8:14pm

A Friendly Game Of Life

THE FILM GAME

When the Hip Hop Motivation team and I began working on our film The Secret to Ballin' Journey, I watched how we all turned into different people at the end of production. Speaking for myself, not only did I raise my vibration mentally by interviewing so many dope people, but I also had a shift in my overall outlook on the rhythm of the pendulum swing, which represents the ups and downs of life. I learned many lessons about patience and deep breathing that turned me into a better translator of God's work. There were a lot of tests of character while developing and filming The Secret to Ballin' Journey that would have sent the average man to prison for assault or running for the hills. For example, there was few disagreements that went down between me and a couple of my partners that would have caused the old mentally immature Kenyatta to charge them to the game without looking back. But I remained calm when the pressure was on and I kept my temper in check.

I learned that daily improvisation is a significant part of living a "Good" life, meaning that we have to practice controlling our negative reactions through emotion manipulation. After consistent practice of emotion manipulation, you will find yourself in control of what you allow to affect you whether it's positive or negative. This type of practice for me turned me into a producer with mental agility that kept me focused on the bigger picture to finish no matter what obstacle was in front of me. On the real, for everyone reading this chapter planning to film your first feature film, I have to tell you that in the end, there's nothing like finishing what you set out to do. Don't sleep, it'll open your mind to the infinite possibilities of creating. As we all know, Dame has a great catalogue of movies connected to his name like Paid in Full, State Property, Streets Is Watching, his new film Loisaidas, Too Honorable, Bukowski, and Dressed to Kill. I've seen Dame develop many things over the years, but in my opinion, I feel like where he excels the most is in the film game because of his affinity for creating movies.

On a dope sunny day in Malibu, I asked Dame what's different in producing films today in comparison to when he did Paid In Full over thirteen years ago.

"Well now, I'm using my own money. It's completely independent, so it's not like I have to be told what to do. I don't have to make something for someone else's agenda because when someone puts up the money, like, I always say they're the boss, and the reason they want you to make a film is so they can make money off of you. I just got back on my feet where I'm able to fund my own movies again. I like being a one-hundred-percent creative, so I'm not really trying to be administrative these days. I'm done with that. I just want to direct for a little while because I'm really enjoying it. And the way I approach movies is not just the movie itself; it's the merchandise you can sell, the toys, and the videogame. I want to turn a movie into a franchise and have it 'waterfall' money, which means it'll make money forever because I can license it. There's so many ways that you could make money off movies if you make them yourself. The movie companies generally don't like the exposure of development because it takes money to get it written, and then it takes money to get the actors, and all those things—to even say 'action' cost a lot of money. So if you take that headache away from the movie company, they're more inclined to want to work with you because there's no financial exposure on their part. See, if you have something already done,

they'll license it from you. You can rent it to them, and they can't really tell you what to do, and they're happy they're not exposed. They're happy they did not have to put up any money to get it to that finished point. So, if you can do it yourself, there will always be a way to make money off of your movie from licensing."

Just a few days prior to this interview, we watched both State Property movies and I noticed that both of those movies showcased all of Dame's brands. I said, "I noticed you did a lot of merchandise placement in State Property 2. You had Armadale in there. You had the clothing lines, Rocawear and State Property visual in every scene. That was dope."

"Yeah. A movie is the best commercial. Like, to be honest with you, when I filmed all those movies, we were really wearing that, and that's what we were drinking at the time. Everything was organic. So yeah, it's a commercial for your lifestyle, whatever you're really using. Not something that you're getting paid to use, but something that you use on a regular basis. The difference is that I try and own everything that I enjoy. The reason why I make the clothes is because I enjoy wearing good clothes, so I might as well make it perfect, and I know how. Why should I build someone else's brand when I'd prefer to build my own? The same with the liquor, which is why I created Dusko whiskey, and that's why there's the Dusko Blu wine. Instead of selling someone else's wine, I'd rather make it perfect, package it the way I want, and sell it, for me, I'm not trying to really compete with the whole world. I'm not trying to sell a billion dollars. Like twenty, thirty million is good for me. I'm an independent, and my margin is better. I find that putting things in stores is just like marketing, and you don't make any money because it takes so much time collecting from the stores, and you have to re-up to get more goods. When you put things in stores in order to re-up and make more product, you have to collect money, but it usually takes thirty to sixty days, so the timing is always fucked up. Being in a store is for everyone else to make money. I find that a direct to consumer relationship is the most profitable because you have full margin. There's no sales commission. You're not selling it at a wholesale price; you're selling it at full price, and you never have to sell it off-price. You never have to fight for real estate, and what I find is if your product is good, people are going to find you, so I don't worry about marketing. I don't worry about any of that. I know that what I make is portal, so people will find me. There's this spot in the Lower Eastside that I eat at, and they make pancakes. They don't advertise; they don't do anything to promote. Every single time I go into that spot, there's a two and a half hour wait every time, every single day. It's off the beat with no advertising, so it's not like you'll know about it. They don't take credit cards, they only take cash, and those pancakes are moving. Again, I heard about them because their product is good. The point I'm making is that they're so good they don't have to advertise. They don't have to use credit cards. People wait two and a half hours, but it's all because the product is good. As long as your product is good, you don't have to really worry about putting money into marketing. It's like having a hit record; it sells itself. That's why my thing is to just make sure my product is good.

The illest shit in the world for an independent is selling products direct to consumer. Like, even with this movie that I'm shooting Loisaidas, it's a very violent movie. It might be so violent that in a responsible way, I'm probably not going to put it in theatres, but I'll have to make it available "On Demand" because I want people to watch it from their house, so that it won't be a bunch of violent people getting into a theatre where something could happen, and then the culture looks crazy. But they can enjoy the same experience right at home for ten dollars. It's just easier to watch a quality film in the comfort of your own home. Like, I might put it in a theatre or two for perception, but other than that I prefer the people to see it and pay for it in a safe way.

But, for perception getting your movie into theatres is still good. I mean theatres in an old way, of course, makes things look bigger than they are. So yeah, you might put something in theatres so it'll have better DVD sales, or better licensing, or so that the toys could sell, or that the merchandise could sell, or the videogame could sell. The movie is usually just a commercial to sell all the ancillary things. It's just like an album; it's approached the same way. Then it's a good move to submit your film to film festivals so that you can get seen, or to do a screening where someone will buy it or license it from you. The reason you submit to film festivals is because you have the whole movie industry there where they get to see it. But again, that's the only purpose of a festival. My plan is to shoot three quick movies, direct them, and put them in festivals just because I'd like to get the accolades of it or the perception of it. Or I'll just screen it to launch the fact that I have my own film company and my own film division.

Like I said, the whole industry is there, so you have the eyeballs where everyone can judge it and build a buzz that will make people buy it or increase the anticipation when it comes out. Making movies is all I'm really focused on. That's my passion right now, and that's where I feel I can be an artist, and that might be why my perspective about what's going on outside of the world isn't a concern of mine. When I'm in movie mode, I'm in a bubble because I'm completely focused on making sure it's the best. Filming a movie is just like making a record, or when a painter's painting. It's the same thing. So this is my art that has lots of moving parts, and there's a lot of people that have to do certain things to make those parts work. We all wear different hats. It's a very focused thing, and I'm enjoying that focus. That's what I want to be for a little while. I just want to be creative with stuff. I have a couple of clothing lines coming out on an independent level, and I was doing a t-shirt thing for a minute, and I didn't really like that business model that much. It's too much collecting money. There's this brand, 'When We Once Were Fiends,' that I'm working with and I'll just collaborate with them. So I'll show it in Paris at Capsule, and I'm a show it at New York Fashion Week by doing a presentation. But again, it's just really to show people how good the quality of the work is and that we have the ability to make something at a designer level. But that's just something I have a passion for, like getting fresh. I like getting fresh. I like being able to make quality fashion. I like to be able to monetize it. But again, it has to be fresh and I have to love it. Then when I make music, it's more or less for passion. I put it in the movies where we can film videos with the artist, which will help build their brand. But really I just want to be creative for a little while."

No matter what business venture Dame enters, I know there's going to be some music involved, so I asked him how he was preparing music for the soundtrack.

"Well, usually what I do is put a studio on the set, so whatever music is created on the set can be recorded right away. Whatever happens there, I try to shoot the video right there while I'm shooting the movie. I'm not wasting a second when the lights are on. I have mics, cameras, and the artist there, so while we're setting up one scene I'm like, 'Yo, playback some music,' and of course you know we got it lit. My idea is that you might as well just shoot—get a lot of footage—that way as well because music is all a part of it. It's like one artistic pot that I'm cooking. And from there, I look at what I got, from the music, the clothing, to the actual visual. Like, all of that is an art to me which dictates the way I put it out. Right now, that's where I'm at. I'm just twisted in art right now."

Already aware of the answer, I asked Dame what the first concentration of any film production was.

"Well, the first move is the script. You have to get that script right, and then for some people, they have to worry about the financing. But I've dealt with that, so now I can just organize it, get it shot. The script has to translate to everyone first. See, in my crew everything is legit. It's one-hundred percent independent, but it's just as big as anything anyone else is doing. It's probably a little smarter, a little leaner and a little faster. I don't waste any time. Plus, I know my consumer, I know who I'm talking to. I'm not really trying to make something that's going to fit any particular format, I'm just making what I enjoy making and what I enjoy watching, and whoever doesn't enjoy what I create doesn't have to watch it."

Gems:

Movie companies generally don't like the exposure of developing a movie because it takes money to get it written and to get the actors. If you take that headache away from the movie company, they're more inclined to want to work with you because there's no financial exposure on their part.

When you have a movie that's already done, you can license it which means the studio rents it from you.

A movie is the best commercial; it's a commercial for your lifestyle, whatever you're really using.

I find that a direct to consumer relationship is the most profitable because you have full margin. There's no sales commission. You're not selling it at a wholesale price; you're selling it at full price, and you never have to sell it off-price.

You never have to fight for real estate when your product is good. People will always find the person that has a good product.

Releasing a movie in theatres of course can help make the film look bigger than it is, which increases DVD sales, provides a platform for better licensing, and the sales of all merchandise connected to the theatrical release.

Screenings at film festivals are a good way to get seen by the people that can buy or license your film.

Damon & Kenyatta
Malibu, CA
5:19pm

DIGITAL BENEFITS

"It's a lot easier to shoot now that everything is digital. There's no film; it's way easier to monetize. It doesn't have to necessarily be seen in a theatre. You can make more money through direct to consumer. It's crazy how much you can achieve through that medium. Because all of my films are independent, It's a real easy set. Like, it's really no stress or pressure because it's not like anyone's really worried about who's going to be mad because I'm going to be the one that's mad if things don't go correct. And it's going exactly the way I want it to because usually what would happen is I want one thing and the person paying for it will want what's more cost-effective and not understand the value of taste, which would be our issue. And then you have the person that wants to do what's creatively right, but they have to do what they're told because that person is paying them. There's always that struggle.

So, it was always tension on the set because they were

listening to different people, plus they had to listen to me, and that was always my issue even at Roca-A-Fella. It was always worrying about Def Jam trying to order around the people that work for me, and then I'm telling them here's something different to do, so it always put them in a funny position. It's like parents putting their kids in a funny position when they get divorced; it's a fight where they're a causality of war. They're just there by default, and their parents are emotional, and they're sending messages through them, and they're using them to get back at each other, and it puts you in a funny place, always making them want to be on one side or the other. And that's not happening because now everyone's on one side. We're all fighting the same fight.

When you're putting up the dough, you don't have to argue at all. There's no arguing when you're putting up the money. It's just like when you're in a cab; if you don't like the way the guy is going, you tell him to pull over and you get out. You never think about that person again. If you choose to pay the cab driver to go the wrong way or the long way, as long as he's getting paid, he shouldn't really have anything to say, and he doesn't, and if he does, kindly tell him to pull over. Here's for your time, and you're in my rearview mirror, just like I'm in yours, so there's no argument when you're putting up the money. If you don't like what I'm saying, that's it, you're gone, no argument. Only time I'll argue with you is if I'm trying to save you. Like, 'Yo, dog, you keep talking, man. I don't have to worry about this. Just get off it.' Other than that, life is easy when you're putting up the dough."

Gems:

The good thing about making a movie today is that everything is digital and it's easier to monetize. A movie today doesn't necessarily have to be seen in a theatre; a person can make money selling their film directly to consumer.

The person that puts up the money never has to argue. That would be like arguing with a cab driver if you don't like the way he's going. If you choose to pay the cab driver to go the wrong way or the long way that's your prerogative. If not, you can kindly tell him to pull over, pay him for his time; he's now in your rearview mirror. It's the same way in business.

You can't become a boss until you learn how to care about other people more than yourself.

Damon, Kenyatta, & John Robinson
Malibu, CA
11:19pm

THE INVESTMENT GAME

My boy John asked Dame what are some of the smartest things people can invest in today? Without hesitation, Dame said, **"Themselves."** He allowed his answer to breathe before he added: **"You have to invest in your own dreams, B. People are always trying to invest in someone else. You have to make money off your own. Stop trying to make money off other people all day. Get good at something and invest in your own dreams. Stand up. Stop looking for other people to make money off of and make money off yourself.**

Today I'm living my dreams. The experiences I gained in making a movie like Paid In Full was good for me. I went through a lot of bullshit. So, from Paid In Full, I said I was going to make my own movies and because I was a little mad at the Weinsteins, I wanted a little bit of their money. That's why I invested in the Woodsman so I could get an artsy movie that could be in the Oscars, which is also why I invested in Lee Daniels. I had two million for my own indie movies that I put into him because he

Culture Vultures

was another black man, pause, and it worked out.

Money came back. But when he wanted me to invest in Shadow Boxer, which was just a platform for him to showcase his directing skills, the script was retarded. It was nothing that was commercially viable, but he guaranteed me that I would get my money back, and I was like, 'You know, this is my money to invest in my movies.' And he was like, 'Look, man, Oprah wouldn't give me any money,' and he said all the other black people that were investing in movies at the time wouldn't give him any money. He made the point that as black people we need to stick together. I was like, 'Alright.' So I looked out. I was like, 'Alright, dog, I'm gonna let you get this two, but I need my money back.' He was like, 'You're going to get my money back next week. I promise you.' The movie ended up costing too much, like twelve million dollars, and I ended up having no say in how it got released. Nothing was done in the best interest of the people that put the money into the movie and because of that, I was tight, but I figured I would be able to get my money back at some point. Then another movie came around; I forgot the name of it, the one starring Mariah Carey."

It wasn't Precious. It was the one before that; you don't hear about that one to much. But I knew the people that were investing in it and one asked me to cosign for him. Then I was like, 'Dog, all I can do is be honest and tell them that I put up this money, and I haven't got it back yet.' And he was like, 'Well, I'm going to put you on as a producer for every movie until you make your money back.' And I said, 'Alright, I respect that.' So he put me on to that bum movie that didn't do anything to the extent that I forgot, and I didn't even watch it to be honest, but the same people that invested in that movie also invested in Precious and I wasn't listed as a producer. And then all communication was cut off, and I was like, 'Damn!' But I was busy doing other things, and I really thought he was going to come back around and do the right thing, but I never got that call. I never even got invited to an Oscar party. I never got a shout out, nothing. Basically it was, like, fuck my money.

Then, on another level, I later found out that he was getting money from selling the foreign, which meant he was making money. So I would be going to wrap parties and he was also having condominium parties. Like, he just bought a condo and I'd be like, 'Yo, you owe me two million. How you buying shit?' I finally had to holler at whoever his manager was; some girl named Simone who talked to me crazy on the phone, and I don't know why because she didn't have anything to do with it. Then when I finally talked to him, he acknowledged that he was wrong and said, 'The money is not in movies anymore. I'm hired as a director, the money is in television, and when I finish this movie The Butler I'm going to put you down with this thing with Brian Grazer.' And I was like, 'Alright, cool, fine, that's cool,' and I didn't even bother him anymore because my lawyers checked in every now and again and he was cool. Then one day I got this call from that same woman Simone and she was like, 'Are you going to jail?' And I was like, 'Why are you asking me that?' And she flipped out, like, 'You could've just answered the fucking question!' Boom, she hung up on me. Damn. And then they sent me a letter of disparagement and whatever, and I tried to talk to Lee again and was like, 'Yo, I don't know what more to do, but that's two million dollars, man. You kind of stopped me from making movies independently.'

I just got to a place where I can do it now, but the answer to your question, 'What's my dream business?' It is movies, and now that I'm back in a position where I can invest in movies, and I can be a filmmaker, and put up the money in Dash Films, and I can do whatever I want. That's my dream, to be freely creative at a professional level, and that's what I am right now. I'm more creative. The businesses are set up so they can run on their own. I still trust other people. Like, I'm not running the day to day of the clothing line I'm wearing right now, which is called 'When We Were Fiends.' This hoodie I'm wearing cost three-fifty. I didn't make it; Ally of 'When We Were Fiends' made it, and I don't have to be there. It's executed well. I'm good with it. All I have to do with certain businesses is show up. If I want to be in fashion, I'm still going to showcase at fashion week at Paris and New York. The Poppington Art Gallery is still there, but I have people that run it. That's what I've been doing is making it to where the businesses can sustain and run on there own because to me a good CEO's business should not only run well when they're around, but should also run smooth when they're not around. If that business can only run good when that person's around then that person is a bad CEO. It's a bad business. A business is supposed to be able to run on its own beacuse a good CEO teaches people how to run the business on their own so that the CEO can just check in to see if shit is running right.

So this is my dream scenario: I can make movies now; the clothes are doing well, and we make music that also goes with the movies. I'm not trying to monetize music. I just want to make music and put it in my movies. I want to have the flyest music in my movies, and I know a lot of people that make good music. Like, when people come around like a Smoke DZA, or Low, or Murda Mook, they're from Harlem. They're new and they're doing things honest. I like how they're doing what they do, and again they're from Harlem. I'm going to assist them, give them a platform, and they get to utilize all of my resources as well. I'll give them that cosign, and if there's some money that can be made, we'll monetize it. But that's not my business model. I'm proud of what they're doing, plus I like to be a part of cool shit before everybody else is. That's generally what I do. I was kicking it with Wiz Khalifa way before 'Black and Yellow,' but I wasn't trying to make any paper off of him. You can ask him. All I wanted to do was give him the right advice, and when we see each other now, it's all love. It is respect because I'm happy that he became successful, and he's young enough that if he's made any mistakes, he can apply it to his future. Plus he's not doing anything that's negative, so I'm cool with it. But my point is I know a lot of people. I knew The Black Keys before they got famous. I've made music with them. When cool people are, I'm going to make music with them because I like making music. But even with them, I've told them, 'Yo, we're doing this as art. I'm not trying to do this as a career, but if we make music, I will put it out'."

I said, "There's definitely magic in doing things for love."

He conclude by saying, **"That's the dream scenario: to be able to do things when you want to and monetize,"** Dame said. "To make money off of things that you love is the trick, but it takes a lot of respect. Like, even when you don't know which way to go, just let respect guide your actions, and anytime you don't understand something, ask yourself what would be the respectful thing to do by my partner and my people. Also, you have to learn how to care about people before you care about yourself. You can't be a boss if all you care about is yourself. A boss's job is to care about everybody else like a dad's job. Your job as a father is to make sure your kids eat first. It's the same in business. If you don't have the ability to do that, or if you're working for someone that doesn't have the ability to do that, then you're in the wrong place. People really don't even understand that. That's also why it's hard for an artist to become a boss because it's hard for them to not be focused on their own agenda. They're used to that. It's hard for an artist to care about other people. They care about their art; they're supposed to. Trying to make an artist administrative and also get them to be articulate about business almost never works out. That's the key to success: "Learn how to care about other people more than yourself." You can't be a boss unless you do that, and for me that probably comes from being a dad at nineteen…"

Marc Brownstein & Damon
DD172
Tribeca, CA
6:14pm

Gems:

The smartest investment is when a person can invest in their own dreams.

A good CEO's business should not only run well when they're around, but should also run smooth when they're not around. If that business can only run good when the boss is around then it's a bad business being run by a bad CEO.

To make money off of things that you love is the trick that makes success appear.

Learn how to care about people before you care about yourself. On the real, you're not a boss if all you care about is yourself.

The job of a mother and father is to make sure their kids eat first. It's the same in business. If you don't have the ability to do that, or if you're working for someone that doesn't have the ability to do that, then you're in the wrong place.

Trying to make an artist administrative and also get them to be articulate about business almost never works out.

The Master Key that unlocks the door to success is to first and foremost "Love Yourself."

Damon, Edan, Jonah
DD172
Tribeca, NYC
1:43am

Wiz Khalifa, Curren$y,
Citizen Cope, & Damon
DD172
Tribeca, NYC
11:29pm

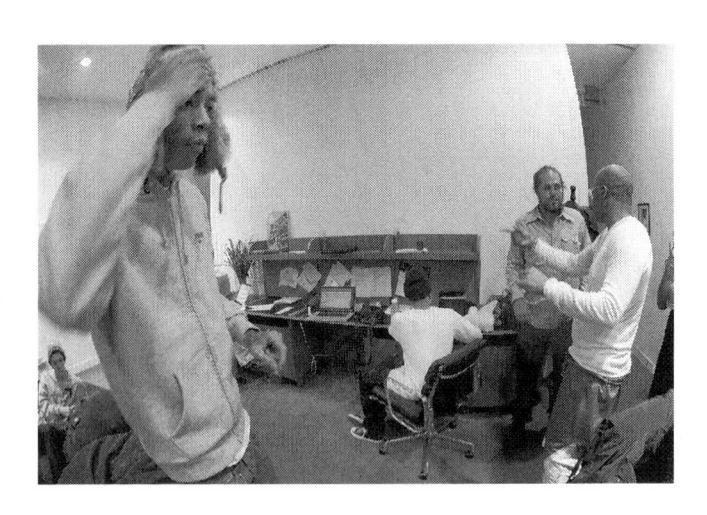

Gallery Opening
DD172
Tribeca, NYC
8:21pm

Curren$y, Damon, MOs Def
DD172 / Under 100
Tribeca, NYC
11:11pm

Dam Funk
DD172 / Under 100
Tribeca, NYC
10:22pm

Erykah Badu
DD172 / Under 100
Tribeca, NYC
1:28am

The London Souls
DD172 / Under 100
Tribeca, NYC
7:12pm

DD172 Staff
Tribeca, NYC
12:15pm

Honor up filming
Harlem, NY
9:30pm

Filming Fancy Commercial
Damon & Cam'Ron
Long Island , NY
5:59pm

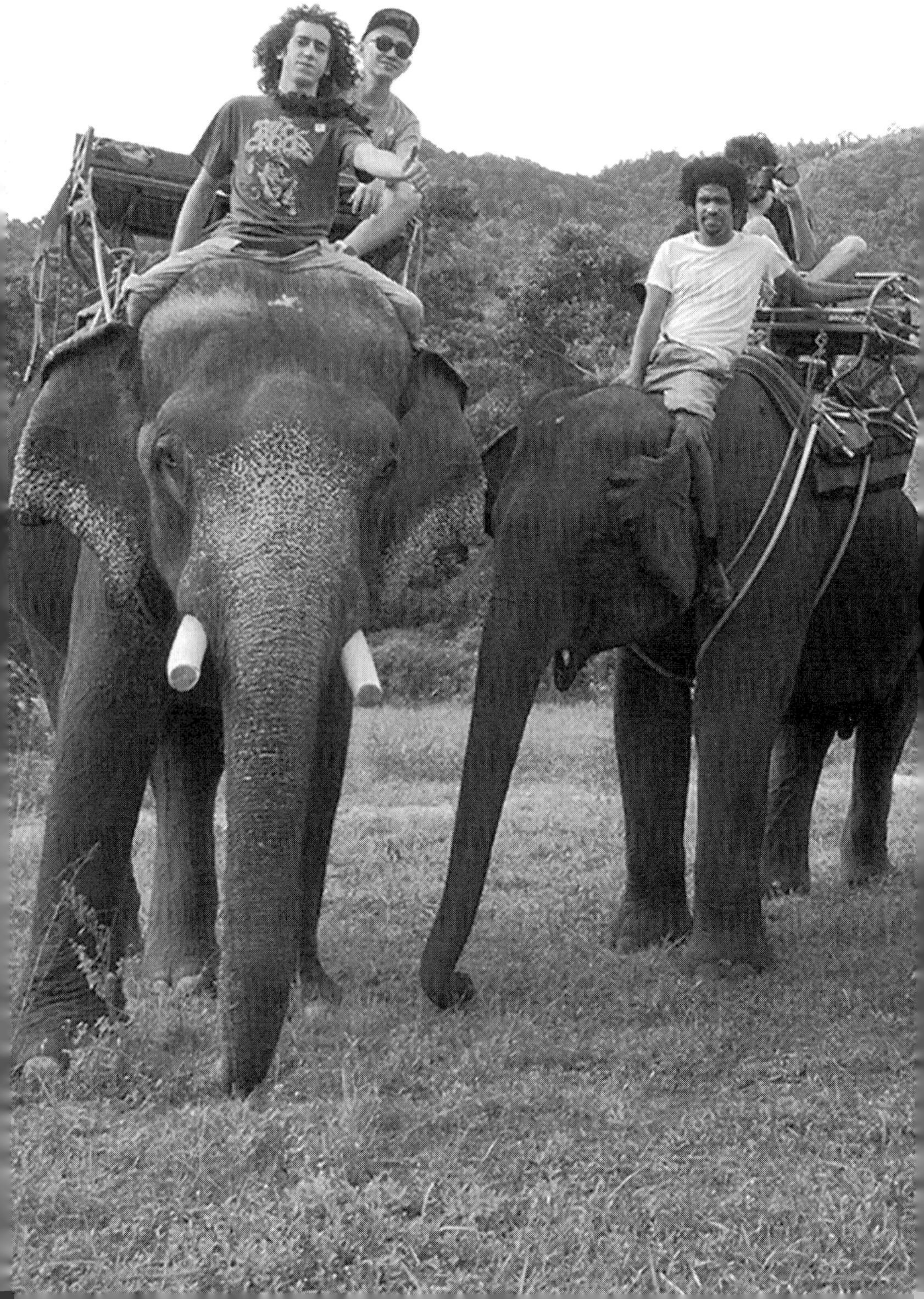

Damon Dash, DJ Wordy, Boogie, The
London Souls, Raquel M. Horn
Ko Samui, Thailand
4:23pm

Kenyatta, Cam'Ron, E-LUV
Malibu
12:15am

Dusko
Venice, CA
11:32am

Lucky & Boogie Dash
Malibu, CA
11:39am

Damon Dash
Sullivan's Island, SC
12:15am

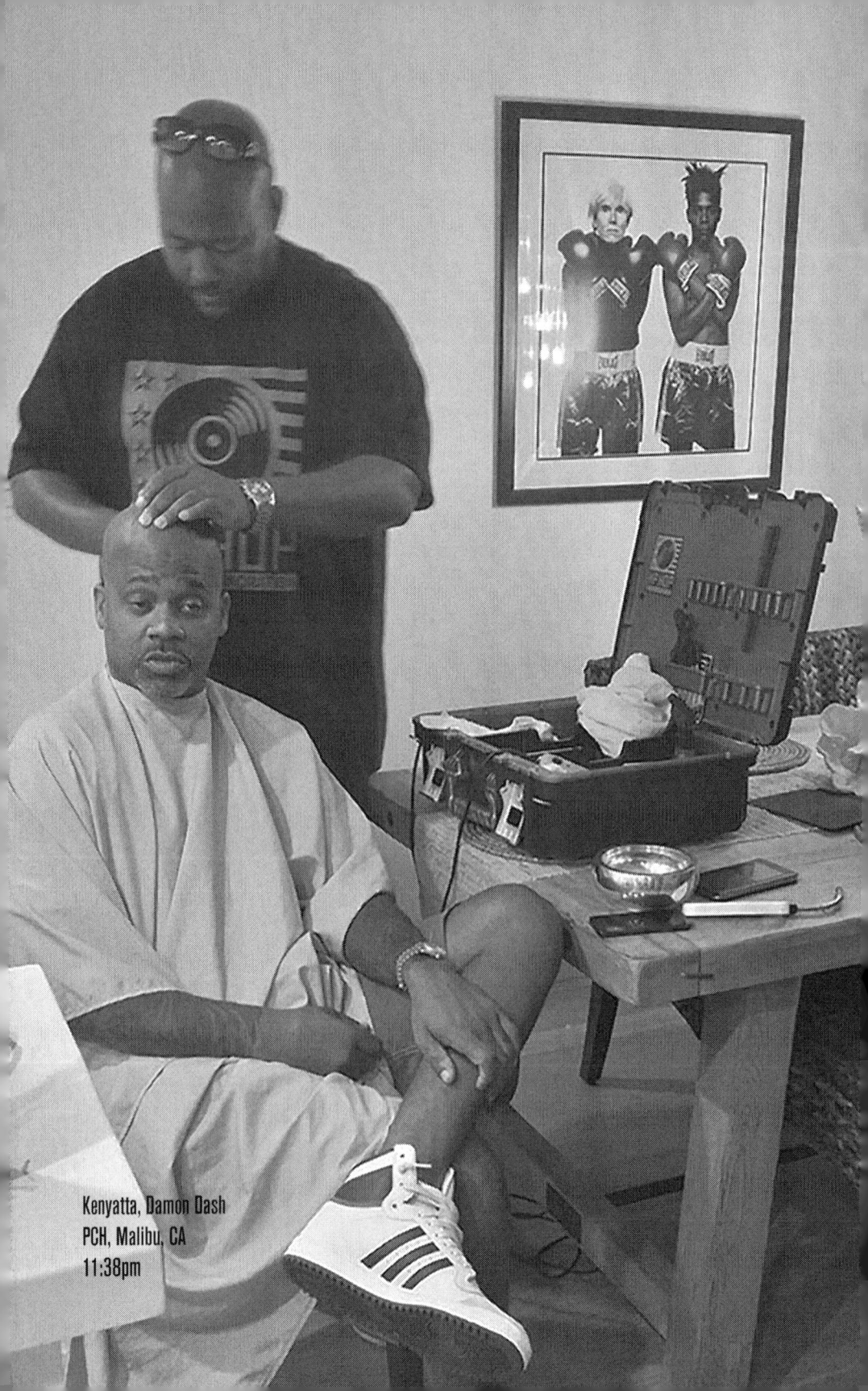

Kenyatta, Damon Dash
PCH, Malibu, CA
11:38pm

Kenyatta, Damon Dash
PCH, Malibu, CA
12:13am

Kenyatta, Damon, Redman
PCH
Malibu, CA
11:02pm

Method Man, Damon, & Kenyatta
Los Angeles, CA
9:23pm

Irv Gotti & Damon
Malibu, CA
1:09pm

Kenyatta Griggs, Damon Dash
Malibu, CA
11:36pm

Damon, Vlad, Kenyatta & Jonah
Malibu, CA
11:08am

Raekwon, Kenyatta, Dame
Culver City, CA
1:24pm

CLASS of
CULTURE VULTURES

LYOR COHEN

ALAN GRUNBLATT,
BARRY KLARBERG

JOEY I.E. MANDA,
TODD MOSCOVITZ

STEVE STOUTE,
CHARLIE WALK

THINK AND BALLOUT
A HIP HOP MOTIVATIONAL

THE SECRET TO BALLIN
Journey

HIP HOP MOTIVATION CORPORATION

Dr. Michael Bernard Beckwith   Snoop Dogg   Kelly Rowland (Destinys Child)   Chris Brown   Rza (Wu Tang Clan)   Timbaland
Professor Kaba Hiawatha Kamene   Redman   Bishop Clifton Edwards Jr   Faith Evans   Dj Quik   Virgil Roberts esq
Travie Mccoy (Gym Class Heroes)   Method Man (Wu Tang Clan)   Norman Brown   BJ The Chicago Kid   Dame Dash
Frank Gatson Jr.   Dr Farid Zarif phd   Bishop Don Magic Juan   Baby Bash   B Real (Cypress Hill)   Luke James
Rev. Eisha Mason   Raekwon (Wu Tang Clan)   Mindless Behavior

THE SECRET TO BALLIN
Journey

HIP HOP MOTIVATION CORPORATION IN ASSOCIATION WITH DAMON DASH STUDIOS PRESENTS "THE SECRET TO BALLIN" CASTING BY CAROLYN GENTLE
WARDROBE STYLING BY JAKIA HANDY   MUSIC BY JONATHAN VANGALAPUDI REGGIE "REDMAN" NOBLE MICHAEL ROBINSON & KENNY MORENO   ORIGINAL SCORE BY BRONSON BUSKETT   EDITED BY CAROLYN GENTLE
DIRECTOR OF PHOTOGRAPHY STEWART HOLLINS   ART DIRECTOR KIRK WEBBER   CO-PRODUCED BY DAMIEN "PIC VAN EXEL" CARTER   PRODUCED BY KENYATTA GRIGGS   MICHELLE GENTLE   JOHN ROBINSON & CAROLYN GENTLE
EXECUTIVE PRODUCED BY KENYATTA GRIGGS jr.   DAMON DASH   REGGIE "REDMAN" NOBLE   WRITTEN & DIRECTED BY KENYATTA GRIGGS

HIP HOP MOTIVATION CORPORATION   DAMON DASH STUDIOS   WWW.DAMEDASHSTUDIOS.COM

WARNING: Many People Have Lost Their Lives Trying To Reveal This Secret... This Secret Has Been Hidden From The World Far Too Long... But Now... They Can No Longer Keep It From Us...

www.thesecrettoballin.com

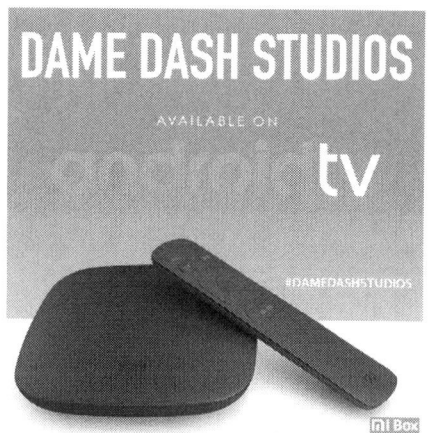

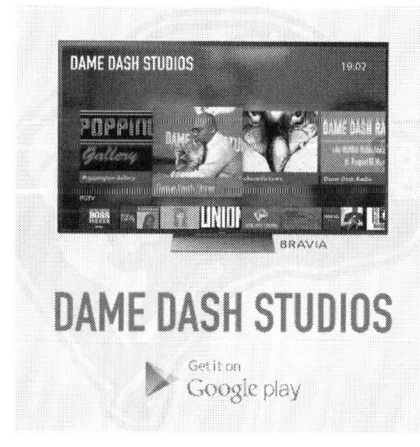

WWW.DAMEDASHSTUDIOS.COM

dash diabetes network

DASH DIABETES NETWORK

Dame Dash, Type 1 diabetic, hosts a lifestyle network showing you how to eat waffles and still keep your blood sugar below 120 thanks to Afrezza.

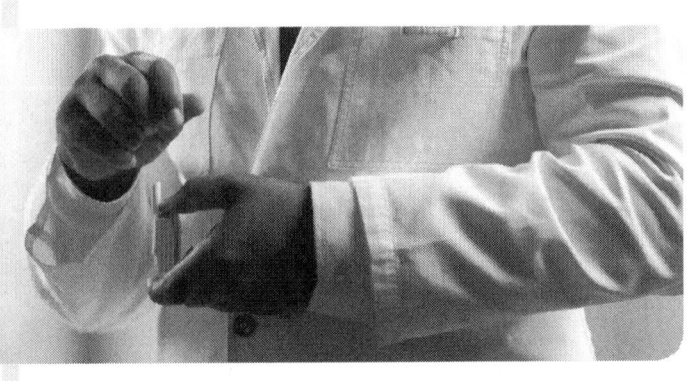

www.dashdiabetesnetwork.com

DUSKO
WINE & SPIRITS

www.duskowineandspirits.com

POPPINGTON

DUSKUS POPPINGTONIUM

1971

www.poppington.com

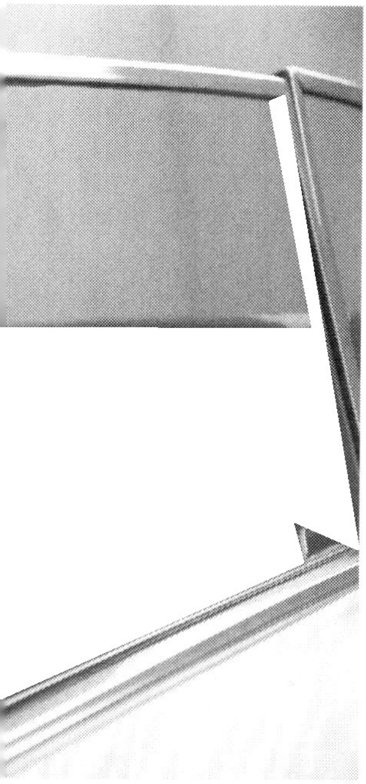

Made in the USA
San Bernardino, CA
13 August 2019